102

3000 800052 78617
St. Louis Community College

Meramec Library
St. Louis Community College
11333 Big Bend Blvd.
Kirkwood, MO 63122-5799
314-984-7797

D1126675

St. Louis Community College
at Meramec
Library

The Ancient Mounds of Poverty Point

Native Peoples, Cultures, and Places of the Southeastern United States

Florida A&M University, Tallahassee
Florida Atlantic University, Boca Raton
Florida Gulf Coast University, Ft. Myers
Florida International University, Miami
Florida State University, Tallahassee
University of Central Florida, Orlando
University of Florida, Gainesville
University of North Florida, Jacksonville
University of South Florida, Tampa
University of West Florida, Pensacola

Native Peoples, Cultures, and Places of the Southeastern United States
Edited by Jerald T. Milanich

The Apalachee Indians and Mission San Luis,
by John H. Hann and Bonnie G. McEwan (1998)

Florida's Indians from Ancient Times to the Present, by Jerald T. Milanich (1998)

Unconquered People: Florida's Seminole and Miccosukee Indians,
by Brent Richards Weisman (1999)

The Ancient Mounds of Poverty Point: Place of Rings, by Jon L. Gibson (2000)

The Ancient Mounds of Poverty Point

PLACE OF RINGS

Jon L. Gibson

University Press of Florida

Gainesville · Tallahassee · Tampa · Boca Raton

Pensacola · Orlando · Miami · Jacksonville · Ft. Myers

Copyright 2001 by the Board of Regents of the State of Florida
Printed in the United States of America on acid-free paper
All rights reserved

06 05 04 03 02 01 C 6 5 4 3 2
06 05 04 03 02 01 P 6 5 4 3 2 1

First cloth printing, 2000
First paperback printing, 2001
Library of Congress Cataloging-in-Publication Data
The ancient mounds of Poverty Point: place of rings / Jon L. Gibson
p. cm. — (Native peoples, cultures, and places of the southeastern United States)
Includes bibliographical references.
ISBN 0-8130-1833-1 (alk. paper) — cloth
ISBN 0-8130-2551-6 (alk. paper) — paperback
1. Poverty Point State Park (La.). 2. Poverty Point culture. I. Title. II. Series.
E99.P84 G5 2001
976.3'83 — dc21   00-061518

The University Press of Florida is the scholarly publishing agency for the State University
System of Florida, comprising Florida A&M University, Florida Atlantic University,
Florida Gulf Coast University, Florida International University, Florida State University,
University of Central Florida, University of Florida, University of North Florida,
University of South Florida, and University of West Florida.

University Press of Florida
15 Northwest 15th Street
Gainesville, FL 32611–2079
http://www.upf.com

Contents

Foreword

For more than a century, the Poverty Point archaeological site in Louisiana has drawn the attention of visitors eager to unlock its secrets. With its six huge concentric earthen rings and a like number of mounds, Poverty Point is unique. There are no similar sites anywhere. Who built these curious earthworks, and what exactly are they? When were they built, and what activities occurred at the "Place of Rings"?

In this popularly written study, author and archaeologist Jon Gibson, who has spent a lifetime investigating Poverty Point, provides the first book-length overview of the site, relating how it came to be and what it represents. He also describes and explains the array of extraordinary artifacts found there, some made of stone brought from more than a thousand miles away.

Gibson's cogent explanations of the site's economic, social, cultural, and ceremonial milieus are intriguing and fun to read. He takes us back and forth in time, allowing us to experience the site as the people who lived there 3,500 years ago did. Drawing on the latest archaeological findings, *The Ancient Mounds of Poverty Point: Place of Rings* paints an engaging picture of this American Indian site and the pre-Columbian world of which it was a part.

An extraordinary example of our Native American heritage, Poverty Point today is a Louisiana State Commemorative Area open to the public. I hope Jon Gibson's colorful account will persuade readers to visit Poverty Point and its remarkable earthworks, a monument that has attracted people for nearly four millennia.

Jerald T. Milanich,
Series Editor

Acknowledgments

Books are invariably born in debt, and this one is no exception. Dennis LaBatt, Poverty Point Commemorative Area manager, has my unceasing gratitude. His friendship and help over the years have been major reasons why Poverty Point is such a special place to me. Dennis has shared research materials, reported sites, interceded with landowners and collectors on my behalf, seen to my fieldwork needs untiringly, and spoiled me so badly that I have become nearly unfit for fieldwork anywhere else. He facilitated access to museum collections so photographs could be made; when I wanted more pieces to illustrate he arranged for loans of private collections. Without Dennis, this book would be considerably thinner and plainer and my Poverty Point experience much poorer.

My friend and colleague David Griffing, who helps Dennis run the Commemorative Area, contributed directly to this book by sharing his firsthand knowledge of Maçon Ridge archaeology, especially from places south of Poverty Point. He, too, enabled photographic access to private collections.

David Hurst Thomas, curator at the American Museum of Natural History and fellow traveler along old Paleoindian paths on the Llano Estacado, furnished copies of James Ford's Poverty Point excavation and analysis notes and related correspondence. He also provided photos from Ford's 1955 excavations. Robert Connolly, with the Mississippi Department of Transportation and formerly with Poverty Point, provided copies of Jacob Walter's journal, Clarence Moore's field notes, and other useful materials.

Bo Boehringer, communications director of the Louisiana Office of State Parks, permitted photography of state-owned museum pieces. Charles

Parker, University of Louisiana anthropology alumnus and veteran of Poverty Point fieldwork, did the on-site photography. Steven Carricut, University of Louisiana anthropology major and a Poverty Point field-school veteran, produced illustrations of artifacts loaned by Dennis and David, redid poor photographs, and worked out details with the staff at the press in the curious dialect spoken in the graphics world. Additional photographs were made by Gordon Maxey for the late Clarence Webb, pediatrician and long-time Poverty Point researcher; others were furnished by my associates. Credits are detailed in illustration captions. Uncredited illustrations are by my own hand or camera.

Sarah Mertins, University of Louisiana anthropology student, proofed the manuscript. Joe Saunders, regional archaeologist for the Louisiana Division of Archaeology, and an anonymous reviewer offered constructive commentary. Their efforts improved science and prose without condescension.

Working with Jerry Milanich, series editor, Meredith Morris-Babb, editor-in-chief of the University Press of Florida, and Judy Goffman, project editor, has been a tutorial as well as an enjoyable experience. Thanks for both.

I continue to draw inspiration from the spirits of Clarence Webb and Mitchell Hillman. To me, they will always be synonymous with Poverty Point research and advocacy. Thanks, old friends, for walking with me to the Bird Mound and for facing me into the gentle breezes that rustle the leaves atop it.

Aliens, Atlanteans, and American Indians

This Old Barn

The forty-watt bulb dangling from the naked cord dimly lit the interior of the old barn. The milk cows had been sold years before, and glass cases replaced the hay and feed-grain bins. In the case closest to me, thousands of cooking balls were bathed in the amber glow. They were sorted by shape—cylindrical, melon, biconical, spheroidal. The next case held projectile points, hundreds and hundreds of them. No, thousands. The next, soapstone fragments; then came a case of plummets, or net weights; and beyond—well? By the time my eyes adjusted to the dimness, I was overwhelmed by the magnitude of what lay before me. This old barn held King Tut's treasure, and I knew how Howard Carter must have felt.

"I'll have to move the light bulb. I've got a few more things back here," Carl Alexander solemnly understated, exposing another anteroom, "Might keep y'all busy a spell."

Trying to act nonchalant, I ambled out through the barn door, squinting in the sunlight streaming through the young foliage on the pecan trees. Over at our makeshift lab table, Clarence Webb was busy sorting cooking balls. He didn't look up or say anything. His smile said it all.

"I'll start on the plummets," I said settling into the rickety cane-bottomed chair.

The Place Where Carl Found the Artifacts

A mile north of Carl Alexander's old barn sits the Poverty Point site, where Carl found the artifacts. It is a quiet place, far from assault by traffic and checkout lines. Some days you can hear the whine of an Ag-Cat spraying cotton or the drone of a John Deere cultivating fields, but most of the time there is quiet—quiet so profound you can hear stirrings from thirty-five centuries ago.

Earthworks distinguish the site. They hug a precipitous bluff that doubles as the western bank of Bayou Maçon and the eastern edge of the Maçon Ridge, which is a long narrow finger of high land rising out of the Lower Mississippi River floodplain in northeastern Louisiana. Six low man-made rings of earth arc away from the bluff like a set of giant nested Cs. In addition to the rings, there are several mounds, including two large ones thought to be figures of birds. The biggest mound reaches the ear-popping height of more than seventy feet and is said to be the second-tallest Indian mound in the United States. All together, the earthworks and core habitation areas cover more than a square mile.

Fig. I.1. This old barn housed Carl Alexander's collection of artifacts from Poverty Point. Located on the banks of Bayou Maçon about a mile south of the rings, the barn saw many notable archaeologists gather there to study the remarkable holdings. Rephotography by Steven Carricut.

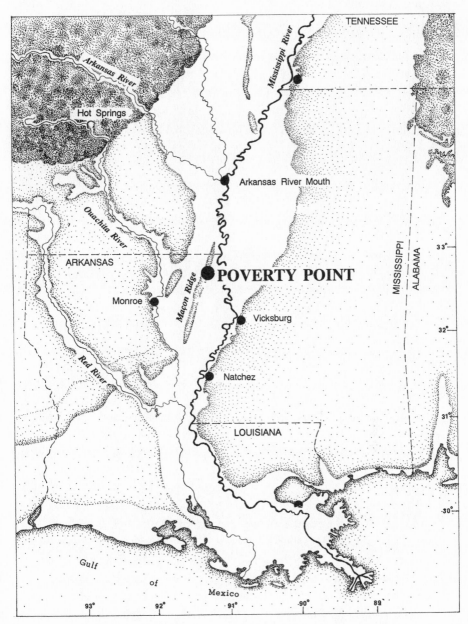

Poverty Point is located in the Lower Mississippi Valley in the northeastern corner of Louisiana, only a score of miles from the present-day Arkansas and Mississippi state lines.

Commemorative Area

The State of Louisiana purchased 400 acres of this site in 1972, and in 1975 the Poverty Point State Commemorative Area opened to the public. The modern complex includes a museum where many of Carl Alexander's artifacts are displayed, a viewing tower where visitors see Poverty Point's earthworks more easily, a small but efficient laboratory where archaeology students process artifacts dug from the earthworks, and hiking and tram trails where visitors experience the earthworks up close and personal. Back in the woods, next to a twisting, steep-sided bayou, and off-limits to tourists, lies a coed dormitory designed to house forty students, the historic site manager's residence, a maintenance shop, and an artifact-storage building. The mailing address is Poverty Point State Commemorative Area, P.O. Box 276, Epps, Louisiana 71237; its e-mail address is povertypoint@crt.la.us. Callers may dial 1 (888) 926-5492. The Commemorative Area is open to the public from 9:00 A.M. to 5:00 P.M. every day except New Year's Day, Thanksgiving, and Christmas.

The creation of the Poverty Point State Commemorative Area was the culmination of a lengthy effort to promote Poverty Point's historical prominence and ensure a measure of protection. James Ford and his American Museum of Natural History crew dug at Poverty Point in the early 1950s and showed just how large and unusual it was for its 3,500-year age. Its reputation outgrew the cotton, which had been grown and picked in its dusty fields since the 1830s when the land was part of Philip and Sarah Guier's Poverty Point plantation. Sarah is buried here on top of a mound named after her, Sarah's Mount. Although promoters have talked often about changing the site's name, the old plantation name has survived.

At first, efforts were launched to make Poverty Point a national monument. Thrusting the effort into the national spotlight elicited a mixed reaction. Archaeologists believed Poverty Point deserved recognition because of its historical importance. Town councils and police juries sought recognition for Poverty Point because they believed it would bring economic benefits to the area. Landowners worried that the federal government would use it as an excuse to take their land away. Other residents fretted that having outsiders come into their rural community would upset the status quo. They all disagreed on how best to secure recognition yet still preserve landownership and the status quo.

The first attempt to secure monument status was made in 1960. John Griffin, Southeast Regional Archaeologist for the National Park Service, made the recommendation, but Congress took no formal action, assuaging landowners' fears. The second attempt was almost thirty years later, in 1988. This time, a bill creating the Poverty Point National Monument passed Congress, but the site was never officially transferred into federal ownership. Today, Poverty Point remains in state hands, showcased as one of Louisiana's premier tourist attractions and listed on the National Register of Historic Places as a National Historical Landmark.

It is the most widely known prehistoric site in Louisiana. It attracts attention—lots of it. Annually, between 10,000 and 15,000 visitors pass through its museum and board the summer tram for the two-and-a-half-mile ride through the earthworks. Demonstrations of earth-oven cooking, stone-bead drilling, and spear throwing with atlatls captivate young and old; the staff sponsors popular programs such as Native American dancing, storytelling, and flint knapping. Schoolchildren from all over the state take field trips to the site, and a learning-activity guide for elementary and middle schools has been written by Deborah Buco and published by the Louisiana Division of Archaeology. Each year, more people attend Archaeology Week activities at Poverty Point than at any one of the dozens of other locations throughout the state. Also, since the commemorative area opened in the 1970s, hundreds of college students have participated in field schools conducted at the site.

Visitors have probably been coming since at least A.D. 1200, when a daring man from Mounds Plantation on the Red River in the northwestern corner of the state came and removed some of the site's ancient objects. Antiquarians and archaeologists have been traipsing over its earthworks and picking up its artifacts since the 1870s. Archaeologists have been digging here since 1912.

A Wide Appeal

Poverty Point appeals to all kinds of people. During a séance held in Baton Rouge in the 1970s, a group of visionaries remotely sensed beneath the big mound a burial chamber appointed with Egyptian hieroglyphs and Old Kingdom furniture. In a paper delivered to the 1994 annual meeting of the Society for Scientific Exploration, geophysicist Andrei Apostol described how strong geophysical stimuli originating from Poverty Point presumably cause blindfolded biolocators' forearms to twitch when they cross the site. In a book entitled *Sacred Sites: A Guidebook to Sacred Centers and Mysterious Places in the United States,* New Age travel guide Frank Joseph notes that certain people—particularly reincarnated Atlanteans capable of past-life regression—succeed in releasing Poverty Point's psychic energies by splashing purified water on the ancient oak atop the largest mound; unfortunately, the tree blew down in a recent storm. Both Joseph and lost-continent advocate John Ward, in his 1984 book *Ancient Archives among the Cornstalks: Twenty-seven Century Old Documents on Stone Revealing a Commercial Enterprise of Mediterranean Colonists in the Wabash Valley of MidAmerica,* contend that Poverty Point is the New Atlantis. Ward believes it was founded by a wave of refugees hunting lead ore who rowed their way up the Mississippi River after the old Atlantis was destroyed in 1198 B.C. Extraterrestrial-contact advocate Erich Von Daniken, author of *Chariots of the Gods* and *Gods from Outer Space,* visited Poverty Point and inspected a reputed UFO landing site west of the big mound. He was enthralled by a cooking ball shaped like the Gemini space capsule. Paranormal investigator Dennis Hauck, in his book *The National Directory of Haunted Places,* claims Poverty Point is haunted by ghosts; and in an interview given to the *Lake Providence Banner Democrat,* the Yap family, Pentecostal missionaries from Kuala Lampur, Malaysia, claimed that evil emanations originate there. Poverty Point is the setting for Jean DeCato's Harlequin Romance *Delta Nights,* a story about Alisa Fairlight, an archaeological field-school participant who set out searching for indications of Mesoamerican contact and instead found love with local farmer Pace Lofton.

Even those of us with less imagination find Poverty Point stimulating. Indigenous peoples, especially shamans, come to Poverty Point to find inner peace and spiritual power. A photographer from the *New York Times,* visiting my university field school in 1988, shot two rolls of film with two different cameras around Sarah's Mount, and the film came out blank. I shot a roll at the same spot and at the same time with the same result. Heat-spoiled film, undoubtedly. Apparitions are common sightings on Sarah's Mount, as they are on the big mound. Three girls walking to the big mound in late afternoon stopped; one of them snapped a picture of the other two. The clear print shows three people: two girls and a third figure standing beside them. Emulsion problem, probably. A hollow tree on one of the western rings beats a slow drum cadence when the moon is full. Five minutes after I set up my mapping equipment on the first day of the first field season I ever spent at Poverty Point, a funnel cloud passed directly overhead, pelting the mapping crew with hail, enveloping us with a bluish umbra of static electricity, and playing havoc with the magnetic needle in our alidade. Our Poverty Point experiences have included dancing rabbits, bellowing alligators, hooting owls, and a menagerie of other woodland creatures. We have had foxes, or maybe The Fox, a yellow-furred Spirit Fox prominent in both ancient design and modern folklore (the one John Calhoun writes of in his short story "Season of the Fox" for the 1989 issue of the literary journal *Helicon*). We've had fire ants, ticks, redbugs, and poison ivy. Nature is just full of wonder.

Place of Rings

While these contemporary happenings make Poverty Point much talked about, its past is what makes it truly special. In its heyday, Poverty Point was a bustling place—big, busy, important. This book is about Poverty Point during its heyday. It is also about its encircling countryside, the domestic-economic support territory that encompasses almost 700 square miles. I even discuss lands up to 250 miles distant—too far away to be considered part of its familiar domestic-economic hinterland but close enough to have had political-economic relations or reactions. This book is about Poverty Point culture as seen from the Poverty Point site.

The residents who lived at Poverty Point were Native Americans, descendants of hardy Asian immigrants who came to America across the frozen Beringian isthmus twelve to fifteen millennia ago—maybe longer. Poverty Point residents were removed many generations from these immigrants and from the early settlers in the Lower Mississippi Valley, who—according to linguist Julian Granberry—may have spoken a now-extinct language anthropologists refer to as Gulf. That language connection seems quite plausible to me because certain symbolic elements in myths, artistic displays, and earthworks were shared widely by tribal peoples whose languages evolved from ancient Gulf speech. On the other hand, Canadian anthropologist Gene Denny thinks that speakers of Algonkian, another ancient language, may have influenced Poverty Point language and culture. If so, then rock exchange with Algonkian-speaking midwestern groups may have been involved.

Can we trace Poverty Point descendants to any historic tribe or group of tribes? In a word, no. Yet, there is a word that provides us with the best clue as to their identity—Colewa. Colewa, pronounced Co-wah or Co-le-wah, is the name of the largest creek immediately west of Poverty Point. If Colewa is a corruption of a tribal name, then Poverty Point descendants may have been the Koroa, Tunican-speaking traders who lived in the Poverty Point vicinity before vanishing from history in the eighteenth century.

The Place of the Rings sits amid cotton fields and woods. Crop dusters buzz the rings, and air-conditioned harvesters raise clouds of dust at cotton-picking time. Tobacco-chewing men run trotlines in Bayou Maçon's green waters, pull thirty-pound catfish off steel hooks, and, clad in starched overalls, gather at the gin every Saturday to tell whoppers about the big one that got away and to complain about the week's commodities market. Schoolchildren run and play at the park's picnic tables and ooh and aah over miniature owl pendants in the museum displays. Archaeologists scratch their heads trying to figure out why the walls of this test pit do not look like the walls of that pit dug only six feet away. They count löess cooking ball fragments from each excavation level, tally them up on analysis sheets, and argue about whether staples were provided by corn farming, starchy-seed gardening, or hunting and gathering. Sensitives expect the unusual and make much ado over rumors of strange happenings.

And thirty-five centuries ago, Native Americans hauled ton after ton of dirt to build massive mounds and embankments. They secured stone for their tools from foreign places, some more than a thousand miles away. They pulled thirty-pound catfish from lakes and bayous and hoed roots on the banks of Joes Bayou. Their way of life is discussed in the pages of this book.

1

Conceptual Matters

On Theory

Whether emphasized or not, theory is basic to archaeological practice. Without it, archaeologists are fated to collect curios and marvel at mounds. With it, they can begin to unravel the past.

Since research started at Poverty Point over a century ago, archaeology has undergone several theoretical transformations. At first, a culture-history orientation guided research and interpretation. Culture history helped to dispel the idea that Poverty Point was a cultural enigma by recognizing its basically Late Archaic nature. But the site's massive earthworks and tons of exchange rocks were not typical of Archaic culture and prompted cultural historians to attribute its origin to Early Hopewell occupation troops from Illinois or Ohio or to maize-planting Olmec missionaries from Vera Cruz. In the 1960s, a processual orientation began to share the theoretical stage with culture history. Processual archaeology upheld deductive science as the one true way to discover the facts of the past. It caused archaeologists to stop thinking of Poverty Point solely in terms of diagnostic artifacts, radiocarbon dates, and trait resemblances to other archaeological cultures, and to begin thinking of it as a multitribal event or a closed society with economic, social, political, and religious institutions and inseparable adaptational ties to its hardwood forests and swamps. Despite these new interests, there remained a strong feeling of déjà vu: that what archaeologists were really doing was still primarily classification only of sociopolitical forms instead of artifacts. Since the late 1980s, a postprocessual orientation has affected Poverty Point archaeology. This orientation has archaeologists searching for symbolic meaning in earthworks, glyphs, and charms as well as for the power source behind the earthworks. Postprocessualism's oft-intuitive logic has touched off resistance from processual hardliners and evolved culture historians.

The point of the matter is that no single theoretical orientation provides the sole truth about Poverty Point's past. Culture history, processualism, and postprocessualism give archaeologists different perspectives on the past. Archaeology gains on its ultimate goal of comprehending the past by degrees. Unless researchers make recording errors, use flawed methods or logic, or discover contrary cases, they cannot automatically dismiss interpretations proposed under previous theoretical frameworks. They can and usually do disagree, for that is the nature of archaeology and people, but normally interpretations just fall from favor. Where archaeologists seem to be gaining ground in understanding Poverty Point is in the better-informed questions they ask each time a new theoretical orientation sways the field. As archaeology enters the twenty-first century, I am convinced that Poverty Point is better known today than it was three decades ago, but I am just as convinced that the next three decades will bring even greater understanding.

On Present Specifics

Theory or what passes for theory—that is, a set of fundamental tenets that underlies interpretations—is liberally spread throughout the remaining pages. It is not identified as such and may not even be obvious, because it is given in memoir or life-snippet form at the beginnings of more speculative chapters. For example, the snippet "A Different Fox" illustrates the shortcomings of scientific theory when applied to events that seemingly defy scientific explanation. The old Choctaw belief in the Shilombish better explains the selectively visible fox, and, to me, native explanations of symbols and glyphs are more appropriate than modern scientific, religious, or astrological ones. The snippet "I Owed Him One" illustrates how generalized reciprocity works, and I use reciprocity to explain political economy. "Souse and Chops," a composite childhood memoir, conveys the salient power of reciprocity—the power of kindness. I use it to explain how Poverty Point distributed its foods and other resources, leveraged labor to build its massive earthworks, conducted its vast exchange system, and managed other extraordinary endeavors within a basically egalitarian organization. A composite memoir, "Sixteen Hateful Miles," attests to a general pugnacity that exists between small, neighboring southern towns and is used to gauge intercommunity relationships among Poverty Point and surrounding settlements.

There will be some who will claim that these ideas don't really qualify as theory—that they are simply observations on life perhaps mixed with too much folk wisdom to be generally applicable to other situations, especially as guides for explaining aspects of Poverty Point culture. To those dissenters, I reiterate: Theory is a set of fundamental tenets that underlies interpretation.

Another fundamental theoretical point deals with perspective. I assume a broad view of Poverty Point, one in which operation and change in one aspect of culture affect and are affected by operation and change in other aspects. Had I not been able to show how Poverty Point data could have resulted from specific, interconnected cultural operations, I would have had little reason to consider Poverty Point an integrated community or closed society but rather would have deemed it merely a unique event or specialized practice. I realize how self-serving this sounds; it's like saying that if the parts fit, then that has to be the way things happened. But shacks can be built out of mansion materials. Fortunately, archaeologists have a quasi-independent means of support for their reasoning: They can draw on studies of traditional peoples.

Fishing furnishes a good illustration. Even bountiful warm waters like those in the Lower Mississippi Valley produce both good and bad fishers. Among simple peoples food is shared, and sharing is nearly always reciprocal. Good fishers do not need or want return gifts of fish, but other kinds of gifts would have kept sharing from getting too one-sided. Reciprocity works by creating obligation, and therein lies opportunity to manipulate payback. Technological improvements, such as adding weights to fishnets to make them work better during winter and spring flood, not only intensify food acquisition and reciprocity but promote acquisition of iron ores from the Ouachita Mountains. Exchange instantly expands as other rocks from the Ouachitas and from all over the midcontinent are acquired. Technology accelerates with the feedback.

These are only the interrelated economic effects, but other aspects of culture are affected, too. Exchange exposes home folks to foreign lands and peoples and to real and imagined threats to community well-being, especially strangers, witches, and evil spirits. Earthworks and charms are fashioned to protect residents, their size and number compatible with the perceived dangers. Labor for construction comes from the very same sharing ethic that permeates domestic economy. Social organization and leadership are tied to the same principle, and no sources of power and motive other than reciprocity and animism (belief in ghosts, spirits, and orenda) are necessary to forge a community like Poverty Point, which raised egalitarian principles to their fullest.

Such interpretations are compatible with function and change in many southeastern native societies. This lessens the possibility that Poverty Point was a unique or periodically staged affair.

These theoretical considerations leave only a handful of archaeological facts: Poverty Point flourished in the middle of the second pre-Christian millennium; its domestic economy was based on fishing, gathering, and hunting; it used sizable quantities of many kinds of exotic rocks; and it erected massive mounds and embankments. All else is interpretative, some would even say speculative.

The implications of these facts are what drive interest in Poverty Point prehistory. They are what evoke allusions to its unusual nature. Those attributions always came from lack of understanding, not because Poverty Point culture was out-of-sync with the rest of native culture. Poverty Point culture always "fit"; it was archaeological explanations that did not.

Lately, researchers have begun to realize that Poverty Point hunter-gatherers attained levels of organization and integration once thought possible only by advanced farming cultures. Earthworks the size of Poverty Point's, which rival the largest constructions ever built in North America above Mexico at any time, were just one of Poverty Point's achievements. An exchange system that spanned more than a thousand miles and that fulfilled basic stone needs in a nondiscriminatory manner was another. Even having to move around to get food and provide life's other necessities, once considered normal for hunter-gatherers, was curtailed by the way Poverty Point organized and conducted its domestic economy. Its technological cup runneth over in terms of innovation, gadget and appliance richness, and absolute tool numbers, creating feedback loops that pushed Poverty Point toward the upper limits of simple society. Poverty Point never invented writing, but its representational system of imagery in earth and stone was not only symbolic but communicated the dominant role that supernaturalism played in everyday life.

On Writing

Poverty Point archaeology consists of a few facts, lots of interpretations, and much that is not known. Interpretations fill the following pages, and most reflect my views or preferences. I do not try to disguise that fact by using passive voice or third person or by presenting them in language so equivocal as to weaken what they are—reflections of current thinking. Everyone knows interpretations are not direct observations or explanations of the past. They are simply expressions born of interaction among data, prevailing theoretical frameworks, and personal preferences.

This brings to mind a conversation I recently had with a trial lawyer. After reading a popular booklet I had written about Poverty Point, he told me he would never defend a case that had as much qualified evidence as that booklet. He continued, "I'd never be able to convince a jury with that kind of evidence." Of course, there's no shadow-of-a-doubt clause to deal with in archaeology, but my point is this: Why qualify interpretations with words such as "appears," "seems," "maybe," "probably," and "possibly"? Interpretations are already qualified by being what they are.

There's another point to be made, and that's the obvious one that most interpretations herein are merely asserted without systematically eliminating alternative possibilities or offering compelling empirical support, and that may not seem very scientific. Most interpretations have already endured scientific trials and are nakedly exposed in the professional literature. Some cannot be put to empirical tests—at least not easily—and therefore must stand on their own until better ones replace them. I am not writing science so that the few can judge the veracity of interpretations for themselves. I am writing a plausible account for the many.

So as not to interrupt the narrative, I have not used citations or footnotes. Where I quote someone or use their idea directly, I mention them by name. I have tried to keep this book from becoming a memoir or a list of citations of my work but will not deny that it primarily represents my personal views on Poverty Point. Most archaeologists prefer their own views anyhow, but I have been involved with Poverty Point matters for so long that I have a hard time separating self from science.

Then there is the matter of writing a general book, of trying to find common ground between professional archaeologists used to reading professional literature and nonprofessional readers used to reading for interest and entertainment. The harder I try, the more I have become convinced that there is no common ground, at least not one that will completely satisfy both groups of readers. I have written about topics that interest archaeologists in a style as free of specialized archaeological terms and theoretical discussions as possible. Just in case, a glossary has been included.

I also have let the vernacular and folksy side of Poverty Point's rural Louisiana setting drawl into the narrative in places—especially in the little parables at chapter beginnings. My reason for conveying theory this way is twofold: to maintain a familiar, nontechnical tone and to convey a feeling for the backdrop in which fieldwork has taken place. Besides, the way people say things often says as much as what they say. Taking self out of science may be laudable, but it doesn't express how personal archaeology is; it never expresses its human side. I've written this book much as I would tell stories around a crackling campfire waiting for the fish to fry. Listen, is that an owl hooting or a Shilombish?

2

From Then Until Now

"Strewed in Grate Profusion"

On my a rival at the place of my destination, on bayou Mason at which place I had been informed lead ore had been found. But on examination I soon discovered how the lead ore came to this place. & with this discovery, all hope of finding a lead mine disapate. Instead of a lead mine, I found myself on the site of an old indian town. The surface of the earth at this place, for several acres around, were strewed in grate profusion, with fragments of indian crockery. & a large number clay made by the indians for edible purposes indicating the fact that the inhabitants who located the town were a tribe of clay eating indians. The clay balls were the size of a green walnut & had been baked in fire. Some were as red as a Salmon brick. I have some of them in my cabinet which were brought home with me as curiosity. The lead ore (?) to had been brought by the indians from parts unknown to us & (?) lost by them. Thus disapointed in the discovery of a lead mine, I mounted my horse. I rode out to look & see what the country looked like in the vicinity of this old town site. I soon discovered a mound of colossal size. The figure of the base of the superstructure was a rectangle twice as long as wide & about 1000 long by 500 broad & 150 feet in altitude with (?) top or terrace, of 20 feet wide & 500 feet long (this estimate is guess work I did not measure it. This mound has an inclined plain attached to one side, with a grade, so as to enable one to ride up on it with ease. I did pass up this inclined way on my horse. This is one of the largest mounds I have ever met with & from the peculiar shape of its apex I judge it to be entitle to the digni fyed indian title of a "Teo(?)lli" of the first order.

Jacob Walter, passage in his unpublished daily log, ca. 1830–40

Settler Jacob Walter had ridden a long saddle-weary way from his south Louisiana home on Bayou Ramos seeking a legendary lead mine at Poverty Point. He was disappointed. There was no mine. The lead turned out to be galena, a native ore derived from ancient Indian diggings in the Upper Mississippi Valley.

Before Ford and Webb

Walter's journal entry was the first known written account of Poverty Point, but the site had attracted visitors during the ages. An anonymous Caddo Indian, probably a *Konah*, or medicine man, from Mounds Plantation—a twelfth-century village on the Red River in northwestern Louisiana and about 150 miles west of Poverty Point—was the earliest visitor to leave a record. He was buried at his Red River home with his medicine bundle, which held two red stone beads, a slate pendant made from a two-hole gorget, and a perforated hematite plummet. These charms had been collected either from the ruins of Poverty Point or from some other long-deserted Poverty Point encampment, where they had lain undoubtedly gathering power for centuries until collected by the brave adventurer from the Red River.

The first published account of Poverty Point, which appeared in 1873, was penned by Samuel Lockett, Confederate officer, engineering professor, and head of the Louisiana Topographic Survey. Well-traveled archaeologist Clarence B. Moore steamed up Bayou Maçon in a sidewheeler named the *Gopher* during the winter of 1911–12 and quickly published his discoveries. His report of strange artifacts and huge mounds drew considerable interest as archaeologists began to realize how extraordinary his discoveries were. In 1926, the Smithsonian Institution sent Gerard Fowke down to investigate, and he made another unusual discovery—a concentration of soapstone fragments, which he surmised came from a single large vessel.

Fig. 2.1. A youthful James A. Ford developed the Lower Mississippi Valley's first chronological outline. Here he relaxes at the WPA laboratory in New Orleans around 1939. Later he explained that he ignored Poverty Point at first because it did not fit. Photography by A. R. King; courtesy of Bob Neuman; rephotography by Steven Carricut.

Fig. 2.2. Clarence Webb was a principal Poverty Point researcher in the mid-twentieth century; Ford was the other. In 1969 and 1970, Webb and associates Thomas Koehler, John Connaway, and Sam McGahey conducted excavations at Teoc Creek in Mississippi's Yazoo swamp. Hot, dusty, but still raring to go, Webb emerges from Teoc Creek at day's end. Courtesy of Clarence Webb; rephotography by Steven Carricut.

Nothing further was written about the site for a decade and a half after Fowke, but interest didn't die down. James Ford, a pioneer of modern archaeology, was aware of Poverty Point in 1933 during his first attempt to develop a chronological sequence for Lower Mississippi prehistory. He actually visited Poverty Point but chose not to include it in his seminal book *Analysis of Indian Village Site Collections from Louisiana and Mississippi.* He did describe the immediately adjoining Neal farm, which had

Fig. 2.3. Mike Beckman, a Shreveport oil man, was a longtime friend of Clarence Webb. In the 1940s and 1950s, he amassed a large collection from Poverty Point and collaborated with Ford and Webb during the American Museum of Natural History's excavations in the early 1950s. Courtesy of Bob Neuman.

more-familiar artifacts. In 1935, pediatrician and self-taught archaeologist Clarence Webb began his long involvement in Poverty Point research. Intrigued by Fowke's report of the broken soapstone vessel, Webb stopped off while returning from a deer hunt. Taken to the spot of Fowke's find by local farmers, he excavated a pit containing thousands of soapstone fragments broken from hundreds of vessels (not just one large one as Fowke thought), and he described the deposit in an article published in *American Antiquity* in 1944.

During World War II, the area around Poverty Point produced another kind of treasure when oil and gas were discovered underfoot, and later, in 1946, Shreveport oil man Michael Beckman initiated his search for oil and artifacts. Beckman, a friend of Webb's, amassed a large surface collection, and it provided much of the artifactual information used in Ford and Webb's American Museum of Natural History report a decade later.

Ford and Gordon Willey, who ran Louisiana's WPA archaeology laboratory for a year during the Depression, ignored Poverty Point in their discussion of southeastern culture history in 1941. James Griffin did, too, in his first culture histories, published after the war, as well as in his later synthesis published during the Vietnam War. And the classic Philip Phillips, Ford, and Griffin volume on Lower Mississippi Valley prehistory, *Archaeological Survey in the Lower Mississippi Valley, 1940–1947*, published in 1951, started Lower Mississippi Valley chronology with the culture period that followed Poverty Point. Ford and Webb subsequently explained why they chose to ignore Poverty Point: It didn't fit into the chronological outline then being developed.

Poverty Point did not seem to fit because of the way Ford and associates thought about prehistory in the early twentieth century, not because it was a developmental quirk or cultural anomaly. Poverty Point had stone tools that looked like those made during earlier Archaic times, but it had little of the pottery that was so prevalent during later Early Woodland Tchefuncte times. Archaeologists convinced themselves that Poverty Point must have existed before pottery was made. But it was a huge place and its earthworks were colossal, and in mid-twentieth-century thinking, lack of pottery and presence of large earthworks were regarded as incompatible traits. Archaeologists attempted to make them compatible by contending that people had lived at Poverty Point long enough for materials that appeared at various points in prehistory to wind up inadvertently mixed together or that Poverty Point was occupied late enough to have been influenced by midwestern Hopewell culture, which did incorporate large geometric earthworks and pottery. In the archaeological thinking of the day, there were no other ways to explain the apparent contradiction represented by existing earthworks and missing pottery.

Clarence Webb was the lone voice heard in the silence. Four years after his short report on the soapstone deposit, he recommended in another *American Antiquity* article that Poverty Point be considered not only a site but a widespread culture transitional in time and content between Late Archaic and Early Woodland Tchefuncte cultures. Webb's work refocused attention on Poverty Point, and among the eyes it attracted were Ford's. Actually, Poverty Point had never been out of his sight. In 1951, Ford, along with Phillips and William Haag, excavated at Jaketown in western Mississippi about a hundred miles east of Poverty Point. In their report of the dig, entitled *The Jaketown Site in West-Central Mississippi* and published by the American Museum of Natural History, they confirmed the pre–Early Woodland age with the first radiocarbon dates ever determined on Poverty Point culture. Webb visited the Jaketown excavations, and the Jaketown gang visited him at Poverty Point. While driving across Arkansas en route to the 1952 Caddo Conference in Norman, Oklahoma, Haag and Webb decided to pool their data on microliths, small blade tools so common at Jaketown and Poverty Point. In their co-authored article, which appeared in *American Antiquity* in 1953, they

Fig. 2.4. Clarence Webb (*left*) and William Haag (*right*) collaborated on a seminal study of Poverty Point microliths, which they planned on this trip to the 1952 Caddo Conference in Norman, Oklahoma. Courtesy of Clarence Webb; rephotography by Steven Carricut.

prophesied that archaeology would have to revise its thinking by admitting that mound building, large populations, prepottery corn agriculture, and microlith manufacture were Archaic traits. They turned out to be right about everything except agriculture. Poverty Point did cause later archaeologists to revise their views on agriculture, but not the way Haag and Webb anticipated. Contrary to their expectations, Poverty Point's subsistence economy proved to be based on wild foods, not on maize or native southeastern domesticates. Poverty Point showed that *some* Archaic groups built large earthworks without corn agriculture.

During Ford and Webb

After the Jaketown report appeared, James Ford brought his genius to Poverty Point. He borrowed long-time friend Robert Neitzel from the archaeology museum at Marksville, Louisiana, in exchange for his help designing museum exhibits. They put in three excavation seasons at Poverty Point in 1952, 1953, and 1955. Junius Bird, Ford's coworker at the American Museum of Natural History, joined them for a month in 1955, and George Quimby of the Chicago Field Museum, who had been with Ford during his WPA work, came and helped for a fortnight. Webb and Beckman visited, often bringing artifacts they had surface-collected at Poverty Point and sharing their firsthand knowledge of the site. The 1955 dig was like a prolonged working conference and culminated in Ford and Webb's classic volume *Poverty Point, a Late Archaic Site in Louisiana,* which was published by the American Museum of Natural History in 1956.

Although given short shrift in technical publications, the human side of a dig often determines what is written and how. Human-interest stories frequently are as informative and decidedly livelier than tables full of numbers or long lists of measurements. Ford's 1955 excavations are no exception.

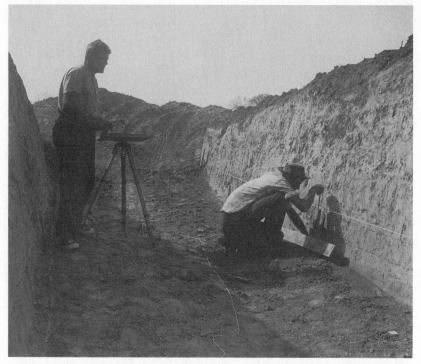

Fig. 2.5. Robert "Stu" Neitzel was Ford's right hand during the 1955 excavations at Poverty Point. Here he draws the profile of one of the trenches through Mound B, while the tractor-driving Ford was busy digging others. Courtesy of David Hurst Thomas.

Fig. 2.6. Set in the edge of the woods near Mound B on the banks of Harlan Bayou, this trailer was home to Jim and Ethel Ford during the 1955 Poverty Point excavations. A squad tent for fellow excavators and visitors was pitched next to the trailer. Courtesy of David Hurst Thomas.

Ford's field camp in 1955 was a busy place. He rented a house trailer and parked it at the edge of the woods just east of domed-shaped Mound B. He and Ethel, his wife, lived in the trailer. Next to the trailer, he pitched a sixteen- by thirty-two-foot squad tent, where Neitzel, Bird, and Quimby, as well as many other visitors, carried on and did some sleeping. One memorable get-together occurred in March. Neitzel, Bird, and Quimby were already encamped. Webb came over from Shreveport, William Haag from Baton Rouge, and Robert Greengo from Harvard's Manny dig in western Mississippi. James Griffin, Albert Spaulding, Charles McNutt, and Art Jelinik drove down from the University of Michigan. Spaulding and McNutt busied themselves setting up leveling stations and mapping Motley Mound while Griffin and the others inspected open dig areas. Griffin was not at all impressed with Ford's ingenious mechanical shaker screen, which Quimby was using to sift dirt from one of the test units. Griffin told me that the shaker simply balled up dirt into small pellets, which looked like "rabbit pills." Actually, Poverty Point's silt loam looks like "rabbit pills" anytime it is dry screened. At night, when the crickets started singing and the owls started hooting, out came Griffin's banjo and the libations. One night, twenty-five-cent-a-pound chuck steaks were thrown on the grill tended by Michigan graduate students McNutt and Jelinik, who got an earful of Spaulding and Ford's famous disagreement about the reality of types (Ford arguing that types were created by archaeological methods, Spaulding arguing that they were real and discovered by the archaeologist). McNutt actually got more than an earful. After he lobbied too loudly for Spaulding's cause, the six-foot-four Ford tossed the five-foot-eight McNutt out of the trailer and ate his steak. Repentant in recent years, McNutt told me that since it was Ford's steak in the first place, Ford had every right to eat it. Ford and Spaulding kept their argument cerebral. Griffin stayed out of it.

William Haag recalled Junius Bird's departure for New York on the morning after McNutt's lost supper. Bird hired a local crop duster to fly him to Vicksburg so he could catch a flight north. The pilot landed in a cotton field, picked up Bird, and took off. Without warning, he banked steeply and buzzed the throng gathered to see Bird off. "If that pilot had not pulled out, southeastern archeology would have been wiped out," Haag quipped in a videotaped conversion with George Quimby in 1988.

Poverty Point witnessed some of the first experimental archaeology done in North America. Working under the tent by campfire light, Bird and Ford molded dirt into the shapes of Poverty Point objects (PPOs) figuring out how they were made. Ford wrote to Webb: "I helped at first but my enthusiasm vanished before his did." Bird and Ford performed no use experiments, since PPOs had been found packed together in fire pits indicating their use in pit baking. Back at the American Museum, Ford wrote to Neitzel telling him of his efforts to create microlithic perforators, or small key-shaped drills, by scraping pieces of bone and antler with narrow straight-sided flakes, or bladelets; he wrote that fifteen minutes' worth of scraping produced an object indistinguishable from perforators, while deliberately chipping the edges of bladelets left microscopic hinge fractures not present on archaeological specimens.

The Ford and Webb volume did not start out as a collaborative effort but wound up as one. After fieldwork, Ford wrote to Webb from New York: "The letters get fatter as seems to be inevitable in long distance collaboration. In the end we may decide to publish the correspondence and throw the report away." But they did not, and their correspondence showed just how the report evolved. The chapter on projectile points in particular went through several collaborative revisions. The final volume truly was a joint effort. They even shared the same culture-historical vision of Poverty Point—almost.

Ford and Webb surmised that Poverty Point had been inhabited by a resident population of several thousand people who possessed an agricultural economy and that it was organized and run by religious figures. They concluded (actually Ford concluded, Webb was tepid to the proposal) that there had been a war with northern aggressors and that invading Hopewellian war parties from the Midwest had conquered a local Archaic group and forced it to build massive earthworks. Webb tried to convince Ford to play down his thoughts about Hopewell connections. In a letter, he reminded Ford that apparent Hopewellian traits such as Motley points, bird motifs, mound building, clay figurines, and microliths were only generic and vague, whereas Late Archaic traits were close and specific. Webb suggested that general Hopewellian resemblances might have been assimilated through trade with midwestern peoples and that Poverty Point was essentially a Late Archaic culture. He doubted that Poverty Point sprang from an early Hopewell group that had come south picking up Archaic traits en route, telling Ford: "I am . . . not too strong in my convictions as to how P. P. [Poverty Point] acquired the Hopewell-Adena traits, or vice-versa, and maybe we just need more information." Ford wrote back, "[I] Don't see how a society that was not stratified and rather tightly organized could have produced those useless earthworks. . . . If so the guess follows that probably the bosses were Hopewellian and the underdogs local Archaics." Ford's version prevailed.

Gordon Willey, Ford's old friend who was then teaching at Harvard, objected. Claiming as Spaulding had before that Poverty Point was not a town but a succession of trash piles left by periodically convening mound builders, Willey likened Poverty Point to Hopewell or Adena sacred circles, which were presumed to be vacant ceremonial centers. But his Mesoamerican leanings led him to suggest that the impetus for Poverty Point came not from Hopewell but from south of the border down Mexico way.

Later, Willey recanted his vacant-center theory. He and Philip Phillips, in their influential culture-historical synthesis *Method and Theory in American Archaeology*, identified Poverty Point as a Formative development instead of an Archaic one because of its massive earthworks, implied large and stable population, and the prevailing belief that such achievements were possible only through corn agriculture. The assumed link between mound building and agriculture was so ingrained in archaeological thinking that investigation of Poverty Point's food base was actually suppressed for a long time.

On the question about whether Poverty Point was a vacant ceremonial center or a permanent town, opinions continued to be split. Ford and Webb got back into the thick of that argument, first semi-independently and then together. Armed with new data both from Webb's extensive inventory of Poverty Point sites and traits across the Gulf South and from Ford's inventory of Formative sites and traits in Central and South America, they proposed that Poverty Point arose when some Lower Mississippi Archaic groups got caught up in a burst of religious and agricultural reforms emanating from the heart of Olmec country in Vera Cruz. Webb and Ford were working on a new study detailing this proposal when Ford passed away in 1968.

After Ford and Webb

Such was the state of Poverty Point research when Webb asked me to help him analyze a large controlled surface collection, which he and local resident Carl Alexander had gathered from Poverty Point between 1968 and 1970. Our collaboration began in January 1970, neck-deep in a test pit that we had dug at Caney Mounds, a Late Archaic mound site far south of Poverty Point.

Back on January 24, 1970, when Dr. Webb and I had put in the test of midden and mettle at the Caney Mounds site, we had talked about the Poverty Point site and what needed to be done. Overzealous and full of Binford, Levi-Strauss, Jim Sciscenti, and the new archaeology, I proceeded to tell Dr. Webb . . . that what was really needed was a study of artifact distributions throughout the different parts of the earthworks. Such a study, I avowed, was the only way we would be able to truly understand the site. . . .

Patient and kind, he told me that he and Jim Ford had already thought of that back in the 1950s. They believed a distributional study might show if different parts of the earthworks had been used for different purposes and perhaps even reveal the building and occupational succession. Interesting, I thought, considering that was pre-Binford. They had already devised a labeling plan for artifact locations. . . . Not only that, but Webb told me that he and Carl

Alexander had, for several years now, been marking the artifacts they were surface-collecting by this sector and ridge system, and that tens of thousands of provenience-designated artifacts were at our disposal. (Jon Gibson, published in *Louisiana Archaeology*, 1992)

In April 1970, Webb wrote me: "I talked with Carl [Alexander] about doing a study of distribution, of the kind you and I had discussed. . . . I wished to find out whether you would like to participate in such study." I liked, and thus started our quarter-century-long collaboration on Poverty Point matters.

Webb used our findings to refine chronology and define intrasite activities. I used them to reconstruct social organization, which then was the current rage. I claimed Poverty Point was a chiefdom, mainland North America's first. I construed Poverty Point as the chiefdom's center and

Fig. 2.7. Carl Alexander allowed archaeologists to study his provenience-controlled collection. In 1970, Clarence Webb and Jon Gibson analyzed the collection on a makeshift lab table Carl set up under the pecan trees in the family graveyard beside the barn. Carl (shown here with a table full of PPOs) did the preliminary sorting while awaiting his weekend visitors. His sister, Mrs. Harry Rusk, ensured the visitors' weekly return with her delicious catback biscuits and thick, homemade cane syrup. To this day, I'm not sure whether the collection or the biscuits were main attraction. Rephotography by Steven Carricut.

Fig. 2.8. Carl Alexander's barnyard witnessed many visitors in 1970 when his collection was being analyzed. Here Clarence Webb (*far left*) and Jon Gibson (*second from left*) discuss raw-material identifications with Hiram "Pete" Gregory (*second from right*) and Sherwood "Woody" Gagliano (*far right*). Courtesy of Carl Alexander; rephotography by Steven Carricut.

envisioned dozens of smaller surrounding encampments as social and economic affiliates. I thought I had detected correlates for several chiefdom characteristics such as a large, sedentary, hierarchically organized population managed by a small chiefly elite; a surplus-producing economy and redistribution; and craft specialization. I argued that Poverty Point subsistence was based on hunting and gathering and that Poverty Point developed all by itself without Mesoamerican contact or stimulation. The chiefdom argument was pretty persuasive for a while.

Interpretation stalled here while new investigations got off the ground. Webb and Alexander had dug a few test pits in the northern and southern rings during the late 1960s, but otherwise Poverty Point had not felt the spade since Ford's last dig. State plans to turn Poverty Point into a com-

Fig. 2.9. Vivid, multicolored, basket-loaded fill was revealed in Poverty Point's largest mound during William Haag's excavations in 1976. Deborah Woodiel (*far left*), Clarence Webb (*crouching*), William Haag (*white T-shirt*), and Robert Neitzel (*far right*) discuss the stratigraphy and the surprising discovery that the mound was built over a filled-in depression. Photography by Bill Spencer; courtesy of Debbie Woodiel; rephotography by Steven Carricut.

memorative park prompted a new round of fieldwork in the early 1970s. Professor William Haag led the way, putting in four summer seasons between 1972 and 1975, digging areas where park buildings and roads were to be constructed. Carl Kuttruff, then affiliated with a community college in St. Louis, put in an icy winter season in 1972–73, digging test pits alongside one of Haag's excavations in the northern rings. Deborah

Woodiel of the Louisiana Office of State Parks tested additional park construction areas in 1978, mainly places where the laboratory, parking lot, and museum now stand. Other spots outside construction-mandated ones were tested in order to assist with museum and site-tour interpretation.

Everybody was looking for evidence of houses in order to prove Poverty Point was a big village. Ford and Webb contended that plowing had destroyed house remains, so not finding any was not proof positive that they had not existed. If plowing had not been responsible, then maybe archaeologists simply had not dug in the right place, maybe they had not uncovered a wide enough area, or maybe the Indians had used flimsy construction material that disappeared without trace. But finding a house, just one, or even a few lines of wall-post holes was tantamount to proving that Poverty Point had been a place of residence. One razed house was as good as a thousand, under the prevailing sentiment of the day. Besides, nobody except maybe a few vacant-center advocates believed that a place having so much construction really lacked substantial housing. Haag excavated what he thought were ruins of a thatched house, but it turned out to be a lens of burned cane. The large postmolds he found in

Fig. 2.10. Carl Kuttruff dug in the northern rings during the icy winter of 1972–73. Later, he joined Jon Gibson for several seasons of excavation in various parts of the rings. Here, he shaves the walls of a test pit for profiling during the 1993 field season.

the western plaza formed no recognizable patterns. Sharon Goad reported house patterns from the first northwestern ring, but Robert Connolly's reanalyis failed to confirm them. The 1970s and early 1980s came and went, and still convincing evidence of housing was lacking.

Haag contended that the large plaza postmolds were astronomical markers, and he and his physics colleague Kenneth Brecher claimed that the southwestern and northwestern aisles, which transected the rings, provided sightlines to solstice sunsets. They also pointed out that the southern aisle came pretty close to the setting position of Canopus, the second-brightest star in the sky. Robert Purrington, an astronomer from Tulane University, disputed these claims and proposed that Poverty Point's layout was simply geometrical, not stellar. Disagreement hinged on the location of the site's center, ostensibly the observation point. Both views used Clarence Webb's hand-drawn map traced from an aerial photograph. Many angles could be projected through the aisles on the drawing. Even if one of the small-scale engineered maps of the earthworks had been used, it would not have made any difference. The aisles were too wide and too difficult to follow on the ground to resolve the issue.

So, was Poverty Point astronomically aligned? I said so in a public talk I gave in 1984, perhaps with a little more assurance than was warranted. Afterwards, a Cherokee medicine woman in the audience suggested I might want to reconsider. She was convinced that Poverty Point's Old Ones would not have wanted their earthworks pointing to the west, the direction of death and evil. Her conviction lacked the weight of science, but when science had provided no answer, her belief backed by millennia of native tradition was pretty convincing.

Subsistence emerged as a hot topic in the 1970s and 1980s. Everybody wanted to find Poverty Point food remains in order to resolve the unsettled issue of agriculture, especially whether or not native seed plants had been grown. Starchy and oily seed plants had replaced maize as the most likely domesticates in theory. Kuttruff looked in vain, Woodiel found a few, but it was Prentice Thomas and Janice Campbell's investigations of various natural gas-injection well locations outside the rings that produced food remains in abundance. Zooarchaeologist Kathleen Byrd recognized fish, turtles, and small mammals as primary meat sources but identified no deer remains. Paleobotanist Andrea Shea found remains of hickory nuts, acorns, walnuts, pecans, persimmons, grapes, and pepo squash. She also identified rare doveweed, knotweed, and goosefoot seeds

Fig. 2.11. Jan Campbell and Prentice Thomas in 1978 conducted extensive excavations at several core encampments lying outside the rings. Their work resulted in the first substantial recovery of food remains from Poverty Point's core. Jan's nimble fingers transform facts and figures into narrative for their report, *The Peripheries of Poverty Point*. Courtesy of Jan Campbell.

and suggested that because of their small size they probably came from wild rather than cultivated varieties. She proposed that squash grew wild, but since the only pit that contained squash remains also contained later Coles Creek pottery, it was not possible to resolve the issue of Poverty Point horticulture. Despite continued uncertainty about horticulture, remains of foods finally had been identified, and they showed that Poverty Point's subsistence was based strictly on fishing, gathering, and hunting.

How exchange was conducted had been an unresolved issue ever since Webb first discussed the subject. In his master's thesis, Ted Brasher proposed that exchange involved a complex net of interregional interactions. Poverty Point, he said, was the ultimate or penultimate destination for dozens of circulating exotic stones, but other encampments along trade routes often had higher proportions of the rocks that moved along those particular routes than did Poverty Point. Trying to figure out where the exotic rocks came from was another area of concern. In his thesis, Thomas Conn used visual comparisons and identifications by experts to pinpoint exotic flint sources. Sourcing by means of elemental analyses was limited initially to soapstone and only later broadened to include galena, copper, magnetite, hematite, catlinite-like rock, obsidian, and Dover flint.

Brasher's findings led me to propose that Poverty Point exchange had been directional—that is, personage-controlled transfers between gateways, or outposts, and Poverty Point. Sandra Bass disputed the gateway model in her thesis: She doubted Poverty Point had been involved in any kind of exchange on the grounds that presumed exotic rocks had been collected from local gravel deposits. She was right about that. The rocks she identified were all used to make microliths, and they were almost always local Citronelle gravels.

In the mid-1970s, Clarence Webb synthesized available data on Poverty Point and on Poverty Point–like materials throughout the Lower Mississippi Valley and South in general. His synthesis was longer on data than interpretation, which says worlds about his science and personality. Webb always pinned his archaeology on data he could hold in his hands or see in the ground or add, subtract, multiply, and divide. He was an empiricist, tolerant of those who chose to offer interpretations based on little evidence but always cautious about accepting interpretive fads. Poverty Point archaeology was fortunate to have him as a stabilizing influence at the moment when culture history was giving way to culture process in archaeological thinking. But he was much more than just a timely physician looking after the health of Poverty Point archaeology: For many years, alone or with others, he was responsible for documenting Poverty Point archaeology. He equated Poverty Point culture with a generally coherent group of stylistically similar artifacts distributed throughout the Lower Mississippi Valley, but encampment-to-encampment variability bothered him and eventually led to his scheme for determining *definite, possible, and related* encampments. In historical perspective, his breakdown was a giant leap forward because it emphasized differences while everyone else was emphasizing similarities. To even acknowledge that differences existed was simply another indication of Webb's medical training, his reliance on data—on symptoms—to make diagnoses. He went along with my chiefdom model because at the time it was the handiest way to account for Poverty Point organization, but he was never comfortable with it.

As the 1970s came to a close, the chiefdom idea began to flounder. Why? Mainly because mainstream archaeology had detected signs of sedentism and cultural complexity in hunter-gatherer societies. Before, sedentism and complexity always had been regarded as attributes of agricultural chiefdoms. Discovering that these conditions occurred indepen-

Fig. 2.12. Sharon Goad oversees the excavation of five large blocks on the north-eastern end of the first northwestern ridge in 1982. Her digging exposed one of the largest contiguous areas in the rings. She unearthed numerous postmolds and hearths, but house patterns remained elusive.

dently of other chiefdom characteristics rendered the model unsatisfactory and made attempts to correlate archaeological situations with ethnographic archetypes essentially nonproductive. Archaeologist Jay Johnson was one of the first to question the idea when he discovered that exchange in the Yazoo swamp conformed to a simple falloff pattern rather than the complex directional pattern usually associated with chiefdom societies. But Johnson pointed out that just because Yazoo exchange was simple did not necessarily mean that exchange around Poverty Point was. Sharon Goad also opposed the chiefdom hypothesis. She maintained that the rather complete range of work tools and ornaments she recovered from a small section of one of the rings meant that occupational and social segregation typical of chiefdoms did not exist. Edwin Jackson applied the *coup de grâce* with his trade-fair proposal. He suggested that Poverty Point was a neutral campground where independent groups periodically met to trade and forge social and economic alliances.

I did not try to rescue the chiefdom hypothesis, staying quiet as it went under for the third time. By the early 1980s, Mitchell Hillman, Clarence

Webb, and I had become more interested in what appeared to be glitches in the architectural symmetry of the earthworks or in descriptions of them. We decided we needed to check out these glitches, many of which Hillman spotted during his daily rounds of the rings. With his urging and Webb's backing, the first season of this campaign to ground truth these features was launched in 1983. With help from Edwin Jackson and a geophysical company, I set up five permanent locational benchmarks by conventional ground survey and satellite translocation and had a new fifty-centimeter contour map of the rings produced by aerial photogrammetry. I spent that season plus seven more with University of Southwestern Louisiana field schools during the 1980s and 1990s investigating dozens of problematic architectural features throughout the earthworks. Field schools from the University of Akron, led by John Marwitt, joined us in 1985 and 1988, and Carl Kuttruff, Thurman Allen, and Arville Touchet lent a hand each season. Hillman also persuaded Glen Greene

Fig. 2.13. Jon Gibson cools off in the depths of one of his 1988 units excavated on the southeastern edge of the plaza near the end of the first southern ring. He spent eight excavation seasons at Poverty Point investigating the constructional and architectural makeup of the rings.

Fig. 2.14. Glen Greene
spent several field sea-
sons excavating and cor-
ing the northern portion
of Poverty Point rings
and plaza, primarily re-
cording the distribution
of fill dirt and undis-
turbed native soil. In
1991, he took a moment
to talk to a group of ar-
chaeology students about
his excavations on the
end of the first northern
ring.

and his field schools from Northeast Louisiana University to join the efforts in 1983 and 1991. A University of Alabama at Birmingham field
school, led by Roger Nance, helped Greene in 1991. Between field
schools, Greene put in three seasons in 1988, 1989, and 1990, systematically coring the northern half of the plaza and some of the northern ridges.
Hillman conducted an excavation off the edge of the plaza near the inside
southern ring. Civil engineer James Marshall did extensive transit survey-
ing on the earthworks between 1978 and 1985. His measurements, along
with others furnished by the Corps of Engineers, the state of Louisiana,
and me, provided the bases for a 1:6000 contour map.

When the dust from these tests settled, a lot had been learned about
soil, construction, architecture, and chronology and about time's ruinous
effect on the proud earthworks. But hard questions about organization or

Fig. 2.15. Mitchell Hillman was curator of the Poverty Point Commemorative Area opened by the state in the 1970s. He kept track of spots that needed excavation and usually managed to talk other archaeologists into investigating them. He carried out his own excavations off the southeastern edge of the plaza near the southern rings in 1985. Here, he demonstrates the use of darts and atlatl in 1983. Rephotography by Steven Carricut.

political economy were not even asked, much less answered. Poverty Point archaeology settled into a period of normal science, which is a polite way of saying that archaeologists stayed busy acquiring routine information they could manage in-house with little funding.

Edwin Jackson's 1981–82 excavations at the nearby Copes site resulted in the first really large-scale recovery of subsistence remains from a small, permanent swamp village on Poverty Point's periphery. He found that pecans and acorns were the primary foods, supplemented by persimmon, honey locust, wild bean, wild plum, portulaca, and a few wild seeds. Fish, deer, small mammals, turtles, waterfowl, snakes, and frogs provided meat. He concluded that Copes residents ate pretty well and that they exploited a fairly undisturbed swamp environment—one that had not been degraded because of its proximity to Poverty Point. To him, this indicated that Poverty Point must have had fewer residents than the thousands previously suggested by some estimates, or otherwise Copes occupants would have been forced to eat less desirable foods and far less venison.

Jackson's detailed food analyses and emphasis on site-to-site differences led to a fresh interpretation that Poverty Point was a place where independent groups came together seasonally to trade and then went their separate ways after the gathering. Sherwood Gagliano had offered a similar idea a quarter-century earlier, but it was abducted by reputed alien encounters, encounters of the Mesoamerican kind. But with Mesoamerican and chiefdom models falling into disrepute, Jackson's proposal won support.

On other fronts, researchers continued looking into exchange and mound building. Comparing amounts of exotic rocks with distances transported upheld earlier conclusions that Poverty Point was the major exchange enabler in its hinterland as well as lands to the south. Quantity comparisons showed that neither local nor regional exchange showed a simple falloff (or *distance-decay*) pattern. Function or more precisely activity intensity turned out to be a better gauge of how much exotic material wound up on a given encampment than did distances from either rock sources or Poverty Point. Johnson remained steadfast in his earlier view that exchange in Yazoo swamp was simpler than exchange around Poverty Point. Lehmann's graphic analysis of Yazoo swamp exchange revealed a heavy and continuous use of central Arkansas's Ouachita Mountain rocks but a fickle and generally diminishing use of midwestern materials through time. Marvin Jeter and Jackson asserted that exchange in southeastern Arkansas was ad hoc and subject to distance falloff. They also proposed that exchange around Poverty Point was of this unassuming nature.

The upshot of these studies was the perception that exchange was not one big unified system controlled or administered from Poverty Point but was instead a variable and changing web of intergroup relations that spanned large physical and social distances in order to get high-quality rock into the hands of the general populace. Large numbers of common tools or tool materials were exchanged, not just prestige objects or goods. Poverty Point stone exchange did not benefit elites alone even though prime movers undoubtedly gained social standing. Social importance and exchange operations probably were directly linked, but elites did not keep all the exotic rocks for themselves. Exchange benefited everybody directly. Poverty Point exchange made high-quality foreign rock and local gravel available to those who needed them most.

Although understanding of Poverty Point's architecture and construction grew by leaps and bounds, it was chronological and functional details that gained the most attention in the 1990s. Investigations by Joe Saunders and his associates at Hedgepeth, Frenchman's Bend, Watson Brake, and other Middle and early Late Archaic mounds in northeast Louisiana, as well as by other mound investigators elsewhere in the Lower Mississippi Valley, proved that earthworks had been built since early in the fifth millennium B.C. Poverty Point's earthworks no longer shouldered the burden of being the largest *and the earliest* earthen buildings erected by Archaic peoples; they turned out to be only the largest. Just knowing that mounds had been built before Poverty Point made its earthworks less precocious. Lower Jackson Mound, long assumed to be part of Poverty Point's overall layout, probably was erected hundreds, if not thousands, of years before the rings. It provides a precedent on Poverty Point's own grounds.

But why build earthworks? Poverty Point's mounds were not primarily tombs or temple bases. Ford and Webb suggested that the rings were house foundations, an interpretation supported by dark middens lining their lower fore and aft slopes. But *how* rings and mounds were used and *why* they were built were separate questions requiring different answers. Poverty Point's biggest conical mound, Mound B, did not contain burials, although it was raised over the ashes of a huge bonfire, which had consumed at least one person. Probes and test pits in the two giant bird mounds failed to turn up either burials or house patterns. Postmold patterns were found on several building stages in Dunbar Mound, one of the three platform mounds. Although often idealized as either burial or temple mounds, they were actually used for many purposes, and geometric constructions were something altogether different.

I proposed that Poverty Point's earthworks comprised a vast security system, an invisible shield protecting the social and political heart of its folk. Native oral tradition contains allusions to mounds as metaphors of cosmos and creation. It contains inherent references to the ability of encirclements, or "broken circles," to guard against dark forces and evil spirits lurking on the outside. It implicitly testifies to the power of symmetry and alignment as barriers against those same supernatural forces. In short, it looked to me like Poverty Point's inhabitants had turned to architectural magic in order to ensure safety against malevolent supernatural forces and spirits, and the scale on which they laid out their magic indicated how fearful they had become, showed how much protection they felt they needed. That the massive security system was installed at the same historical moment that long-distance exchange intensified suggests that exchange was a major source of up-welling fear and stress.

In 1995, the state established a regional archaeologist position at Poverty Point, and Bob Connolly was appointed. He set to work testing several spots slated for park improvements and cleaning up around fallen trees, using his findings to check for horizontal differences in the rings. He also took floral remains from soil samples taken during Goad's 1980–82 work and had them identified. Analyst Heather Ward found that nuts and acorns were the most common remains, identified in up to 80 percent of the samples. Cane, persimmon, cucurbit, and little barley were recognized in fewer than half the samples, and goosefoot, spurge, and maygrass also were present. She suspected the cucurbits were probably wild gourds and not cultivated squash and that little barley was probably wild, too. Remains were too skimpy to settle the question of whether or not Poverty Point people cultivated native starchy and oily seed plants. Even if they did, they never gave up their fondness for nuts and acorns, and these staples suggested that Poverty Point plant foods were provided largely, if not wholly, by collecting. Anyway, the question of cultivation was always of more interest to archaeologists than it ever was to the inhabitants of the rings.

Investigations had continued at other core and periphery components ever since Webb dutifully started recording private collections in the 1960s. During the 1980s and 1990s, local farmers and friends found, surface-collected, and reported many periphery encampments. Mitchell Hillman, Dennis LaBatt, David Griffing, Irving Arledge, Orvis Scott, Stanley Morgan, Henry Hendrix, Terral Lewis, J. W. Copes, Francis Thompson, and Mark Fox all helped in data recording. T. R. Kidder's survey and testing of sites in the Boeuf Basin, well west of the peripheries of Poverty Point, disclosed other encampments bearing general and specific resemblances to Poverty Point. Kidder proposed that the Boeuf River encampment cluster and other nearby clusters exhibited a hierarchical settlement pattern—large important places ranging down to small unimportant ones—but he doubted that any of them fell under Poverty Point's political jurisdiction.

Only two periphery components were excavated after George Beyer's digging at Insley in 1900 and Hiram Gregory and associates' excavations at Terral Lewis in 1966–67. Jackson's Copes dig was the most extensive. In 1992, I tested another, Orvis Scott, a small encampment on Joes Bayou only three miles southeast of Poverty Point. Its stonework showed signs of having been intensively conserved, suggesting that tools were hard to re-place—a circumstance I attributed to shortfalls created by ongoing con-struction at Poverty Point. In addition to these digs, David Griffing moni-tored land-leveling at another periphery site, Insley, making extensive surface collections and inventorying a rich trove loosed from overturned midden.

Core components—those lying within two and a half miles of the rings—attracted little attention after Prentice Thomas and Janice Camp-bell's investigations in 1978. Dennis LaBatt faithfully monitored a couple of encampments after spring plowing each year, but generally landowners kept people out of their fields. In 1992, a two-mile-long strip immediately south of the rings changed hands, and the Farmers Home Administration required that a cultural resource investigation be undertaken. I performed the search and discovered four core encampments and nine isolated Pov-erty Point artifacts. Adding these and previously reported locations made a total of twenty-five core encampments and isolated finds less than two and a half miles from Poverty Point's outermost ring—a substantial num-ber considering how spotty intensive search has been.

No encampments or isolated finds were recorded between two and a half and four miles or so beyond the rings. While sampling may be respon-sible for the gap, many encampments were found more than four miles from the rings, particularly along Maçon Ridge bluff, Joes Bayou, and small creeks in the West Swamp (a poorly drained section of Maçon Ridge a morning's walk west of Poverty Point). Core encampments were scat-tered outside the rings in all directions except east off the bluff. Other than a light scatter of plummets, points, and other tools, and a low artificial ridge found directly across Bayou Maçon from the rings, I am unaware of other Poverty Point encampments in the swamp between Maçon Ridge bluff and the high meander-belt ridge occupied by Joes Bayou. Incomplete sampling might be blamed except that Robert Pace and a student crew from Indiana State University searched an old crevasse ridge connecting Maçon Ridge and Joes Bayou ridge in the winter of 1983–84 and found no Poverty Point encampments. The crevasse ridge was the highest land in the swamp close to Poverty Point, which would have made it attractive and easily accessible to campers and workers. That Pace found no Poverty Point camps suggested either that the ridge was unsuitable for utilization or that there really was a gap between the Maçon Ridge and Joes Bayou encampments. Artifacts recovered by Pace show that the ridge was already in existence by Poverty Point times. Whatever the case, I use the gap to separate core from periphery encampments.

Poverty Point has attracted archaeological interest since first investigated in 1873. Still, less than three-tenths of 1 percent of the ringed enclosure has been excavated, and only a handful of the three-score core and periphery encampments have received more than passing attention. While having so few facts has made speculation easier, it has made it harder to figure out just what transpired at Poverty Point. As archaeological practice has changed over the past half-century, so have interpretations. From being envisioned as a victim of Hopewell conquest or a precocious chiefdom to an occasionally used fairgrounds or a corporately organized hunter-gatherer residence, changing interpretations have simply mirrored archaeology's shift from culture-historical to culture-processual and postprocessual interests.

But no matter how many versions of Poverty Point's basic nature have been or ever will be proposed, there is but one reality, only one correct interpretation. All other versions will prove to have been wrong. Archaeology will continue to be driven by the quest for truth, although it is doubtful that it ever will know whether or not it finds the truth. The interpretations that follow are presented in the spirit of that quest.

3

Roots

"Yokni Chishinto"

It [the mound] was raised and made level as high as a man's head and beat down very hard . . . women and children and all the men, except the hunters, carried earth continually . . . constituting a mound half as high as the tallest tree.

The work was not yet completed. Yet it was sufficiently so to allow them to suspend operations for a season. . . . The people must now scatter into the forests and collect the rich autumnal fruits which were showering down from every tree. That done, the people must return to the encampment. . . .

Then . . . the nation could again prosecute the work on the mound, and so on, from year to year. . . .

Then having nothing else to be working at, a thoughtful old man, pointing to the great unfinished mound (*Yokni Chishinto*), said, "the weather is cool and pleasant, and the grave of your dead kindred is only half as high as a tall tree." Taking the timely suggestion of the man, thousands went to work, carrying dirt to the great mound. Afterwards, it became an honorable thing to carry and deposit earth on the mound at any time they were not engaged in their domestic pursuits.

. . . [T]he work on the mound was regularly prosecuted; and at the eighth green corn dance celebrated at Nunih Waya, the committee who had been appointed at the commencement, reported to the assembled multitude that the work was completed and the mound planted with the seeds of the forest trees in accordance with the plan and direction of the minko at the beginning of the work.

The minko then instructed the good old Lopina, who had carried it so many years to take the golden sun to the top of the great mound and plant it in the center of the level top.

Gideon Lincecum, in *Publications of the Mississippi Historical Society*, 1904

Centuries of Experience

Native people first came to Maçon Ridge more than 11,000 years ago and disappeared after the arrival of the white man in the eighteenth century. Poverty Point people inherited centuries and centuries of social and economic experience. Many Poverty Point customs, styles, and ideas were not new but passed down. Even earthwork construction was an old vocation, although its scale was unprecedented. Poverty Point's forefathers had carved stone ornaments, but not as many as their descendants. Their forefathers had cooked with hot rocks; their descendants with hot löess balls—same principle, different materials, except that hand-shaped löess balls helped regulate cooking-pit temperature as well. Forefathers used a few quartz crystals and points made of novaculite from the Ouachita Mountains, but their descendants used exotic rock from dozens of far-off places. Old-time exchange was like a trickle before a floodtide. Poverty Point people clung tenaciously to old stories about creation and how things came to be. The stories were their literature, told around flickering campfires on cold dreary evenings. Their stories were preserved metaphorically in silt loam and clay. Rings and mounds were not representations of a new foreign ideology but an old worldview built to glorify the past, protect the present, and ensure the future.

Styles set off Poverty Point material culture from preceding material culture. Motley points, cross-grooved cooking balls, and the fox-man design were pure, unadulterated Poverty Point styles, and so were dozens and dozens of other forms and renderings. Unique stylistic and technological changes made Poverty Point so different from preceding and neighboring cultures that modern stories about it having dropped in from a foreign land, lost continent, or distant planet gained favor in some circles. Yet the greatest difference among Poverty Point people, their neighbors, and their ancestors was in how they organized themselves.

So much of Poverty Point culture came from the Old Ones that telling what was new and different from what was old and traditional requires a close look. Poverty Point culture may have been born in the löess of Maçon Ridge, but its pedigree came from the lives that came before.

Clovis, the First Old Ones

The first Old Ones were Paleoindians, only a few generations removed from Mongolian immigrants. Their grandfathers had made the crossing to America braving frigid waters in skin-covered canoes or trudging across Beringia, a wind-swept isthmus of ice and tundra that joined Siberia and Alaska when sea level dropped. And that happened several times during the Ice Age, when continent-wide ice fields crunched slowly, incessantly southward. Maçon Ridge and the Mississippi Valley were different places then.

The Mississippi River was more than a stream. It was an event, an event that shaped every aspect of these pioneers' lives. When the great ice sheet started melting for the final time, sometime between 12,000 and 11,000 years ago, the river angrily accepted the slush carrying three to five times its usual summer discharge. Cataracts and falls dotted its canyonlike upper reaches. In its lower reaches below present-day Memphis, muddy waters slowed and spread out over a much larger expanse of land dropping their heavy load of glacial outwash gravel, sand, and silt, and branching into many separate but interconnected channels. During winter, the river froze, exposing its nakedness to howling north winds. Enormous dust storms raged, expending their fury along the river bed and blowing themselves out within a two- or three-day walk beyond the scoured bed. During summer thaw, the river went on a wall-to-wall rampage, bent on washing away as much of the midcontinent as possible.

But Maçon Ridge remained high and dry during the worst floods, affording refuge for man and beast, while the torrent raged only yards away. Winter dust clouds settled out as soon as they crossed the bluff-lined eastern edge of Maçon Ridge. A blanket of löess one to two stories thick formed along the bluff but thinned and gradually disappeared some fifteen to twenty miles westward. Vegetation in the löess belt was parklike with waving meadows interspersed with fluttering gum-oak-hickory woods. The western side of Maçon Ridge beyond the löess was heavily forested. So was the floodplain off both sides of the ridge—at least, where trees had not been uprooted and strewn about by the furious waters. Mammoth, mastodon, big-horned bison, ground sloth, tapir, and other now-extinct animals roamed the land. Archaeologist Paul Martin and other investigators blamed Paleoindians for the extinction of many of these animals, claiming that hunters killed them faster than they were able to reproduce. But evidence of overkill was lacking in the Lower Mississippi Valley, as was direct evidence that Paleoindians had even hunted the beasts. Climate was warming quickly, and although ice readvances periodically stalled the warming, the continental ice sheet thinned and broke up, permitting cold Arctic air to reach Maçon Ridge and other parts of the South. Four seasons replaced the long winter/short summer cycle, bringing rapid and widespread changes in forest makeup. Many big animals simply could not reproduce quickly enough to keep pace with the tumultuous remaking of their pastures and browsing lots and died without a single spear ever being thrown at them.

The first Paleoindians on Maçon Ridge were wandering bands of Clovis people, their passage marked by a few lost spearheads characterized by lance-shaped bodies, concave bases, fluted faces, and ground edges. Clovis points were the ultimate utility tool, used for just about every imaginable job in addition to killing game. If Maçon Ridge knappers made scrapers, knives, awls, and other tools like their cousins did out West or elsewhere in the East, they have not been identified as Clovis handicrafts. Not even flakes resulting from point making have been recognized. Perhaps, they were buried by dust and mud or simply sank into the löess as it weathered. The land trod by Clovis hunter-gatherers was buried under several feet of löess along the Maçon Ridge front. Almost one-third of the Clovis points Hillman recorded from Maçon Ridge were found in the wind shadow of an ancient hill, which had diverted the biting dust clouds. The remaining two-thirds came from West Swamp, where dust failed to reach.

But even if time and nature had not hidden evidence of their presence, Clovis peoples' land tenure would have. Always on the move, never staying in one place for long, and traveling light meant that their campgrounds did not get strewn as much as those of later less-mobile groups. The wide scatter of their points and the lack of other residue vouched for constant wide-ranging movements. The Clovis way of life lasted for 200 to 300 years, long enough for a trail of lost or discarded broken points to map the relentless march through the wilderness. Camp debris never had time to accumulate, but point losses mounted as first one group and then another passed over the same area.

Completely surrounded by lowlands but above high-water level, Maçon Ridge offered near-perfect living conditions. Game populations were swollen for several months each year by swamp animals driven onto high ground by the fury of the waters, creating a hunter's paradise, at least temporarily. Fish, turtles, snakes, and frogs abounded in the swamp. Upland woods were overrun with running, hopping, climbing, crawling, slithering goodies to eat. Nuts, acorns, seeds, roots, and other plant foods grew in profusion. Although direct evidence of foods is lacking, Maçon Ridge Clovis hunter-gatherers probably ate some of practically everything edible when in season. Simplicity, practicality, and fluidity shaped their economy and sharpened their palates; if they could not find enough to eat in one place, they went on to another and then another until they filled their bellies. They moved where they wanted, when they wanted. Land was open and free, and the horizon beckoned. Nothing stood in their way except the great river, the mighty Mississippi.

Generally, Clovis bands did not grow attached to particular territories, but Maçon Ridge was an exceptional place. It was rich in food for most of the year, super-rich for the remainder. Its bands did not need to move around as much as peoples passing through poorer lands in order to consume equal calories. Its physical prominence made it a landmark and offered flood protection as well. These assets not only attracted mobile hunter-gatherers and kept them well fed, but having a more or less permanent population (although not necessarily the same population) acted like a magnet. Finding mates always was chancy for people who spent their entire lives on the move. The buildup of population on Maçon Ridge ensured that everybody knew where to come courting, even folk who were just passing through. Although never crowded, the long narrow landform concentrated movements, making it easier for people to find one another.

Maçon Ridge was the land of opportunity. It had everything an enterprising Paleoindian could want: dry sleeping furs, plenty of food, and mates. Well, there was one thing it did not have—rock. It had no rock. All rock had to be carried in. Mitchell Hillman found that more than half of the Clovis points from the Poverty Point vicinity were made from

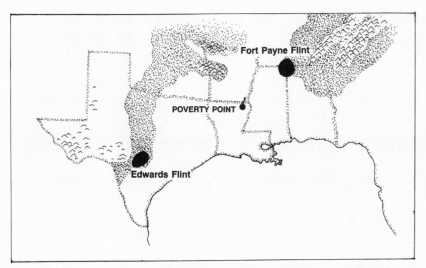

Map 3.1. The distance to Edwards flint outcrops in Texas was nearly twice as great as to Fort Payne flint deposits in Mississippi, Alabama, and Tennessee. Nonetheless, Clovis points from Maçon Ridge predominantly were made from Edwards flint. Did the rampaging Ice Age Mississippi River prevent Paleoindians from using the nearest high-quality flint, or was this merely a reflection of what direction Clovis nomads had come from when moving onto Maçon Ridge?

Edwards chert, which outcropped in the hill country of south central Texas some 500 miles southwest of Poverty Point, and from white rock probably from Oklahoma or Missouri. In a distributional study, Sherwood Gagliano and Hiram Gregory found that three out of four Clovis points throughout the entire state of Louisiana were made from exotic stone, usually Edwards chert. In a similar distributional study, Sam McGahey reported that most Mississippi Clovis points were also made of exotic rock, such as Dover, Fort Payne, and other gray flints. Yet there was a big difference from one side of the Mississippi River to the other. West of the river, rock came mainly from Texas; east of the river, it came from sources that outcropped on that side of the river. Local gravels were used more often as the Mississippi River neared the Gulf of Mexico.

Maçon Ridge Clovis people used Texas flint even though it had to be brought from twice as far away as Fort Payne flint, probably because having a wild and unruly river between them and Fort Payne supplies put a damper on using the closest bedrock. The river was nearly impassable. Crossings were feasible only in the dead of winter, when ice water trickled down its branching arms. But the peril of frozen feet or drowning and the sting of yellow-brown blizzards was enough to make even the hardiest adventurers stay in their tents warming before a cozy fire. During the warm season, floods made fording impossible and boat crossings treacherous. The Mississippi River was a physical barrier some of the time and an economic and social boundary all the time.

So how did Edwards flint wind up on Maçon Ridge? Did wide-ranging foragers go all the way to Texas hill country during their seasonal round? No, hill country was over 500 miles distant—too far away for a yearly migration to reach, even though high-quality flint beckoned. Besides, there undoubtedly were several Clovis bands using the land in between, and the unspoken law of the forager was not to trespass on another's grounds, eat his food, or cause bodily harm. Encounters were probably pleasant affairs or were avoided altogether. Also, Maçon Ridge and Texas were about as different as daylight and dark—too ecologically diverse for the same people to manage economically. Low population densities everywhere ruled out trade as a dependable means of getting Edwards chert to Maçon Ridge hunter-gatherers, especially for such a basic resource. Some rock possibly passed through cascading mating networks as bride compensation or gifts between bands loosely joined by matrimony. But to me, the most likely explanation is the simplest: that Edwards chert simply was carried in by one group of migrants and then another as they headed toward the rising sun. It meant that Maçon Ridge groups came mainly from Texas or Oklahoma or descended from ancient Texans or Oklahomans and that when their shiny flint tools wore out or got lost, knappers resorted to local brown gravels. Clovis people were never very numerous, but since Clovis tradition persisted for some 200 or 300 years or more, it afforded more than ample time for an archaeological presence to build up in an area, even though any one band lost or threw away only a few points and carried their other tools into oblivion with them.

The end of the Clovis tradition coincides with a brief return of cold climate, the extinction of large Ice Age mammals, and the completion of continentwide colonization. By 10,900 years ago, Clovis nomads had explored America from sea to shining sea and moss-covered tundra to moss-draped swamp. They did not fill up the land—their numbers were lost in its vastness—but their presence was felt. The never-ending search for food and mates made sure of that. Still, as people swept across the land, big migratory pushes gave way to smaller ones. Some bands chose to remain in especially productive locales, some were forced to stop in poorer terrains by wild rivers and shorelines, and a few lucky ones like the Maçon Ridge nomads got stalled in a land of milk and honey. As Clovis people calmed their wanderlust and settled down, they changed the way they used the land, and their tools showed it.

Dalton and Late Clovis Traditions

Clovis tradition did not end everywhere at the same time. Migrants at the front of the still-advancing population wave kept the old tradition alive. They made their sleek spear points in the old style, although the further they traveled, the freer that style became. By the time they reached sunny Florida, they often fashioned points with waisted bodies, deeply indented bases, long ears, and more than one flute or sometimes no flute whatsoever—all departures from classic Clovis style.

New migrants and daughter bands fell in behind the Clovis vanguard. Generally, they followed the same trails and foraged across the same old grounds, but they also explored pockets of land bypassed or underused by previous generations. They did not completely settle down, but many groups began to restrict their rounds, moving only as often and as far as necessary in order to wrest a living from the land. Movements were more like shifting than resettling. On Maçon Ridge and elsewhere in the Lower Mississippi Valley, these revamped ways of life were called Dalton culture and the persistence of these ways became the Dalton tradition.

The Dalton tradition appeared around 10,500 years ago, or possibly a century or two earlier, and lasted until 10,200 years ago or slightly later. The important thing to remember is that Dalton tradition was already under way in lands vacated by Clovis nomads, while Clovis tradition was still thriving on the ever-widening migration front and in some cul-de-sacs.

Dalton people used the land differently from their Clovis forebears. They made some equipment changes, but perhaps the biggest adjustment was to having neighbors. No, the land was not crowded. There were still huge tracts where nobody lived or hunted, and population densities everywhere probably were lower than when the Clovis wave pushed through. Nevertheless, if Dalton bands ranged far enough in any direction, they would have encountered other bands. They no longer could go where they pleased, whenever they pleased, and as far as they pleased, and sometimes

Fig. 3.1. Paleoindian points from the Poverty Point vicinity are numerous. The top row consists of two Dalton Y-drills (*left and middle*) and a Dalton point. Two more Dalton points make up the middle row. Another Dalton point (*left*) and two Clovis points comprise the bottom row. The Clovis point on the bottom right is 2.8 inches long. Photography by Steven Carricut.

they wound up making their living on terrains that did not offer nature's best.

Maçon Ridge was blessed and cursed. It had enough food for an army but lacked even one small stone. After waves of migrants stopped coming in and ridge dwellers found themselves caught between a big river and encircling groups, they had little choice but to make do with what was at hand. They turned to Citronelle gravels obtained from deposits in the hills some thirty-five to fifty miles west of Maçon Ridge.

Technology adapted to chert gravel without missing a beat. Gravels compromised neither style nor size of projectile points, which were quite similar to those of their neighbors who had settled close to Ouachita and Ozark mountain bedrocks. In fact, converting to gravel boosted economy because Dalton knappers had an abundant, easily accessible raw material that they could use to make all kinds of tools. They no longer had to use projectile points for every job or be so careful about breaking or losing tools. Some archaeologists claim that using Citronelle gravel limited tool sizes. That probably was the reason why specialized tools were small, but it had nothing to do with how big points were. There were plenty of big rocks in stream beds, and if they were hard to find when waters were on the rampage (cold conditions made a brief but spectacular return everywhere during Dalton times), then deposits up in the hills lay above the flood. Any old rock was suitable for small tools, and a few bigger ones were selected for points.

One of the main technical differences between Clovis and Dalton points stemmed from the way they were mounted, used, and resharpened. Both were used primarily as spearheads, although wear marks indicate they also doubled as knives, scrapers, and other tools. Upon leaving knappers' hands, Clovis and initial-stage Dalton points looked a lot alike, but when they broke down, so did their similarities. Dull or broken Clovis points were resharpened on the tip end while still attached to the shaft. Dalton points also were repaired while in the shaft, but instead of just being repointed, they ordinarily were resharpened along both sides. This procedure resulted in steep bevels and triangular bodies and, if carried a step further, created rounded edges and Y-shaped bodies, the Dalton drill. Repeated resharpening of Clovis points left them shorter. Repeated resharpening of Dalton points changed their entire shape.

Dalton tools were recycled to help conserve stone and enhance efficiency, but making smaller tools was also another means of making stone go a long way. Dalton knappers fashioned a variety of small flake tools such as endscrapers, sidescrapers, gravers, spokeshaves, and other edge-retouched implements. They also used flakes without further modification. Abraders and pebble hammerstones were employed, and chipped adzes were common.

Clovis and Dalton tool kits on Maçon Ridge were as different as the lifeways that gave rise to them. Clovis kits were made up almost exclusively of points, and nearly all finds consisted of solitary points. Three Clovis points were found at Poverty Point, making it the most productive location on Maçon Ridge. Other tools were carried away by their bearers to be lost here and there. Only at quarries did Clovis tools occur in reasonable numbers, and Maçon Ridge had no quarries. On the other hand, Dalton kits contained tools other than points, which suggests that knappers found favor in local gravels and that Lower Mississippi colonization essentially was finished.

On Maçon Ridge, Dalton peoples struck an acceptable compromise, giving up high-quality flint for high-quality food. They managed well with tools made from local gravel. After all, venison tasted the same no matter whether deer were killed with a dull brown or shiny gray spearhead. Dalton bands lived off the land and were not overly particular about what they ate. The aroma of parching nuts and acorns, steaming persimmons, stewing fish and turtles, baking turkeys and other small birds, roasting small game and deer, and other foods wafted on the smoke from their cooking fires. The short-lived blast of Arctic cold that set back the general warming trend at the end of Dalton times helped rather than hurt economy. It dropped sea level, which in turn caused widespread erosion in the uplands along the Mississippi Valley. Erosion created copious edge habitat. The edge effect enhanced natural bounty and boosted foraging conditions, especially since cool showers kept Maçon Ridge and nearby hills well watered. Dalton population responded by growing and expanding.

Dalton tradition was clearly derived from Clovis tradition. Stone-working techniques were similar. So were tools, but tool kits differed, reflecting widespread fleeting use of the land by mobile Clovis groups and more-intensive, prolonged land use by more-settled Dalton peoples. Two things stand out about Dalton equipment: One was the wise and proficient use of stone, and the other was the light and easy-to-carry tool design. Both were accommodations to mobility, and Dalton groups did continue to move around, though not as often or as far as Clovis groups, especially the earliest ones. The earliest Clovis groups were true nomads, rarely foraging across the same territory twice. Dalton bands moved around within set territories, each band having its own. It is likely that Dalton grandchildren lived on the same land as their grandfathers. The same cannot be said for Clovis. Dalton people had familiar places they called home. Clovis people had familiar faces they called home.

Archaeological opinions about Dalton land tenure differed, and for good reason. Land use in one place was not the same as in the next. In his study of Paleoindian settlement patterns around Poverty Point, Mitchell Hillman proposed that logistical mobility was the order of the day and that residential base camps, field camps, and isolated stands were established to take advantage of local conditions. Field camps outnumbered residential bases by about five to one.

Dalton knappers came up with new means for repairing stone tools, an adaptation to settling down and using local rocks regardless of quality or abundance. With mobility curtailed, high-quality stone resources lost their primacy in dictating peoples' movement. Clovis people collected food along treks between high-quality bedrock outcrops. Dalton people collected rocks, whatever the quality, along treks between food patches.

San Patrice Tradition

Joel Gunn, an expert on ancient climates, maintained that persistent drought baked the land for a century or two around 9,900 years ago. Uplands dried out the most, making Maçon Ridge more attractive than ever because the nearby Mississippi River was running swift and full with the last glacial-melt water. The river was throwing a new tantrum, writhing across the floodplain, first one side and then the other and sometimes down the middle, dividing and then reuniting its waters, venting its ugly mud-brown rage in spring, and then, as if in apology, putting on a gentle, pretty green face in summer. Still, for all its changing, the river was a constant force for all who lived along it. Its water sustained life; its overflow renewed it. As long as people didn't try to cross it, the river was their lifeline.

San Patrice tradition developed out of Dalton and persisted for a little while, probably for a century or two around 10,000 years ago. The subtle transformation entailed the kind of changes that affect neighbors who share genealogy and history. In fact, Dalton and San Patrice material culture was similar enough to be regarded as early and late parts of the same technological and stylistic tradition.

On Maçon Ridge, San Patrice culture continued the settling-down trend Dalton launched. Although Hillman found more Dalton encampments than San Patrice camps, he discovered that there were about twice as many San Patrice residences as there were Dalton residences and that they contained about one and a half times more tools than Dalton; both conditions can be hailed as signs of decreasing mobility. San Patrice encampments were equally divided between eastern and western sections of Maçon Ridge, whereas Dalton camps, especially residences, were more prevalent in the better-watered, löess-free West Swamp west of Poverty Point.

San Patrice tool kits contained essentially the same gear as Dalton, and tools looked alike, too. Except for points and beveled bifaces, which David Griffing called "Hillman knives," tools were small and made from flakes or flat pebbles. They included endscrapers, sidescrapers, gravers, notches, spokeshaves, and edge-retouched and -nibbled pieces in various combinations. Griffing found that residential encampments as well as some large field camps contained the entire suite of tools. Three or possibly four projectile-point styles were made: Hope, St. Johns, Keithville, and Cache River. Points generally were smaller than Dalton points. Hopes looked like little Daltons, while St. John points had shallow side notches just above the base. Keithville points were corner-notched but were chipped in a manner like other varieties. Cache River points occurred at about one-fourth of the San Patrice encampments, but no encampment yielded Cache Rivers exclusively or predominantly. Dan and Phyllis Morse suggested that Cache River points were between 5,000 amd 6,000 years old, possibly a little older, but Maçon Ridge associations indicate they were around 10,000 years old. Mitchell Hillman was probably right when he claimed that encampments bearing both San Patrice and Cache River points were more recent than pure San Patrice encampments, although surely only decades and not centuries had elapsed.

Including Cache Rivers in San Patrice assemblages or actually including Hopes, St. Johns, Keithvilles, and Cache Rivers in the same assemblages casts doubt on conventional belief, which holds that each cultural tradition had one and only one point style. That bit of logic was always a product of typological thinking, not of ancient technologies. Points al-

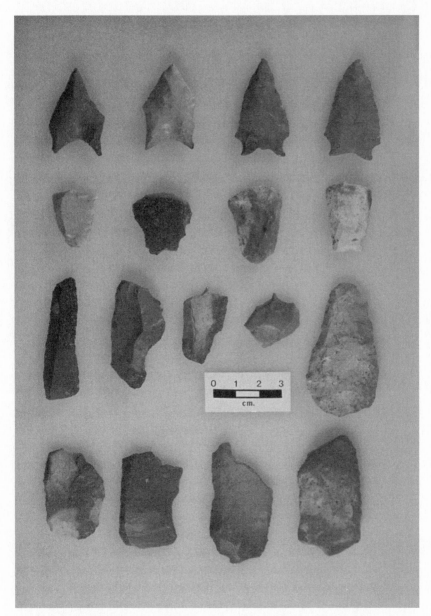

Fig. 3.2. Epipaleoindian San Patrice points and tools are almost as common in the Poverty Point vicinity as earlier Paleoindian materials. The top row consists of San Patrice points (the two on the left are Hope varieties, the two on the right are St. Johns varieties). The second row consists of flake end scrapers. Side scrapers, perforators, and a bifacial Hillman knife (*far right*) make up the third row. The bottom row consists of multiple-edge scrapers, some bearing notches and becs (or projections). The point at the upper right is 1.8 inches long. Photography by Steven Carricut.

Fig. 3.3. Other Epipaleoindian points occur around Poverty Point. The three bottom points are Hardins, as is the first point in the middle row (*far left*). The specimen on the far right of the middle row is a Keithville point. The remainder of the points are Cache Rivers. The Hardin point at the lower left is 2.2 inches long. Photography by Steven Carricut.

ways differed, even those placed in a single type. Why? Because archaeologists emphasized a few general similarities and ignored the differences.

But what did having four distinctive point styles reveal about San Patrice people living on Maçon Ridge, especially when those styles had largely separate geographical distributions but intertwined history? Hope, St. John, and Keithville points were homemade styles, native to Maçon Ridge and much of northern Louisiana. Cache River points, on the other hand, reached their popularity peak in northern Arkansas. Hillman concluded that intermixture resulted from incursions of northern Arkansas people or ideas. Seeking mates would have encouraged incursions. But whatever the reason, what I want to emphasize is that Cache Rivers and the other three styles arose in separate areas, a result of fierce social independence that came from a compelling sense of home and territory. Although they intermarried, San Patrice bands spent most of their lives apart living and dying near where they were born. Wandering Clovis bands simply pressed on when they felt the urge. Wandering did not promote artistic expression, and frequent travel would have made it nearly impossible for point styles with distinctive histories to appear together as often as they did in San Patrice tool kits. A wife here, a husband there, an idea picked up along the way simply did not embellish Clovis material culture as much as San Patrice.

Early Archaic

Drought broke after several centuries, and the final surge of ice water drained from the Mississippi Valley. For perhaps 2,000 years, from roughly 9,500 to 7,500 years ago, conditions anticipated today's but geography differed. The floodplain floor was many feet lower. The river swung back and forth across these lowlands, although later scouring and alluviation erased traces of those swings.

Evidence of land use has been covered, washed away, or simply unrecognized. Yet hindsight leads archaeologists to suspect that Early Archaic groups followed the footsteps of their San Patrice ancestors. Projectile-point styles undoubtedly proliferated but did not spread far. In fact, no Archaic point form ever reached as widely as San Patrice or Paleoindian forms. Whatever points replaced Hopes, St. Johns, and Keithvilles did so less ambitiously, suggesting that the number of bands was increasing but the size of their territories was decreasing. The Mississippi River continued to be a boundary, although the original reason was no longer quite as important since local groups had all turned to using local rocks. Landscape-challenged economics still shaped regional raw-material supplies, but the Mississippi River had become more of a social boundary, a crucial shift toward achieving the geopolitical importance fate had reserved for it.

Middle Archaic

Around 7,500 years ago, climate turned warmer and drier for a while—a long while, probably three or four millennia. Since climate is only a trend, localized and short-term effects varied widely. On Maçon Ridge, woods probably shrank and meadows spread. Swampland off the ridge probably expanded because sea level rose fifty feet, quickly choking the floodplain with sediment and making the river wander around more. The clogged-up valley made it difficult for the river to follow a single course, so it sometimes sent its water down one course and sometimes down two or more.

Technological and organizational adjustments were made everywhere. Social consequences of territorialism kept intensifying. A bewildering array of projectile points was made: big ones and little ones, side-notched, corner-notched, base-notched, unnotched, and stemmed ones. Some even sported extra notches below the first set. Why so many? For one thing, territorialism kept styles from spreading very far. Each little territory came up with its own. For another, small flake tools were on their way out (if not gone already), and points reassumed duties that would have made Ginsu-knife makers envious. Woodworking and nut-pounding gear became more common, and a few polished-stone ornaments were fashioned. No grand economic or technological revolution swept over the land, but small shifts moved local culture inexorably toward the moment when Poverty Point sprang from the löess.

New tools were culture's way of coping with nature's way. They helped upland groups gather and process drought-scattered foods including nuts and acorns as well as small starchy and oily seeds, which eventually became the Lower Mississippi's first domesticates. They helped lowland groups catch and preserve fish and other aquatic foods, guaranteeing something to eat during winter and flood seasons, when food was hardest to get. Fish was the manna that kept Archaic people from starving in the wilderness. Some groups became so good at getting food from streams, swamps, uplands, or some combination thereof that they managed to

Fig. 3.4. Middle Archaic points from the Poverty Point vicinity include large, wide corner-notched and stemmed forms. The three points in the bottom row are Williams points; two points on the top row (*middle and far right*) are Evans points; the point in the middle row (*right*) is a Marcos point; and the remaining two specimens are Sinner points. The point on the lower left is 3.2 inches long. Photography by Steven Carricut.

settle down fully or at least avoid having to shift main living quarters every time the seasons changed.

Work was reorganized. Sometimes residential groups temporarily disbanded, and individual families scattered about, harvesting abundant nuts, acorns, and other dispersed seasonal foods. Sometimes, they disbanded in times of scarcity. In both cases, scattered families regrouped and returned home after harvest or when conditions improved. Sometimes residential groups sent out small parties to hunt and forage while everyone else remained at home. Such practices were merely alternative means of coping with prevailing environmental conditions and were not necessarily confined to one group or another. Practicality and flexibility undoubtedly guided the organization of the Archaic domestic labor sector.

On Maçon Ridge and the edges of nearby hills, foraging and fishing intensified. They had to. Groups no longer had the freedom to move around skimming the best and most accessible foods. Trespass always had been a serious offense, but with more and more groups living on smaller and smaller territories, it became a capital offense. Although each group possessed its own unique blend of foods, food-getting activities, and organizational strategies, one general pattern came to dominate the lower part of the Lower Mississippi Valley above the coast. This broad pattern emphasized high-yield foods—backwater fish, hickory nuts, pecans, and deer, probably in that order.

Around Poverty Point and southern sections of the Lower Mississippi Valley where economies emphasized fishing, exchange was at a minimum. A little Ouachita novaculite and a few quartz crystals circulated: novaculite for projectile points and crystals for fetishes or shamans' healing aids. The tiny amount of exchange carried out—probably as gifting among personages or as payments for brides—differed fundamentally from exchange in the middle and upper parts of the Mississippi Valley. Further north, exchange concentrated on prestige objects, whereas exchange around Maçon Ridge dealt in objects destined for personal use, the hunt and the medicine bag. Up-valley, exchange conferred status directly on those who carried out exchanges. Why? Because only prestige items circulated. Around Poverty Point, social gain did not come from the gift but from the gifting. For example, Jay Johnson and Sam Brookes maintained that fancy turkeytail or Benton bifaces of imported Fort Payne chert brought prestige to their owners. On the other hand, I doubt that owning

Gary points of imported novaculite carried prestige. If it did, social standing came from the act of exchange or from the generosity of the hunter whose skills were improved by it, not from the material.

Exchange and other acts of kindness or veiled ambition were means not just of building prestige but of incurring future payback and earning loyalty in the process, and therein lay power—pure raw power with the capacity to undergird some extraordinary achievements. Not only could kind or ambitious individuals collect and save obligation like money in a bank, everyone knew that payback was just a request away. Callout of collective debt was probably behind communal projects, which turned some ordinary hunter-gatherer groups into affluent mound builders.

A thin line separated gratitude from servitude, and attitude drew the line in the sand—or rather in the silt loam, as was more often the case. Smart or charismatic individuals realized the power in kindness and took advantage of exceptional moments and strong feelings to promote mound-building projects such as those at Frenchman's Bend, Watson Brake, and Lower Jackson. As community symbols, mounds served group interests, but they also served personal ones, too. Working on the mounds not only allowed laborers to satisfy obligations but ensured benefits for themselves and families. Mounds were not merely feel-good projects or means of paying debts. Mounds were magic, and their magic worked for all who had a hand in building them, young and old, man and woman, average person and personage. They generated supernatural power sanctifying and protecting place and person. They were like the flag and divine insurance combined.

The first Archaic mounds were built more than 6,000 years ago. For the ensuing three millennia, a few Lower Mississippi communities built mounds, usually one but occasionally more. Most were small, only waist high and less than twenty paces across, and were raised in a few days. But some were as tall as one- or two-story buildings, up to fifty giant steps across, and took months to finish. Watson Brake, located on the Ouachita River about sixty miles from Poverty Point, was the most ambitious Archaic construction. There, Joe Saunders and his associates found one large mound and nine or ten smaller ones raised atop a circular ring, which was nearly as wide as a football field was long. The amount of labor that went into them was equal to a hundred people working for ten months straight without taking a weekend off. But Watson Brake construction workers no doubt took time to tend to routine matters. Saunders and his team were not sure whether or not mound builders lived at Watson Brake year-round. Arguably, Watson Brake was raised in a manner similar to missionary Gideon Lincecum's account of how the Mississippi Choctaws built Nanih Waiya, presented at the beginning of this chapter.

It did not matter that Lincecum embellished an old Choctaw story about their sacred mound, because historical accuracy is not absolutely crucial to model building. Several matters in Lincecum's account have direct bearing on Archaic mound building. First, everybody helps except hunters. Second, work is suspended while people do their household chores and during fall when families break camp and scatter in the woods to collect nuts and acorns. Third, work continues year after year until finished. Fourth, an old man's reminder of how important the mound is to the people is sufficient to keep everyone motivated. Fifth, working on the mound is considered honorable work. Sixth, the mound is completed in eight years, and trees are planted on it afterwards. Seventh, one of their chiefs plans and directs the project with advice from a building committee. Eighth, the mound is used as a cemetery. And ninth, it also serves as a dais for sacred tribal poles.

Lincecum could just as well have been describing Archaic mound building. His account showed that small sedentary or logistically mobile groups had the necessary manpower, especially if work was scheduled around other jobs and carried out over a number of years. Logistical organization provided ample time for construction. Building required stout backs but no special skills or know-how. An appeal to community or ethnic pride was all that was needed to keep construction going. Complex organization and heavy-handed management were unnecessary since building was a corporate enterprise. Everybody benefited socially from the work, and the mound continued to work its magic long after sweat dried and blisters healed. Modern Choctaws still regard Nanih Waiya as sacred.

Archaic mounds had little in them other than trash from littered campgrounds from which fill dirt was taken. Occasionally, small baked-earth blocks, notched projectile points, or hard-stone beads or pendants were left from some long-forgotten ritual, but these were not buried or cached like grave goods or ceremonial offerings. William Haag and James Ford did find a few burned bones in one of the Monte Sano mounds located on the high bank of the Mississippi River in Baton Rouge 200 miles south of Poverty Point, but they could not be positively identified as human. They

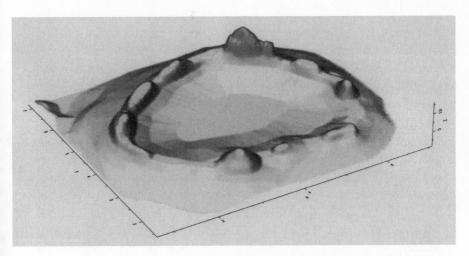

Fig. 3.5. Computer-generated simulation (Terramodel) depicts the Middle Archaic Watson Brake earthwork. The largest mound, which is shown at only half its height compared with the other mounds, stands twenty-three feet high, and the distance across the ring of mounds is about 280 paces. Map data furnished by John Belmont; computer simulation by Ted Hampton.

probably were, but even so, that did not mean that the mound was built as a burial vault. Archaic mounds were not primarily tombs or foundations for temples or special buildings either, despite sometimes being placed over old house ruins.

What, then, were Archaic mounds? Several lines of evidence point to the likelihood that they were earthen models of the Earth Island—the native's cosmological or primordial world—and of Creation—sacred symbols of identity and land rights; highly visible *public* symbols. For example, a Choctaw story tells how first people and locusts climbed out of a long tunnel that opened onto the summit of Nanih Waiya, a metaphor of Earth Mother's womb and the birth process. The Lincecum narrative says that the most venerated tribal totems, the Sun Pole and the Leaning Pole, were erected on the summit of Nanih Waiya and its companion mound. The Sun Pole represented the eye of *Hushtahli,* the sun deity or Great Spirit, and the Leaning Pole was the sacred direction finder, which led the Choctaws through the wilderness during their long march. When the Leaning Pole leaned no more, it signified that they had reached *home.* Sacred symbols for creator and home prominently displayed on top of mounds—what clearer expression of mound purpose could there be? Although these parables were told more than five millennia after the first mounds were built, they contained elements of the ancient creation story shared by native peoples across America, especially those in the South.

Mounds offered a new way of relating old cosmology. They manifested one of the strongest emotions shared by individuals and small communities—the sense of place, or home. Mounds turned meadows and woods, lakes and bayous, houses and hunting grounds into centers of the cosmos and the "Garden of Eden," commemorating and legitimizing that wondrous, unifying feeling of home. Mounds metaphorically expressed the southern native worldview, in which secular and sacred, home and chapel, corporeal and spiritual, and reality and magic were inseparable. That worldview dominated organization and governance of Lower Mississippi societies long after Archaic mounds first celebrated the principle. The principle was more than a guide for living. It was the heart of ethnicity and the soul of relations between groups. It gave people common knowledge and feelings of a shared past. But it was not a writ for friendship. Mounds established, at least, a perception of having common roots, kinship.

Ceremonies gave reason for Archaic groups dispersed by the Hypsithermal drought to gather. Yet ceremonies made poor occasions for transferring technology or style, because they were normally formal, conducted under strict rules of etiquette and diplomacy. Their formality kept local designs from spreading far but provided unparalleled opportunities for orators to spread lore and parables. Speeches and dances did not put meat on the grill or bread in the earth oven, but they promoted friendship or at least equality, created potential marriage ties, and gave hosts opportunities to be patted on the back and to bank obligation, too. Telling how the woodpecker got a red head, how the world was created, where people came from, and other familiar stories evoked common sentimentality that reminded everyone that they shared a heroic past. Why? Because versions of the old stories had come down through the ages from the ancient mother tongue. Cosmic stories represented ancient lore preserved and passed down, albeit selectively, through intervening generations that separated celebrants from the Old Ones who first told the stories. Regardless of how widely bands were separated by kinship, descent, or distance, they still shared bits and pieces of the same ancient stories. Technology and style changed quickly, but teachings of the heart and soul did not. Mounds narrated the old teachings. They were testaments to the time when all people were one big family.

Late and Terminal Archaic

Climate turned cooler and wetter between 3,000 and 4,000 years ago, ending the oppressive Hypsithermal dryness. A rejuvenated Mississippi sent its waters down a single course, which writhed back and forth across the swamp. At times, the river lay less than an hour's paddle from Maçon Ridge bluff, which by 3,700 years ago was alive with the sound of building.

Late and Terminal Archaic peoples ate the same foods as their Middle Archaic ancestors: Fish, nuts, acorns, deer, and other edibles were collected during short forays away from home. Peoples living on Maçon Ridge seasonally exploited both terrestrial and aquatic foods, and water-filled swamps, lakes, and sluggish bayous and rivers promoted fisheries on a scale never seen before. Having plenty of water was only partially responsible for expanded fisheries. Improved gear was the real impetus for growth and made fishing a year-round activity. Nets that worked in moving water were fashioned by adding heavy sinkers to bottomlines, and getting iron ore for those sinkers promoted busy stone exchange with the people of the Ouachita Mountains. Exchange instantly ballooned, and rocks and other goods from dozens of far-off places showed up on Maçon Ridge by the ton. Exploding consumer demand carried political economic consequences, which affected everything from how food was cooked to how people organized themselves. Even supernatural beliefs were affected. Large earthworks were erected to tell the story of those beliefs and to guard against unseen evils, which threatened life and harmony.

Poverty Point was where it all happened.

4

Natural Environment

"That Ol' Grey Dirt"

He leaned over the edge of the test pit and peered intently at the south wall. The strata, the soil, the pavement of clay ball fragments, everything was instantly related to all other subsurface exposures he had seen at Poverty Point, profiles from earlier excavation units, fresh gully heads, slump blocks along the bluff, every armadillo and fox burrow. Everyone waited. The wait seemed interminable. Finally he spoke, "Yep." Then another pause. "Reckon that's that ol' grey dirt, just like over yonder at Deep Six and the Dock," came the soft drawled words everyone awaited. "Another part of the ol' lake shore, you know." And with that Mitchell Hillman instantly clarified another of the mute profiles cut into the anthropic Memphis silt loam of the Poverty Point site. Mitchell knew such things. No one asked how or why. You just knew he knew. Many of us privately wondered if he had not dropped some of the artifacts and dumped some of the fill dirt himself 3000 years before.

Jon Gibson, in *Louisiana Archaeology,* 1990

A Brave New World

Maçon Ridge was the most conspicuous terrain in the Lower Mississippi Valley of northeastern Louisiana and southwestern Arkansas. Everywhere along its 130-mile length, it rose abruptly out of the swamp, its eastern side marked by a two- to three-story-high bluff, which stood out like a freshly painted wall. It was a wall separating Maçon Ridge from Tensas swamp. There was no wall on the opposite edge. The ridge simply merged with Ouachita and Boeuf swamps, twenty to twenty-five miles to the west. Despite standing only a couple of stories higher that the swamp, Maçon Ridge was a brave new world, a world which gave one resident group of hunter-gatherers an opportunity to be different. And in the land of swamps, where even a few inches of elevation mattered, a few stories was like a mountain before a molehill.

A Good Place

Maçon Ridge formed during low sea level. Sea level fluctuated dramatically during the Ice Age, or the Pleistocene epoch, dropping when continental ice expanded and rising when ice shrank. When sea level fell, the Mississippi River entrenched its valley deep and wide, generally removing sediments that had been deposited when the sea was high and rising. With the Mississippi downcutting on the east and the Ouachita and Arkansas Rivers downcutting on the west, a narrow strip of land was left in between. This remnant was Maçon Ridge.

The core of the ridge was composed of alluvial sands and clays. Soil scientists Arville Touchet and Thurman Allen found that bright red and olive clays of the Crowley soil stratigraphic unit reached within seven feet of the modern surface. Beneath them were coarse red sands of the Pine Island soil stratigraphic unit, lying between thirteen and more than twenty-one feet down, which was as low as Touchet and Allen's probes reached. Mound fill itself often incorporated these clays and sands, which meant that laborers took advantage of gullies or the naked bluff itself. None of the ditches between the rings where most of the ridge fill was obtained were dug deeply enough to reach Crowley clay.

The downcutting that carved Maçon Ridge into its present shape took place just prior to 12,000 years ago when continental ice made one final big push southward. Then came the big thaw. Allen and Touchet contend that huge quantities of muddy slush were released during summers but

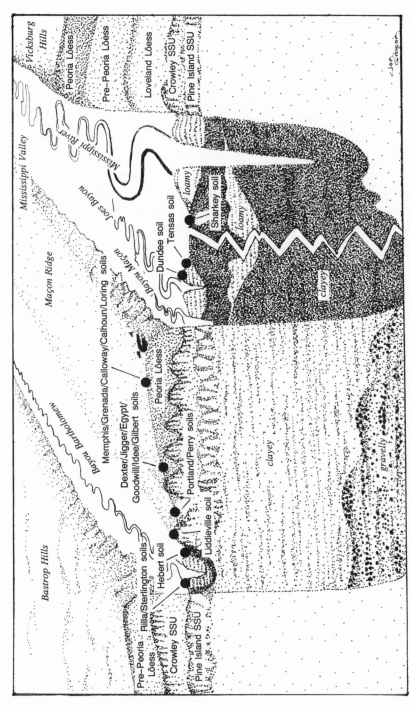

Fig. 4.1. A cross-section through the Mississippi Valley in the Poverty Point vicinity shows Maçon Ridge sticking up above the floodplain between the Vicksburg bluffs (eastern wall of the Mississippi Valley) and the Bastrop Hills (western wall). Soils reveal the effects of parent material (loess or alluvium), landform position, and vegetation cover.

refroze during winters, exposing vast areas of barren floodplain to bitter north winds. Clouds of dust blown out of the denuded floodplain floor settled along Maçon Ridge, at least along its eastern front, blanketing the old Crowley clay, which had been on the surface for millennia. The settled dust layer, or Peoria löess, was seven feet thick at Poverty Point and was referred to as the Memphis soil stratigraphic unit

As soon as dusty conditions abated some 10,000 years ago, vegetation claimed the löess, and weathering began to turn it into soil. Memphis silt loam developed on convex, well-drained areas, Grenada silt loam on convex moderately drained areas, Calloway silt loam on flats, and Calhoun silt loam in depressions. It only took a few thousand years for weathering to alter the löess as much as it was going to. Memphis, Grenada, Calloway, and Calhoun soils were all found beneath different parts of the rings where construction effectively terminated weathering some 3,500 years ago. Yet pickled soils, as Touchet refers to them, were practically identical to Memphis, Grenada, Calloway, and Calhoun soils found on the modern surface.

The patchwork of löessial soils showed that Poverty Point's old preconstruction surface consisted of low ridges, broad flats, and shallow depressions. Gullies cut back from the Maçon Ridge bluff, and deeper gashes exposed Crowley clays and Pine Island sands in their walls. Shallow circular ponds, like the one near Locality Two, dotted the undulating surface of Maçon Ridge, and a large comma-shaped remnant of an ancient Pleistocene stream channel lay immediately west of where the large bird mound would be erected later. One to two miles west of the bluff, Elijah's Creek meandered through the woods, but Harland (or Harlin) Bayou, which today borders the northern section of the rings, was only a gully when the rings were built. As late as 1848, when mapped by federal land surveyors, it ran south of Mound B and headed between Mound A and Mound B less than a half-mile from the bluff. It was probably created by ring construction, or at least the rings caused it to run the way it did.

The bluff was pretty close to its current position when building started, not a half-mile further east like Ford had thought. We know this because builders had draped more than five feet of fill across the bluff lip in the southeastern corner of the plaza and had plugged the ends of architectural swales lying between the northern rings in order to prevent runoff and gullying. If the bluff had not been present, plugs would not have been necessary. They were not used anywhere else.

Standing three stories higher than the swamp, the bluff afforded an impressive vista. Perhaps as related in native stories, open, unblocked vistas provided an entry portal for good spirits, which originated in the beneficent east, and an exit portal for disharmonious spirits, which built up inside enclosed spaces. The vista would have been even more spectacular if a lake rather than a wooded swamp had lain at the foot of the bluff. There is no lake alongside Poverty Point today, but discovery of a dark organic layer in the bluff face at an elevation higher than can be reached by modern still-water levels raised the possibility that one existed long ago.

Mitchell Hillman, Glen Greene, and I puzzled about the layer, which we called "Deep Six" because it was six meters, or twenty feet, below massive artificial fill deposits in the face of Maçon Ridge bluff. How had it formed at an elevation only reached in modern times by rampaging floods? Floods, we knew, carried away fine sediment and organic litter; they did not deposit them. Organic sediments settled out in still water. Geomorphologist Roger Saucier cautioned that Deep Six could have formed in a protected section of a bluff-breeching gully, but Hillman identified sediments similar to Deep Six at the same elevation in several low-lying areas of Poverty Point, showing that high water stand was widespread, not isolated.

How had water come to still-stand at a level higher than flood stage? Probably by raising base level. According to Thurman Allen and Arville Touchet, that could have happened locally by emponding water. The swamp off the front of the bluff at Poverty Point made a perfect water trap. To the west was Maçon Ridge bluff; to the east, three to ten miles away, was Joes Bayou ridge, an old abandoned meander belt; and to the south was the narrow Ranson Slough ridge, which connected Joes Bayou ridge with Maçon Ridge. The narrow ridge was created by high water pouring out of Joes Bayou when the bayou was swollen with Mississippi River outflow. The narrow ridge would have dammed off normal drainage and held seasonal backwater. Water levels could have reached no higher than eighty-six feet elevation without spilling across the lowest point along the narrow ridge. Deep Six reached eighty-three feet.

Other geomorphic features suggested that a lake or at least a long-flooded swamp once lay alongside Poverty Point, but the crucial question was in the timing. A fish-filled lake would explain how a demanding economy met everyday food needs as well as provided potential surpluses without seriously depleting resources. A lake would explain why no Poverty Point camps have been found between Maçon Ridge bluff and Joes Bayou—the area was under water. It would help explain why people abandoned Poverty Point—the lake drained, taking its productive fishery with it. Empty a cornucopia, eliminate a major political economic means for social advancement, and people will seek opportunity elsewhere. But if the lake had existed before or after but not during Poverty Point's occupation, then all benefits ascribed to it would have had no bearing whatsoever on Poverty Point's domestic economy.

Pineywood hills lay within logistical reach of Poverty Point; Sicily Island, an isolated group of hills, lay sixty miles to the south at the end of Maçon Ridge, and Bastrop Hills lay thirty-five miles to the west on the opposite side of Boeuf swamp. Compared with Maçon Ridge, hills were rugged terrain with elevations often reaching more than 200 feet above sea level and summits sometimes winding 100 or more feet above ravine bottoms, especially along the Mississippi Valley wall. Waterfalls plunged forty feet into crystal pools, and small, cold, clear creeks rushed to join large, warm, muddy bayous in Tensas and Boeuf swamps. Pineywood hills, beloved by natives, offered but one attraction for everybody else— rock. Rock was not accessible on Maçon Ridge, and Sicily Island and Bastrop Hills provided the closest deposits west of the Mississippi River.

Citronelle gravels occasionally formed entire hillsides and included everything from pea gravel to head-sized boulders, all rounded and smooth. At Rhinehart, Louisiana, one of the most extensive deposits along the Mississippi Valley wall and just west of Sicily Island, layers of erosion-resistant gravel formed hummocks and vertical faces along terraces. Archaeologist Don Hunter found similar deposits at nearby Manifest, and Sandra Bass recorded more than sixty deposits within forty-five miles of Poverty Point, mostly from quarry symbols on quadrangle maps. Other gravels paved creek beds and bars. Most gravel was brown chert with good chipping qualities.

Fine- to coarse-grained sandstone, ranging in color from lily white to dirty brown, stuck out in creek walls as foot-thick ledges. One exposure near Leland on the southern edge of Sicily Island had two layers, both white coarse-grained Catahoula sandstone. Sandstone outcrops and embedded gravel deposits almost never occur together. They were formed

Fig. 4.2. Citronelle gravels occur in uplands south (Sicily Island) and west of Maçon Ridge. These gravels are the nearest available rocks, even though they lie scores of miles from the rings. The gravelly hummock shown here is at Rhinehart in the Catahoula Hills, just west of Sicily Island.

from sediments deposited millions of years apart and under widely differing conditions, sands on tropical ocean beaches and gravels in Ice Age stream beds.

The hills contained other rocks—silicified wood, geodic limonites or mudstones, ochres, and calcareous nodules and fossil casts. Even a chippable quartzite occurred, but these rocks rarely showed up at Poverty Point. Sandstone and gravel did, but the lion's share of rock used for chipped tools was brought in by exchange from as far as a thousand miles away. Possibly sandstone and chert gravel came from hills closest to Poverty Point, but the large amount of rock brought in from great distances makes this possibility anything but certain.

If there was ever a good place, it was Poverty Point. Land was rich, water was rich, but perhaps the richest asset was its location. The bluff at Poverty Point was one of only a few places in the entire Lower Mississippi Valley where a departing pirogue could have been paddled without portages all the way to the Ouachita Mountains in central Arkansas, to the Ozark Rim in eastern Missouri, or to the Shawnee Hills in southern Illinois. But such a feat was not realized until rocks from those faraway places became primary economic resources, and that happened almost by accident and only once in a large way among Lower Mississippi natives. But once it did happen and all trails converged on Maçon Ridge, Poverty Point awakened to its destiny—a destiny that even a cornucopian environment would not have ensured by itself.

Two Kinds of Forests

Two kinds of forests surrounded Poverty Point, bottomland hardwoods and mixed hardwoods. Stately bottomland hardwoods grew in the swamp off the bluff. Today, the old-growth forest has been felled, but I can remember when a few virgin stands remained. Free of undergrowth except for fern, the woods were shrouded in perpetual dusk, their crowns stretched like a thick blanket 100–150 feet overhead, blocking out the sun. Early twentieth-century forester G. H. Lentz reported old-growth sweetgums over four feet in diameter and more than 300 years old. Squirrels barking up in the canopy could barely be heard and almost never seen, and mulligan wound up mainly as vegetable gravy when hunters stalked squirrels in old-growth woods with a single-barrel twenty gauge.

Old-growth bottomland hardwoods consisted of several tree associa-

Fig. 4.3. Joes Bayou follows an old course of the Arkansas River or possibly a major Mississippi River distributary that parallels the eastern edge of Maçon Ridge in the Tensas swamp. Several periphery encampments were founded on the high natural levees that line the ancient course.

tions depending mainly on degree of flooding. Cypress/tupelo grew in deep swamps where water remained for prolonged periods. Forestry professor Clair Brown found bases on older trees that sometimes measured nine feet across and had knees that stood chest high. Slightly higher backwater zones supported stands of overcup oak/bitter pecan or water oak, and narrow willow/cottonwood fingers lined stream banks. Better drained parts of the bottomland were covered with a sweetgum/water oak association.

Foresters Keith Ouchley, Wylie Barrow, Kelby Ouchley, and Robert Hamilton in their historical study of the Tensas bottomland forest discovered that sweetgum was the dominant canopy species but that dozens of other trees were commonly represented. In sweetgum/water oak stands, Ouchley and his associates found that gum made up nearly 40 percent of the volume, with water oaks comprising another 20 percent and overcup oak about 7 percent. In overcup oak/bitter pecan woods, they found that equal numbers of overcup oak and of bitter pecan comprised about 70 percent of the forest and that water oak made up less than 10 percent. They reported that water oaks make up about two-thirds of the water oak forest. In addition, they found hackberry/elm/ash stands growing where treefalls created openings in sweetgum/water oak woods. Edwin Jackson and archaeobotanist Andrea Shea reported that oaks were common in nineteenth-century land surveys on Joes Bayou ridge and in the swamp west to Maçon Ridge, but Ouchley and colleagues suggested that logging and land clearing favored oak reseeding over sweetgum. Virgin stands, they maintained, contained more gum.

Old bottomland forests continually renewed themselves. Spring winds blew down trees, and old age claimed some. Lightning killed a few, fires destroyed others, and floods uprooted more. Every hole punched in the canopy let in life-giving sunlight, and the miracle spread across the floor of the opening, sowing a new crop of fast-growing species and stimulating growth of standing, slow-maturing trees. Storms and floods made sure the forest recycled annually, and treefall gaps were like stocked pantries to hunter-gatherers.

Except for oak-dominated sections, bottomland hardwoods might seem to have been poor places to hunt and gather, but appearances are deceptive. True, sweetgum balls are not edible, acorns were laced with foul-tasting tannin, and bitter pecans were accurately named. Yet edible plants were widespread and often bountiful. Ouchley and colleagues discovered that white oaks with their better-tasting and easier-to-prepare acorns made up as much as 2 percent of forest volume in water oak forests; hickorys, almost 0.5 percent in the same woods; sweet pecan, 4 percent of sweetgum/water oak stands; and persimmon, nearly 3 percent of overcup oak/bitter pecan woods and around 1 percent each of sweetgum/water oak and cypress/tupelo forests. These nuts and fruits were major Poverty Point staples.

It would be wrong to think of Tensas's bottomland forests as inexhaustible. Many problems could have kept the woods from reaching their maximum potential production of nuts and fruits each year. Yet opponents of the view that nature provides a horn of plenty for industrious hunter-gatherers usually overstate their case by understating it, making it seem that constraints on maximum yields were so prevalent that all species and every plant were affected each year. If that had happened, humans would not have survived very long. People did not tie their livelihood to a promise of sustained maximum yield, but they did not tie them to the poorest production levels either. Living like starving ninnies out of fear that next year might be a poor one was not a prevailing state of mind. Hunter-gatherers lived like either kings or paupers, but they managed to live just the same. Poverty Point folks knew the wild ways, good and bad, as well as anyone could, and they developed a variety of contrivances and strategies to level out ups and downs.

The other major forest grew on Maçon Ridge. Marker trees identified during a 1920 land survey of Poverty Point included ten oaks—three red oaks, two pin oaks, two water oaks, two overcup oaks, and one white oak—and nine sweetgums. Subdominants included two mulberrys and one each of pecan, walnut, hackberry, and locust. By that time, the woods were already second growth; the land had been farmed for nearly a century. More than half of the trees were less than eight inches in diameter and almost nine in ten were less than two feet. Only four trees were broader, with the largest measuring three feet.

Generally, Maçon Ridge old-growth woods were dominated by mixed oak/hardwood stands. Foresters discovered that sweetgum and white oaks such as cow oak, forked-leaf white oak, and delta post oak prevailed, each making up about one-sixth of stand volumes. Water oaks, such as water oak, bottomland red oak, and willow oak, constituted about 15 percent; red oaks, including cherrybark oak, southern red oak, and black oak, around 10 percent; elms, including white, cedar, winged, and red elms, also around 10 percent; hickory, nearly 8 percent; and black gum, nearly 7 percent. Other less prevalent hardwoods included overcup oak and ash, and sweet pecan and persimmon amounted to less than 1 percent each of the volume.

Sloughs, creek banks, and other pocks on Maçon Ridge supported glades and thickets of oaks, sweetgum, elm, ash, bitter pecan, locust, hackberry, and sometimes cypress and willow. Grassy openings occurred, and although some biologists suggested they may have been formed by burning or farming, their mollic topsoil revealed that they had formed under grass cover, suggesting a natural cover or, if due to human activity, one that predated Poverty Point.

Shea found that firewood from Poverty Point encampments surrounding the rings was primarily oak and hickory, a choice understood by anyone who has eaten steak grilled over a campfire.

Virgin forests and full lakes and streams teemed with game and food animals. At Poverty Point and small encampments just outside of the rings, fish and turtle scraps dominated, but deer remains were scarce. Had overpredation seriously degraded game conditions around Poverty Point, or were deer simply not hunted? I don't think that the deer that browsed in Poverty Point's woods were drastically underrepresented. Rather, I think Poverty Point's fishery made deer hunting relatively insignificant. Still, preservation conditions at Poverty Point were so poor that only a handful of burned bone fragments of all species survived.

In contrast, Copes on the banks of Breambrier Lake, an old Joes Bayou cutoff, held forth in typical swampland splendor. Edwin Jackson listed deer, rabbit, squirrel, and raccoon as the most sought-after game; ducks, geese, pelicans, herons and egrets, and turkeys as the most sought-after fowl; snapping, mud/musk, and cooter/slider turtles and rat/king, water, and racer snakes as the most sought-after reptiles; bullfrogs as the most sought-after amphibians; and catfish, bowfin, gar, and drum as the most sought-after fish. He found that fish were by far the most important food source at Copes amounting to nearly three-fourths of the bone counts, and they probably were underestimated because the small bones passed through the quarter-inch screen that was used to recover remains.

The Old Land and Poverty Point

Many places in the Lower Mississippi Valley had environments similar to Poverty Point's: high land surrounded by swamps; löessial soil; juxtaposed upland and bottomland hardwood forests; flanking rim-swamp lake or stream; high meander-belt ridge within foraging distance; water access to Mississippi and Arkansas Rivers; and lack of native rock. Such terrains usually supported population aggregates, but they did not support communities like Poverty Point or others even remotely similar at the time.

Archaeologists used to think they did, but that was when a few general technological similarities were assumed to represent a uniform Poverty Point culture engaged by Lower Mississippi and coastal peoples from Tennessee to the Gulf and from Louisiana to Florida. Thinking back, archaeologists knew there was only one Poverty Point, but they were not looking for uniqueness or variability. They were looking for something—anything, even one or two traits—that suggested that these second-millennium B.C. communities had similar technologies, customs, and even sociopolitical organizations. They searched and searched until they convinced themselves that they had found it. Furthermore, they were all sure that Mother Nature had shaped the outcome. A widespread Poverty Point culture was viewed as an inevitable result of neighboring people's adaptation to a similar environment—the Old South in all its warm, humid, fertile, and raw material–impoverished glory.

There can be no doubt that the natural environment both offered and stifled opportunity, motivated and suppressed effort, and gave and took resources for those who participated in Poverty Point's cultural growth, but Maçon Ridge and Tensas swamp—no matter how bountiful or austere—were not responsible for Poverty Point culture. People were.

5

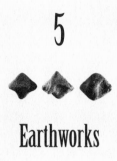

Earthworks

"Look at That Marvelous Earthwork There"

In 1953, he [James Ford] came to Louisiana to plan some excavations at Poverty Point. He came by way of the Corps of Engineers' office in Vicksburg and picked up some aerial photographs, which were the first aerial photographs we had ever seen. And he came over to the Poverty Point site. I met him at a modest motel there, and we sat down to plan what was to be done in his digging. So, it was a good half-hour before he pulled out these aerial photographs and showed them to me and said, "Look at that marvelous earthwork there. Where do you think that is?" I, in my erudition, said, "Why that's got to be in the Ohio River Valley. That's the only place that has complex earthworks like that." And he said, "You've been on that site." I said, "Not I, I've never been on that thing." And then it dawned on me, that's got to be Poverty Point.

William G. Haag, videotaped interview, 1981

The Largest of the Oldest

Poverty Point boasted earthworks, big earthworks, so big that 2,500 years would pass before bigger ones were built. They were old; no, not the oldest known, but they were the largest of the oldest. What made them unusual was that their builders were hunter-gatherers, not some ordinary bunch of foragers, but a group who had strong feelings about who they were, believed in what they were doing, and put communal interests ahead of personal ones.

Six Rings, Six Sections

A C-shaped earthen enclosure formed the central construction at Poverty Point. Its six rings, or ridges, were concentric. Their ends stopped at the bluff edge, and their curving sides arched westward around a large open area. Ridges had lens-shaped cross-sections and stood a head higher than ditches dug between them. Ditches provided dirt for the rings. The outer ring measured three-fourths of a mile from north end to south end, and ends of the inner ring were half that far apart. Rings paralleled one another, their crests between fifty and eighty paces apart, except for the two innermost ones, which lay about ninety paces apart. The inner ring stood from a knee to a waist higher than the others.

Five aisles, or roadways, radiated through the enclosure like spokes of a giant wheel. The western aisle split the enclosure in two and connected the open center to a large mound lying outside. The other four aisles divided northern and southern halves in three parts, each creating a total of six sections—north, northwest, upper west, lower west, southwest, and south—the same as the number of rings. Aisles were formed by a combination of digging ditches and leaving gaps through the rings.

Their original width and uniformity were compromised by modern farmers who used them as roads, driveways, turnrows, and fire lanes. The two least disturbed aisles, the western and southwestern ones, were fifteen and thirty-five paces (a pace being about three feet) across where intersected by the third ring (rings were numbered from inside out). The wide viewing angle possible through today's disturbed aisles lessens confidence that they were sighting paths for summer and winter solstice sunsets 3,500 years ago, as astronomer Kenneth Brecher and colleague William Haag proposed in a 1983 *American Antiquity* article.

A solitary embankment called the Causeway spanned all six rings in the southwestern section. It generally paralleled the southwestern aisle and extended the length of a football field beyond the outer ring, bridging a natural depression and heading toward two isolated core encampments located one-third of a mile and one-half of a mile outside the rings.

Fig. 5.1. A 1938 aerial photograph vividly reveals the six rings at Poverty Point. James Ford first spotted the earthworks on this 1938 image. In addition to the rings, the big mound, the aisles, and the Causeway are visible. Courtesy of Sheila Lewis and the U.S. Army Corps of Engineers.

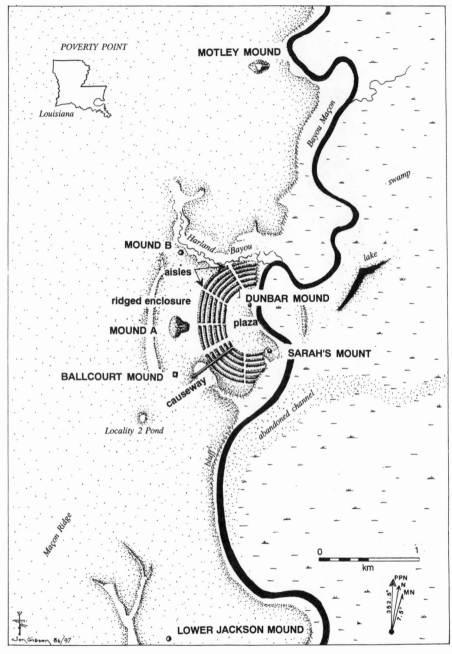

Fig. 5.2. A drawing of the earthworks depicts the extensive layout, which spans nearly four miles from north to south.

Open Center

Bounded by the inner ring and the bluff, the flat open space in the center of the enclosure probably was where dances, ballgames, and all kinds of socials and ceremonies took place as well as where protection from evil spirits was greatest. The horsetrack at Churchill Downs would fit inside. It was free of trash, suggesting that users were careful about littering or else cleaned up after festivities. It was unaffected by construction except for a few places along the bluff—a landfilled gully, a chest-high false front along its southeastern edge, and a few other spots. On the western edge of open area near the inner ring, William Haag uncovered numerous filled-in holes where wooden posts had been set. Some were as big around as three-gallon foot tubs, others as large as washtubs. They formed no recognizable patterns and suggested lots of building and rebuilding. Was this an old living surface that failed to get completely covered over by the inner ring or later ringside building?

Six Mounds

Six mounds were included in the earthworks. Six—six mounds, six rings, six compartments in the rings: coincidence or celebration of sacred directions? One mound sat on the southeastern end of the inner ring, another on the bluff inside the open area, and the other four outside the enclosure—all but one fairly close to the outermost ring. In addition, an older mound located far south of the others was incorporated in the layout.

Of the four outer mounds, the largest was Mound A. Said to be shaped like a bird in flight, the eminence had a two-story-high, flat-topped platform (or tail) joined perpendicularly to ridgelike wings, much higher and narrow-crested; these stuck out past the sides of the tail. The tail ran east-west, the wings north-south. A ramp ascended from the tail to the head, located midway along the wings. The head towered six stories, or about seventy feet, above the rings—higher than the tops of the enshrouding trees. The wing span was just over two football fields long, the body a bit longer, the equivalent of two football fields with end zones. Archaeologist Richard Shenkel calculated the mound held nearly 230,000 cubic yards of fill, about 17,000 big dump trucks full. It was facing away from the rings, as though it were flying out of the end of the western aisle.

Two other mounds were in line with Mound A, but neither guarded aisle entrances like the big mound. Ballcourt Mound was a little over 200

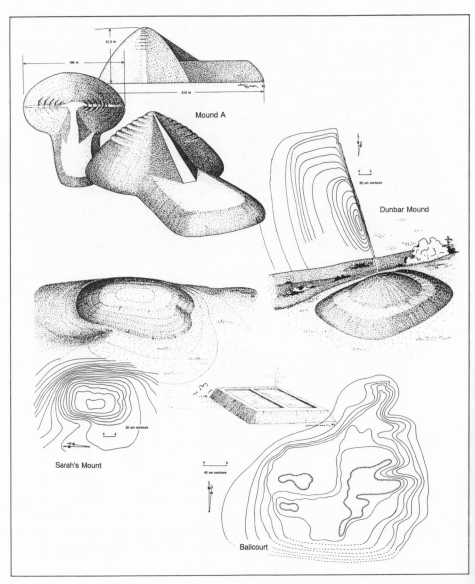

Fig. 5.3. Major mounds include Mound A (the large bird mound), Dunbar Mound (a two-tiered platform), Sarah's Mount (a platform), and Ballcourt Mound (another platform). The second bird-shaped mound (Motley) and Mound B (the conical mound) are not shown.

Fig. 5.4. Ground-level views of the largest bird mound can be best appreciated by noting the height of the mature oak trees that grow on the mound. The mound reaches a height of over seventy feet and contains about 230,000 cubic yards of fill dirt. Courtesy of Clarence Webb.

paces south of the wing tip of Mound A. It was outside the southwest section of the enclosure. If the Causeway had extended far enough, it would have passed just off the southeastern corner of the mound. Ballcourt Mound got its name because two shallow depressions on its flattened top reminded some archaeologists of playing areas in front of outdoor basketball goals, not because they had any revelation about Poverty Point's sports scene.

The mound was nearly square 100 paces on a side and as high as a man could raise his arms above his head. At first, archaeologists considered it to be natural; later, they thought it was natural but that it had been trimmed into shape. Its true nature was realized only after soil scientists Arville Touchet and Thurman Allen discovered lumps of Crowley clay in its natural-looking mass. For lumps of the foreign Crowley clay to have gotten incorporated in the body of the mound, they would have had to be introduced along with the other construction fill. Pronounced soil development had masked its man-made origin.

Mound B sat slightly more than 550 paces north of the bird mound's wing tip and almost 400 paces beyond the nearest ring. It was conical—

Fig. 5.5. Conical Mound B is about 20 feet high and 180 feet in diameter. In 1955, Ford and Neitzel uncovered an ash bed at its base, which contained at least one identifiable human bone. Ford and Neitzel believed the ashes were from a crematory fire and that the mound was a tomb. Recent discoveries in other early mounds suggest that Mound B may have been built for other reasons. Courtesy of Clarence Webb; rephotography by Steven Carricut.

about two stories high, 60 paces in diameter, and filled with almost 6,500 cubic yards of dirt. It was built in four major stages. The first three were successive horizontal layers each about four feet thick, and the last was a domed cap about seven and a half feet thick in the center. Ford and Webb noted that the floor (top surface) of the lowest building layer peeled off cleanly but bore no trash or postmolds. The floors of the next two construction layers were weathered and showed signs that people had busied themselves on them—a dug hole here, a heavily fired pit there, and charcoal and ash scattered about. Rain had even washed dirt into shallow depressions atop the third platform, and a bunch of dirt-filled baskets and bags were piled there, too. Well-preserved pits, impressions of bags and baskets, and an absence of weathering signs indicated that none of the platforms had been exposed for long.

Mound B was built over a bed of ashes. Ford and Webb observed small bone fragments in the ashes, including at least one human bone, the burned end of a femur. Had this been a crematory pyre? Possibly, but burning a dead person—or a live one for that matter—and then piling dirt over the ashes did not necessarily make a mound a tomb. About halfway through construction, builders discarded about 100 baskets and deerhide sacks full of dirt. Leaving perfectly good containers on top of a mound-building stage looks like some sort of ritual had taken place. No bodies were burned or buried during this rite, and despite taking down half the structure, the excavators Ford and Neitzel identified no other human bones.

Mounds that warrant being called burial mounds are those that were used as cemeteries for a long time or that contained a lot of graves. Such mounds came long after Poverty Point and included Early and Middle Woodland structures and occasionally later ones. Neither Poverty Point

Fig. 5.6. In 1955, James Ford uncovered what appeared to be a bunch of discarded dirt-filled baskets and hide sacks atop one of the building stages in Mound B. Courtesy of David Hurst Thomas.

nor Archaic mounds were burying places. A few human bones in a mound, especially one without whole bodies or prepared graves, suggests activities other than mortuary ritual.

Motley Mound was the remaining outer mound. It sat nearly 1,650 paces north of the ridged enclosure. It was not in line with the other three mounds but turned perpendicular to them, an orientation too precise for chance. It lined up with Dunbar Mound, a mound located inside the open area, some 2,150 paces north of Dunbar. The Motley-Dunbar line was parallel to the other mound alignment and 600 paces east of it. Motley was an elongated, oval-shaped eminence, which resembled the wing section of Mound A. It stood five stories high, measured 130 by 200 paces at the base, and contained nearly 131,000 cubic yards of fill, the equivalent of well over 9,000 full dump trucks. Ford and Webb claimed it was an another bird effigy, an unfinished version of Mound A.

Two mounds were built inside the ridged enclosure. The northernmost was Dunbar Mound, positioned on the bluff slightly more than halfway across the open area. It was a double-decked mound, having an upper domed section and a lower flat-topped platform. Its double-decked appearance was due to the fact that its domed cap did not extend all the way to the edges of the basal platform. If dirt had been piled high enough to reach the edges of the basal platform, it would have looked like Mound B and other simple conical mounds. It stood head high and seventy-five paces long. Bluff slumping had cut it in half, and the remnant was thirty paces wide. The complete mound probably held 8,000 or 9,000 cubic yards of dirt, somewhere around 600 dump trucks full.

A succession of horizontal caps lined by hard-packed floors comprised the basal platform. Caps were up to six inches thick, and their topping floors were about as thick as indoor-outdoor carpet. Floors were strewn with charcoal and pieces of löess cooking balls. Post-in-ground buildings had been erected on at least three floors; on two of them, those buildings were rectangular, one with sharp corners and the other with rounded ones. Neither building was oriented with mound axes, but the long side of the mound lined up with Poverty Point's dominant axis, which bore an azimuth of 352.5 degrees.

Mound-top activities vouched for the sacred and ceremonial character of the mound. Making ornaments and fancy groundstone items were activities that engaged mound users, as lots of hematite, magnetite, slate, and granite scraps were left on the floors. I discovered that these particu-

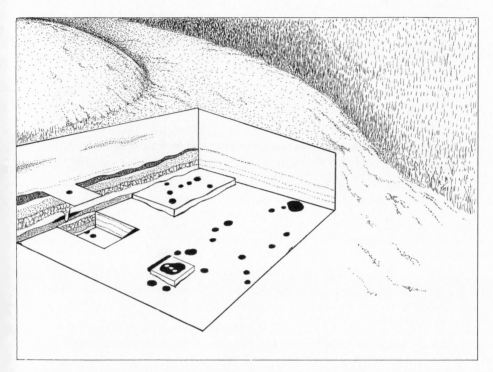

Fig. 5.7. Jon Gibson's 1983 excavations in Dunbar Mound showed that wooden buildings had been erected on several construction levels in the lower part of the two-tiered structure.

lar materials consistently occurred together throughout the rings, too. Another statistical association—kaolinite, red ochre, crystalline quartz, Catahoula sandstone, and galena—occurred as well. These materials probably constituted makeup kits complete with charms. Among historic tribes, ochre, kaolinite, and galena yielded red and white paint, and hematite would have produced a brownish red pigment for those who desired a different shade. Face and body painting were important in dress-up affairs, and paint-bedaubed celebrants led ceremonies throughout the native Southeast. Samuel Gill, a specialist in native religion, considers body painting to be a form of masking, which was believed to transform wearers into supernatural beings. Sandstone furnished a common abrasive, and Catahoula sandstone would have made fashionable emery boards. Quartz crystals probably worked their good luck even back then.

Another indication that special activities took place atop Dunbar

Mound lay in the composition of chipped stone. Nearly three-quarters consisted of Burlington chert, which was a subdominant material everywhere else. Irregularly angular chunks and early chipping-stage flakes made up well over half of the material. Chunks and early-stage flakes were less common than late- and final-stage flakes elsewhere in the rings. Why would Burlington chert, a flawed rock poorly suited for making bifaces, dominate a collection expected to contain the very best? Burlington chert was one of the most distant materials brought to Poverty Point, originating near St. Louis and across the river in Illinois more than 400 miles away (more than twice that by way of the Mississippi River). Poor chipping qualities notwithstanding, it may have carried more social importance than other exchange materials, justifying its prevalence on the mound.

Neither artifacts nor raw materials from the mound were unique. They were all represented in the rings. Painting, wearing ornaments, and breaking white chert showed that people who used mound tops had put on their finery.

Sarah's Mount was 330 paces south of Dunbar Mound on the bluff. It was not in the open space but sat upon the southeastern end of the inner ring. It was a flat-topped rectangular platform with a base that measured 20 by 30 paces and a summit plateau measuring 10 by 20 paces. It was only shoulder high to an observer standing on the connecting ring but was over two stories high when viewed from the foot of the bluff. Its east side coincided with the bluff slope. Its long axis pointed toward magnetic north, not Poverty Point north. Later post–Poverty Point pottery was found around the mound, but it was confined to the plow zone. Some investigators have questioned whether Sarah's Mount was a mound or merely a high spot on the ring spared from plowing because nineteenth-century resident Sarah Guier and two others were buried there. I consider it to be a separate mound. No other protected spot on the rings has such a well-defined shape, and besides, none of the rings are that high anywhere else.

Other surrounding mounds were not part of the Poverty Point earthworks. There were seven mounds on Jackson (or Neal) Place, 300 to 500 paces south of the outer ring, but they were probably built 2,000 years later. All had been bulldozed previously. Infrared remote imagery showed that three of the mounds had been connected by a U-shaped artificial embankment, revealing that this now-destroyed feature, which some investigators attributed to Poverty Point construction, was later, too.

For a while, Lower Jackson Mound, located one and a third miles south of Ballcourt Mound, was considered to be a Poverty Point construction because it lined up with Ballcourt Mound, Mound A, and Mound B—forming Poverty Point's main axis—and because Poverty Point materials were found close by. But those materials actually came from the Morrow–Lower Jackson encampment, 400 to 500 paces northwest of the mound. Objects from immediately around the mound included small baked löess blocks (some with cane-punched ends) and Evans points. Joe Saunders suggests that blocks and Evans points are diagnostic of pre–Poverty Point, Middle Archaic times. Furthermore, soil had re-formed in mound fill to a degree comparable to Middle Archaic mounds excavated elsewhere by Saunders and others. Lower Jackson Mound probably predated Poverty Point's earthworks by hundreds, if not thousands, of years, despite being incorporated by Poverty Point builders into one of the main earthwork alignments.

Building Materials and Loading

Dirt moving was not mindless, back-breaking work—not mindless anyway. Earthworks were fashioned primarily from löess, and löess mantled the entire eastern section of Maçon Ridge. Löessial soils have unique physical properties that would have strongly affected their use as building material. They have low plastic and low liquid limits, which means that it only takes relatively small amounts of water to turn them into mud or muddy water. A prolonged hard rain, for example, can wash away an unconsolidated pile of löessial dirt, and Joel Gunn contends that the climate during Poverty Point times was pretty rainy.

Crowley clays and Pine Island sands lay beneath the thick blanket of löess, and fluvial clays and sands comprised the floor of the swamp off the bluff front. As a consequence, clays and sands were simply not very handy—reaching them would have required either extensive digging or hauling. Exposures of clays and sands in gully walls and bluff faces were too limited to have made a difference.

Löess, despite being prone to meltdown, offered a number of advantages as a building material. In addition to convenience, it was easy to dig and bulked up nicely. Löess could be piled up steeply as long as it didn't rain. Clay, on the other hand, had high plastic and liquid limits, meaning a lot of water was needed to soften and liquefy it. Its hard, firm, or sticky consistency—depending on how wet the ground was—made it hard to dig and poor for bulking. Also, excavated clay would have come out in chunks, and piling up chunky clay would have left lots of room in between—spaces that would have had to be eliminated by packing or long-term settling. Neither would have been a particularly desirable remedy: Packing meant more work, and natural settling eventually did, too, because maintenance would have been required. Still, clay's high liquid limits would have made it the perfect sealant and a durable, scuff- and weather-resistant flooring. A civil engineering degree was not needed to calculate these benefits. Poverty Point builders did their figuring with aching backs and dirty hands.

A lot of löess and a little clay were used to construct the rings and mounds: löess to give mass and clay to seal and protect. Although used mainly as veneer, clay occasionally wound up in bulk fill, which suggested builders were taking fill dirt out of gullies or off the bluff face where löess contacted Crowley clay. Filling baskets with loose, dry dirt crumbled off steep walls of such exposures was bound to mix the materials. Besides, using slopes avoided the difficulty of having to dig up moist clay. Mixing textures created no serious bulking problem. Being fine grained, löess simply filled up voids around clods of clay, and a dense tough aggregate was created, one with higher moisture resistance than löess alone.

Clay and silt worked well together because builders only produced simple architectural forms. After all, a conical mound was just a big pile of dirt. So was a platform mound, only with a flat top. Rings were just piles of dirt continuously run together. Even complex shapes like bird mounds were only composites of piles and platforms. Dirt was not preshaped into bricks but used loose, and neither walls nor special forms were required to make any of the shapes.

I thought I had found a retaining wall in one of the northern rings when a group of long, vertical molds appeared along a construction joint, a seam where several sloping layers of varicolored fill came together. But a clay model I molded forced me to a different conclusion. I mashed different-colored pieces of Play-Doh into thin wafers, stacked them on top of each other, and shaped the stack into a rough ball. Then I stuck all the balls together into a big, roughly conical blob and used a kitchen knife to slice through the blob at various angles. If I had copied directly from actual excavation profiles, I could not have done a better job of showing how Poverty Point building strata looked. That construction joint I thought I had detected was nothing other than where the sloping sides of

Fig. 5.8. Most construction in the rings and mounds was carried out by dumping basketloads of dirt into discrete piles and filling in among the piles to form linear, gently rounded surfaces. Excavations reveal that building on any given section of the rings took place relatively quickly; total construction time may have taken less than a century, possibly only a generation.

three dirt piles merged, and those dark molds—which I tried hard to make into old rotten posts—were more likely tree roots.

Rings were built with run-together piles of dirt, but were they constructed in a modular fashion or as a single continuous exercise? Did they have cores composed of long steep-sided platforms that were subsequently capped or mantled, or were they simple, single-stage constructions from top to bottom and end to end? Apparently, they were neither of these extremes. Construction definitely was incremental but did not result in a series of long, continuous platforms. No single construction surface extended very far in any direction, certainly not for the full length of a ring or even a major segment. Most did not even span ring breadth. Accumulations of trash were discontinuous and did not stack up directly on top of one another. What appeared to be sharp platform edges were places where dirt piles merged. Ford and Webb noted that structural details were obscure. Architecturally, rings were composed of big and small heaps of earth, some stained with living debris, some not; they were not built as a succession of structural modules that formed single, continuous living surfaces from one end of each ring to the other end.

Earthworks were basket-loaded. Most of the time, loads were just dumped, but sometimes piles were spread, and occasionally dirt was strewn, or broadcast. In the Causeway, I calculate that individual loads weighed between 30 and 115 pounds, suggesting a work force that included everybody from children to adults. The full baskets and bags discarded on top of the third platform in Mound B had held from one-fourth to two cubic feet of dirt apiece and would have weighed between 30 and 230 pounds. We know these containers had been full of dirt when discarded, because they only experienced minimal warping where stacked together.

Building Succession and Chronology

The old ground had been occupied before earthworks were built. I found midden underneath nearly every tested section of the rings, except where the ground was naturally low and wet. Calibrated radiocarbon dates on the old ground surface averaged cal. B.C. 1524–1346 from underneath the second northwestern ring, based on a single assay; cal. B.C. 1682–1283 from underneath the third western ring, based on two assays; cal. B.C. 1675–1324 from underneath the fourth upper western ring, based on a single assay; cal. B.C. 1317–349 from underneath the fourth southwestern ring, based on two assays; cal. B.C. 1527–413 from beneath the first southern ring, based on a single assay; and cal. B.C. 1607–1219 from beneath the sixth southern ring, based on a single determination. Standard errors showed that dates belonged to the same statistical population and made it impossible to tell for sure whether one section was occupied before another.

Averaged dates on ring construction included cal. B.C. 1515–1032, on the first northern ring, based on two assays; cal. B.C. 1582–1280, on the third northern ring, based on five assays; cal. B.C. 1636–1233, on the fourth northern ring, based on three assays; cal. B.C. 1432–995, on the third upper western ring, based on five assays; and cal. B.C. 1636–1233, on the fourth upper western ring, based on three assays. Like dates from the old-ground surface, standard errors on construction dates made it impossible to tell which ring was built first, last, or in between. Similarly, it was not possible to determine how long building took overall or how long people lived on the rings after they were finished.

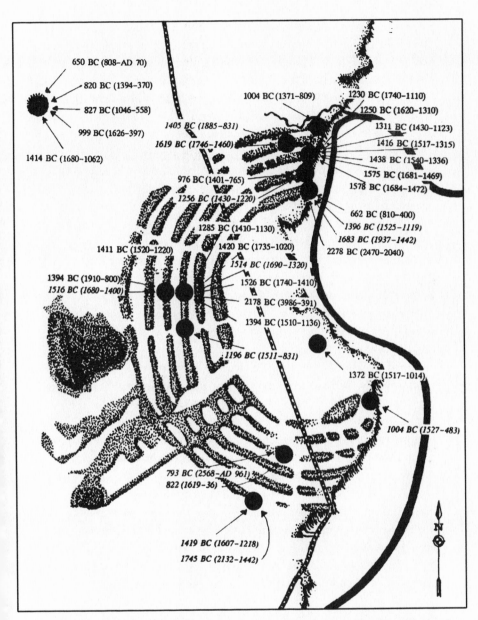

650 BC (808–AD 70)

820 BC (1394–370)

827 BC (1046–558)

999 BC (1626–397)

1414 BC (1680–1062)

1004 BC (1371–809)

1405 BC (1885–831)

1619 BC (1746–1460)

976 BC (1401–765)

1256 BC (1430–1220)

1285 BC (1410–1130)

1411 BC (1520–1220)

1420 BC (1735–1020)

1514 BC (1690–1320)

1394 BC (1910–800)

1516 BC (1680–1400)

1526 BC (1740–1410)

2178 BC (3986–391)

1394 BC (1510–1136)

1196 BC (1511–831)

1230 BC (1740–1110)

1250 BC (1620–1310)

1311 BC (1430–1123)

1416 BC (1517–1315)

1438 BC (1540–1336)

1575 BC (1681–1469)

1578 BC (1684–1472)

662 BC (810–400)

1396 BC (1525–1119)

1683 BC (1937–1442)

2278 BC (2470–2040)

1372 BC (1517–1014)

1004 BC (1527–483)

793 BC (2568–AD 961)

822 (1619–36)

1419 BC (1607–1218)

1745 BC (2132–1442)

N

Fig. 5.9. Radiocarbon dates from various sections and stages in and underneath the rings show a sizable range, but most suggest a span generally from 1600 to 1300 B.C. as the period of busiest construction. Italicized dates pertain to occupation on the old ground surface beneath the rings; the others pertain to building levels in the rings. Date have been calibrated and are expressed as two-standard deviation ranges.

Architect Mark Stielper suggested that the two inner rings were built first, followed by the four remaining ones, then the two bird mounds, and lastly the small outer mounds—first Ballcourt Mound and then Mound B. His proposed sequence was based on a logical architectural progression of forms, spacing, and landscape utilization. Radiocarbon backing for his proposal was lacking. I entertained several other possibilities—that the rings were built successively outward, successively inward, simultaneously progressive counterclockwise, simultaneously progressive clockwise, simultaneously progressive from both ends toward the middle, and without rhyme or reason—but statistical analysis of radiocarbon dates favored none of these either.

Although exact timing and absolute span of construction were not known, radiocarbon dates revealed that folks were living on the grounds while they engaged in construction. When mounds were raised amid all this building frenzy was uncertain, too. Radiocarbon dates from Mound B, the only dated mound, were all assayed a half-century ago using the old carbon dioxide method. Four assays run on charcoal from a single feature—the ash bed at mound base—differ by 800 years, strongly suggesting that they are erroneous.

Statistically analyzing the radiocarbon chronology has kept me from proposing a wrong sequence and ignoring a right one but has not helped me decide whether the earthworks were built quickly or at a leisurely pace. The time from cal. B.C. 1600 to 1300 seems to encompass the span of construction, but telling how much of that time was actually spent building or precisely when various parts of the earthworks were built was simply not possible. The actual amount of time spent in building probably was less than three centuries—a virtual eternity when it comes to trying to figure out what kind of organization was behind the effort. Nonetheless, not being able to tell which of the many possible building sequences was more likely meant one thing to me: that Poverty Point was built in short order. It was not built in a day, but I anticipate that it took less than a century and would not be surprised at less than a generation.

Land-leveling

The rings were built on fairly level terrain, although buried soils revealed it had a few ups and downs. Parts of the old ground beneath the upper west and northwest sections of the rings were low and poorly drained, and deep gullies cut back from the bluff in at least two places underneath the north sector. One was exposed in the bluff face below the end of the innermost northern ring, but the largest ran between where the second and fifth northern rings sit today. It was more than sixty-five paces wide, over 400 paces long, and deep enough in places to hide an eighteen-wheeler. Over 30,000 cubic yards of dirt were needed to level it, some 2,150 dump truck loads of fill. Haag found that the tail of the bird mound was built over a depression. Between low places were broad flats or low sweeping ridges where water drained better. Some higher spots were incorporated in the rings without having to pile much if any dirt on them. I found one high spot enveloped by the fifth ring in the upper west sector and another by the third ring in the north. Haag found still another in the second ring in the north.

Where low spots crossed the path of the rings, they were land-leveled, and rings and sometimes even the swales (or ditches) between rings had to be raised atop these leveled areas. Landfill, like ring fill, was bulk loaded. Basketloads of löess were dumped, and piles sometimes were covered with silty clay loam, silty clay, or clay taken from löessial subsoils or old Crowley clay exposures. Land-leveling was done while the rings were under construction, because it was impossible to tell where landfill stopped and ring fill began. If there had been building breaks between, they were so short that grass did not have time to grow or the sun long enough to bake the earth.

Land-leveling did not achieve a uniform elevation. Neither tops of rings nor bottoms of swales were level or sloped consistently, and that ruled out suspicions that controlling water flow was behind landfilling and ring design. It seems to me that the main reason for land-leveling was to fill up deep holes so rings could go the way they were supposed to.

Orientation and Design

Poverty Point's earthworks formed a large geometric enclosure inside an even bigger square space outlined by in-line mounds. Identified first as octagonal and later as circular, the enclosure was actually elliptical. Mark Stielper found that the radii of ring arcs in north and south sectors were similar, while those of corresponding western segments differed. Ellipses were as easy to lay off as circles. All that was needed were two stakes and a long cord. With ends of the cord tied to each stake, a surveyor holding the cord somewhere in the middle walked out to the point where all slack was pulled out of the cord and then keeping the cord taunt made a full circuit around the stakes. But stakes would have had to be moved each time a new ring was laid off, or rings would not have been parallel. To lay off outer rings, surveyors would have had to lengthen the distance between stakes; for inner rings, they would have had to shorten it. They did not have to know any geometry or the value of pi to get the rings to come out parallel. Trial and error worked as well then as it does now.

If rings had been laid out by the stake-and-cord method, then inward building progression was most likely. Erecting the outermost ring first would have eliminated problems of having to cross standing inner rings. On the other hand, if all rings had been laid off before any were constructed—as implied in the master blueprint idea—there would have been no obstructions to start with. Even if some rings had been raised before others were laid off, there still would have been no problem until houses and other structures were placed on them. Ring masses by themselves were not high enough to have restricted visibility or interfered with cord pulling, no matter which way construction proceeded.

Alternatively, if one ring had been simply chained from another, then outward progression would have been more logical.

All outer mounds—Mound A, Mound B, and Ballcourt Mound—were built along the same north-south line, an alignment bearing an azimuth of 352.5 degrees and considered to be the main site axis. Lower Jackson Mound was also on the same line despite being nearly one and one-third miles south of the Ballcourt Mound and probably centuries older than the other mounds. Lower Jackson Mound could be seen clearly from Ballcourt Mound, providing, of course, that no woods interfered. The north-south line was tangent to the outer ring of the central enclosure and passed through the centers of all mounds except for Mound A, where it passed along the inside edge of the wing. Motley Mound was not on line but lay east of and perpendicular to it. It lined up with Dunbar Mound. The Motley-Dunbar alignment was parallel to the main mound alignment 600 paces away.

The lineup of mounds was not coincidental. The total distance between the four in-line mounds was over two miles. If projected further north to the intersection of the east-west Motley alignment, the line would have stretched over a mile past Mound B, a total distance of more than 5,750 paces. Mathematician William Talley determined that having all mound

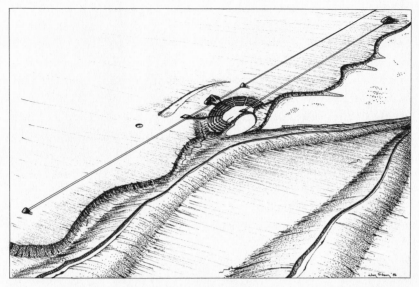

Fig. 5.10. Getting the earthworks to line up as precisely as they do would happen by chance only one time in nearly 250,000 chances. Two mounds—Lower Jackson Mound and possibly Ballcourt Mound—may be earlier Archaic constructions. This suggests that Poverty Point builders incorporated older, venerated structures in the layout, thereby helping to preserve ancient tradition.

positions on-line or tied in perpendicularly over a distance of greater than three miles would have been likely to happen only once in a quarter-million chances. And chances of having two separate paralleling alignments were astronomical.

Function and Raison d'Etre

What were earthworks used for? That question typically got some standard answer such as serving as house foundations, fortifications, ceremonial buildings, or some other common purpose. These uses were conceived as being exclusive and fostered disagreement about whether Poverty Point was a town or a vacant ceremonial center. But residence and ritual were not exclusive among Native Americans. They coexisted.

One of the usual arguments brought up in favor of the rings being residential was how much midden there was. Black-earth midden covered ring crests and lined their bottom edges. Sometimes primary midden thinly capped small areas on building layers; sometimes it was included in basketloads having been transported from somewhere else. Midden veneered the old ground beneath the rings, showing that people were already living in a huge semicircle when building started. But simply arguing that black-earth midden meant long-term residence was not entirely convincing. Why? Because all kinds of ceremonies such as weddings, funerals, dances, ballgames, religious observations, or other events that involved feasting (and they nearly all did) produced trash, too, just like routine domestic activities. Cooking-ball fragments dominated trash.

But it was other kinds of trash that strongly suggested people lived on the rings and did not merely celebrate on them. Trash from every part of the rings included mundane and commonplace items. Whole and broken tools, manufacturing debris, fire-cracked rock, and other residue showed that people were doing all kinds of things—not just feasting or conducting ceremonies, which would have produced limited or specialized groups of material like those I found on Dunbar Mound floors. If people had only gathered to trade, surely they would not have left behind so many perfectly good things or produced so much trash.

Besides, the probable descendants of Poverty Point people—the Tunican-speaking Koroa, Tunica, and Tioux—as well as many other historic southern tribes, staged ceremonies on mounds and in plazas. Mounds and plazas were special set-aside spaces, power places. Politics, spirits, and community pride concentrated in such places. Poverty Point had both mounds and a central plaza apart from the rings.

But why build giant rings to live on? Why not just live on natural ground? Was it too wet? Maçon Ridge never flooded but would have gotten soggy and muddy from rains that fell often during that time. Whether intentional or not, one benefit of living atop rings was having dry feet.

If people really lived on them—a question often asked—where were their house remains? As populated as Poverty Point was, houses ought to have crowded ring crests. But more than a century of digging failed to turn up any house outlines. Were they all destroyed by plowing and erosion? Ford and Webb thought so. But all of them, every single one? Did residents live in simple shelters that failed to leave marks on the ground, like brush arbors, flimsy wickiups, or tents? Did they sleep under the stars? What about the rain? To me, having anything short of post-in-ground houses was inconceivable in light of the wall-posted house patterns that

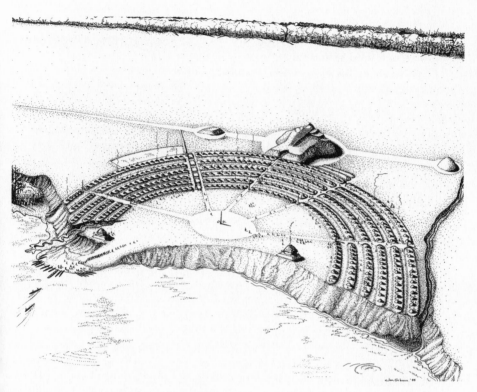

Fig. 5.11. One reconstruction depicts Poverty Point around 1350 B.C. as a large residence having a population of several hundred people, possibly as many as a thousand.

Ford and his excavation team found at contemporary Jaketown, that Haag and Ford excavated at Monte Sano, and that Saunders discovered at Frenchman's Bend. Monte Sano and Frenchman's Bend were thousands of years older than Poverty Point. Although these finds had no direct bearing on Poverty Point, they made it all the more difficult to understand why folks who built such massive earthworks did not build sturdy houses to live in. Or did they, and archaeologists just have not recognized them?

I suspect houses probably did stand atop the rings, just as some archaeologists have thought all along. Hundreds of postmolds were scattered across the rings as well as in the central open space, or plaza, and on several floors in Dunbar Mound. Scores of hearths and pits were found, too. So evidence that houses or some kind of walled post-in-ground structures had been built on the rings was in hand from the moment modern excavations began. The problem was that excavated exposures just were not large enough to reveal complete house patterns or that too many postmolds obscured their recognition.

Goad's broad excavations on the first northwestern ring initially were thought to have uncovered circular house patterns, but Connolly's reanalysis showed that most of the presumed postmolds were shallow stains, root channels, or patches of basketloading. The few real ones were too few to form recognizable patterns. Hard clay patches found here and elsewhere reminded some archaeologists of house floors, but their domed or sloping sides suggested that they were only clay-veneered building piles. Postmold patterns I detected on Dunbar Mound stages were not traced very far, although they seemed to be from square or rectangular wooden buildings.

Still, postmolds scattered throughout the rings and clustered on the western side of the plaza were rare considering how much dirt was excavated. My excavations produced about one postmold every thousand cubic feet. Invariably, they were recognized when they extended through different-colored building layers or when they entered the old ground below the rings. None were recognized on ring surfaces. They first showed up atop building layers below the plow zone or in the old ground surface. The shallowest postmold I ever found originated elbow-deep below the modern surface.

Stratigraphic location suggested that many postmolds had been obliterated and obscured. But land changes other than plowing and erosion, as claimed by Ford and Webb, were involved, too, and Poverty Point's antiquity was behind most of them. Trees have been falling as long as wind has been blowing. Fifteen went down in a recent year alone, and those were toppled by thunderstorms, not tornadoes or gulf gales. Big ones pulled up Volkswagen-sized clumps of dirt and disturbed areas as large as my living room; small ones tore up areas as small as my desktop. At the rate of fifteen a year, big treefalls could have upturned an area of almost 130 acres, or about 60 percent of the ring area since abandonment. At a minimum, an average loss of five small trees per year would have damaged only about 4 percent of the ring area.

The net effect was much greater. Scaling from a 1938 aerial photograph showed that about 160 acres or three-fourths of the total ring area had been cultivated, some continuously for nearly two centuries. Treefall damage was concentrated, therefore, in roughly one-fourth of the rings, the part not disturbed by plowing. Adding treefall and plow damage together suggested that the upper part of the rings ran a high risk of having been disturbed, completely eliminating patterns of all houses built on the rings after they were finished.

As if plowing and treefall damage were not enough, soil and midden development posed another obstacle for finding house remains. Rings were old enough for soil to form in their basketloaded fill dirt, and the soil was organically enriched by tons of trash strewn about. The upper parts of rings, knee-deep down, were transformed into dark midden. Postmolds were not destroyed necessarily by this organically charged weathering, although plant roots, earthworms, and burrowing animals undoubtedly claimed some. Molds simply were engulfed and hidden by midden blackness.

The few postmolds found on temporary surfaces within the rings were probably not from houses either. Some ring segments—perhaps all—were raised without major construction pauses. For example, I found that one section of the third upper western ring contained several building increments with fire pits. Instead of indicating separate construction episodes, these increments indicated rapid continuous building. Seven pits were directly superimposed, and the layers bearing them made up half the vertical mass of the ring. Whoever cooked in each new pit had to know where the lower pit had been before it got covered by a new foot-thick layer of dirt, or else the pits would not have been so perfectly lined up. Good memory, same vista, ESP, who knows? They all pointed to the same conclusion: Building here probably took only a matter of days, not months or years.

Rapid construction was indicated also in the third northern ring. There, analyst James Feathers took a soil sample from a living surface lining one of the lower fill layers and subjected it to optically stimulated luminescence dating. He found that the surface had not been exposed to sunlight long enough to bleach the dirt. Lack of exposure to sunlight may have prevented us from finding out when the surface was occupied, but it enabled us to tell that occupation lasted for less time than it took to get a sunburn.

Building lenses or layers lacking a lot of trash usually were composed of subsoil, and they formed the bulk of most rings. Trash was scattered lightly across temporary surfaces throughout the rings but did not form continuous sheets. Construction workers seemed to have lived temporarily on flatter sections of partially finished rings, probably while they

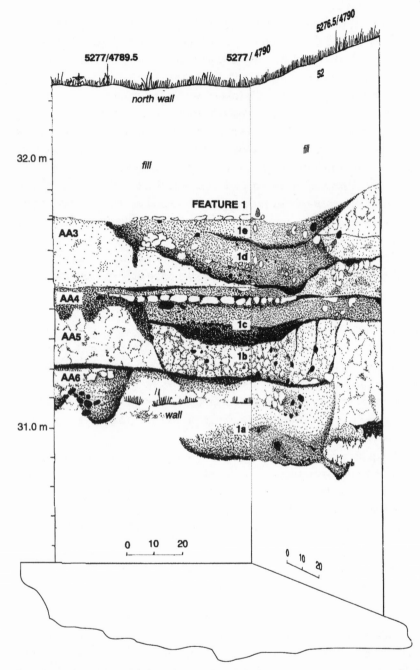

Fig. 5.12. Superimposed fire pits were revealed in one excavation in the third western ring. Precise superpositioning across more than half the ring thickness suggests rapid construction.

labored on other sections. But the lack of extensive living surfaces within the rings did not mean they were built with itinerant labor. As soon as entire rings or sections of rings were finished, residents could have moved onto them, or they could have remained in old living quarters not yet disrupted by construction. The preconstruction living area was huge, the same size and shape as the six-ringed enclosure, so there was plenty of room for people to live and work without ever having to camp on active construction areas.

The absence of abundant housing remains on interim building layers was due to rapid construction. The absence of house remains on top of the finished rings was due to disturbance by plowing, treefalls, and burrowing creatures, as well as to masking by prolonged anthropic soil development. Old living surfaces underlay the rings, and if house patterns are ever going to show up, that is where they will be. Why then were patterns not recognized in excavations that reached old living surfaces? Mainly because narrow trenches and isolated test pits were used, and neither type of excavation opened big enough areas to reveal patterns. Plenty of post-molds were uncovered, but wider exposures were needed to recognize patterns.

Was Poverty Point a residence? I think so—an awfully big one at that, an honest-to-goodness town. But the best proof—evidence of substantial house patterns—has been destroyed, obscured, or not yet unearthed. I realize a hunter-gatherer town sounds like a contradiction in terms, but I also believe wandering sometimes was arrested by resource richness and organization. Poverty Point was one of those stilled places.

Claims that Poverty Point was a vacant ceremonial center are simply not tenable given the extensive midden and its secular-looking trash—trash that resembled nearby core and periphery residences. Since most trash consisted of cooking-ball fragments, it provided little help in distinguishing daily home cooking from periodic, ceremonial-event cooking and feasting. Yet I think that help is provided by evidence bearing on how knappers organized their stone-working technology.

In my view, people periodically gathered for ceremonies would have carried their gear with them. At the most, they would have done minor repairs or made "quickies" (or expedient, throw-away tools). Poverty Point's stonework does not suggest that was the case. For example, on the bluff end of the third northern ring, I found that percentages of local chert flakes bearing no cortex matched up well with those from nine neighboring encampments, which were all small field camps or residences. In addition, I found that local gravels on the third northern ring were handled no differently from exotic exchange rocks when it came to making bifaces: There were between one and three bifaces for every 100 flakes chipped from each of eight different kinds of rock, seven of which were exotic. If Poverty Point had been strictly ceremonial, I would have expected to find more bifaces made out of exotic exchange flint than out of local chert.

Actually, there were so many basic artifactual similarities among Poverty Point and encampments up to fifteen miles away that they graphed as a single group, a group composed of *residences*. British archaeologist Colin Renfrew argued that traditional societies did not separate religion, ceremony, and celebration from routine matters, and there was no compelling reason to think that Poverty Point did so.

Sherwood Gagliano and Edwin Jackson independently raised the prospect that Poverty Point served as the site of a periodically staged trade fair, where independent groups met, traded rocks and other goods, and then dispersed, leaving behind a small contingent of caretakers to mind the grounds until the next gathering. Jackson argued that such fairs, staged by historic hunter-gatherer groups in Canada and Australia, promoted ceremonies and alliances as well as intensified economies. Like the vacant ceremonial center interpretation, the trade-fair idea was posed as an alternative to Poverty Point being a residence. The data simply do not stand up to such an all-or-nothing interpretation.

Exchange obviously took place at Poverty Point but not as a big event or series of smaller events that transpired outside the context of overall domestic activities. Exotic exchange rocks prevailed at encampments out to community edges and were pretty important in a few places located days and days beyond. I suspect some outlying community encampments got their rocks directly through gatherings at Poverty Point, because statistical patterns revealed that tool use generally determined where exchange materials wound up. If rocks had been serially traded—either directly from group to group or preferentially from elite to elite—they surely would have gone to different places in different amounts. More distant encampments probably did get exotics from trade lines, although trips to Poverty Point were not out of the question.

Concluded trade fairs, which would have left the rings largely empty and unused, raised the same basic problems as a vacant ceremonial center: Why did Poverty Point have so much trash; so many tools in good work-

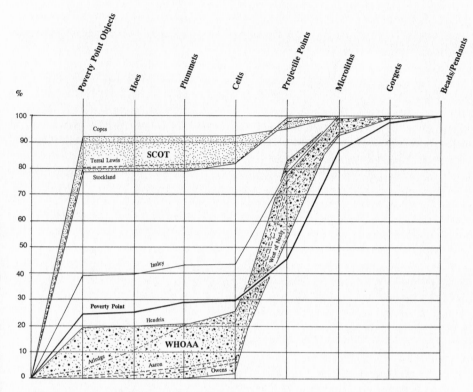

Fig. 5.13. Cumulative graphing of tool inventories at encampments encircling Poverty Point reveals that they form two groups. One seems to correspond to temporary field camps (labeled with acronym WHOAA) and the other group to permanent residences (labeled SCOT).

ing order as well as so many incomplete, resharpened, and recycled ones; so many ornaments, both finished and partly finished; and, most of all, so much exchange rock. Rock exchange was supposedly what brought fair-goers together in the first place. Why would people have left 75, maybe 100, tons of exotic rock behind? I can understand leaving their trash, but there were hundreds of thousands of perfectly good tools, too. I cannot imagine people attending a trade fair in order to acquire hardware and then make, use, break, repair, reuse, and lose or throw away that hardware on the meeting grounds.

Ritual consumption cannot account for the tons of material; neither can it account for its condition or context. The rings had caches and deposits of objects—projectile points, plummets, soapstone fragments, even a bead-maker's kit—but they were uncommon and not convincingly ritualistic. Most exotic exchange rock was treated just like local chert gravel and wound up in general midden. This was very different from the mid-southern Middle Archaic practice, noted by archaeologists Johnson and Sam Brookes, of burying stacks of whole or intentionally broken Benton and Turkeytail bifaces in pits. Those bifaces had never been placed into mundane service, and the pits did not contain any manufacturing flakes or other common trash. Benton's exotic material was ritually smashed; Poverty Point's was routinely trashed.

Massive earthworks also did not play well with the notion of a temporary gathering, especially one involving independent peoples unlikely to cooperate in such a huge undertaking that did not directly facilitate exchange. Still, just because contemporary fair-attending hunter-gatherers did not build anything as massive as Poverty Point's earthworks did not mean that hunter-gatherer groups were physically incapable of such effort. The brute labor required to build the rings and mounds was within the means of even small groups working for a fairly short time. Yet being *able* to build and actually *doing* it were vastly separate issues. The real crux of the matter lay in organization, power, and motivation, not in manpower; and all these things except manpower were minimized at temporary camp meetings, or else competition and rivalry would have reduced them to little more than an uncooperative, haggling, squabbling gaggle. To me, the social and political motives behind earthworks were rooted in home and country. Building earthworks—big ones like Poverty Point's—was simply incompatible with temporary economic incentives and social neutrality. Although trading transpired, Poverty Point was not just a fair. It was a big town.

Why earthworks then? I believe they were expressions of home and soul as well as safety nets for keeping evil spirits at bay. The pattern was old and honored, and I think it came down from stories of the creation told since the time when many, perhaps most, southern native languages were mutually intelligible. The rings were larger than could be detected from ground level. They had to be seen with the mind, not the eye; and in that sense alone, they were extraordinary. The ringed or broken-circle pattern was charged with supernatural meaning. The break in the eastern side gave a direct path to the sun, the primary celestial being of Gulf-speaking groups, and also provided an exit for negative feelings that built up inside the enclosed spaces. But openings—any openings—in geometric figures provided portals for outside ghosts, witches, or evil forces to enter unless, as Robert Hall suggests, they were kept out by water or ash barriers. A stream or lake lay along Poverty Point's open side. Rings arched completely around the western side and, following traditional beliefs, prevented truly evil spirits from the west and north from getting inside the enclosure. Outside evil was barred from gaining entry through the narrow cross-cutting aisles by a second line of protection: the geometrical square formed by the five outer mounds. Yet the aisles, in keeping with traditional beliefs, could have carried away negative energies produced inside the rings and vented them safely past the point where they could upset inner harmony.

The earthworks embodied Gulf language–related metaphors relating to magical protection. I suspect they symbolized creation and cosmos, representations of Earth Mother and the three planes of existence—the upper, middle, and lower worlds. As such, they served as conspicuous expressions of land ties, social identity, and community pride. Earthworks may have been magic, but they also embodied a spirit of unity and pride. Rings were expressions of corporateness; they were manifestations of home.

Effort

Poverty Point's earthworks were large, among the largest ever built in prehistoric eastern North America. They were assumed initially to be the handiwork of many people working for centuries, but an army of laborers was not necessary even if construction had been done quickly. Total volume of the rings and mounds was somewhere between 870,000 and 1 million cubic yards, and an undetermined but sizable quantity went into land reclamation. Based on a two-man experiment in dirt hauling conducted in Mexico nearly four decades ago, I estimated that it would have taken 100 laborers between twenty-one and twenty-four years, working every day, to build the standing earthworks alone. A thousand laborers could have finished in two to two and a half years. If work had been spread out, say for a century or three generations, then 100 people would have needed to work about six or seven days a month to complete the job; a thousand people, only about seven or eight days a year. Earthworks could have been finished in a single generation, or thirty years, if 500 people had worked between one and two months a year. These figures were not intended as estimates of Poverty Point's labor force or population but as expressions of how much work was expended.

Knowing that it was possible for 100 people to build the mounds and rings, even at a leisurely pace within the statistical error range of a radiocarbon date, meant that determining the order of construction would be difficult but that the labor required was well within the capabilities of hunter-gatherer groups. Actually, it was not difficult to decide which possible building sequence was followed; it was statistically impossible. Furthermore, despite long-held assumptions, labor estimates showed that big work gangs were not needed to build big earthworks even when completed quickly. Hunter-gatherers could have built them easily, and they need not have been any more numerous than a local group of a half-dozen families.

Although a small group was capable of building the earthworks within the span of a radiocarbon date—a century or so—does not necessarily mean that Poverty Point was built by a small group. I cannot imagine a construction so massive being done by so very few. There is no evidence of comparable undertakings in eastern North America or anywhere else in the world for that matter. Poverty Point must have served a population larger than a half-dozen families, but just how much larger remains unknown, hidden by a mighty large sentiment—love of place, of home.

6

Gear and Appliances

"The Mother String"

Dec. 14th—Found copper beads in flash flood ditch . . . SE from "cut # 7 & 8 . . . Ford and Webb" . . . 6 copper beads.

Dec. 15th. 4 copper beads, at above site.

Dec. 16th. 3 more copper beads recovered from site above, a total of 13 beads. Please refer to 10 April C-3 (1) copper bead. Exact spot as of Dec. 14th making a total of 14 copper beads.

Dec. 19/61. Found the mother string of what was left of the copper beads, 19 in all, as follows, in two rows 2 1/2" apart north and south, on a horizontal level, 3'10" deep, south of flash flood ditch. In place or two, some fused together. I would say some perishable substance was used for every third bead. Bone or shell or wood but no trace . . . found by me.

Carl Alexander, notes in unpublished field journal, 1961

Carl Alexander's scribbled notes in his journal appear drab and matter-of-fact until you look at the entry dates—Dec. 14, 15, 16, and 19, three days in a row and four in a week—and realize what excitement they harbor. Poverty Point is like that. Expect the unusual and it is likely to turn up. Why? Because Poverty Point is such a well-appointed place.

A Well-Appointed Place

Tools for every imaginable household task as well as objects for the body and spirit were scattered on, in, and underneath rings and in mounds on floors and in fill. Mainly, they were made there. Lots of scrap said so. Many were used right where they were dropped, too, and signs of repair work marked equipment across the rings. Some places had a little more of this or a little more of that, but basically every ring segment yielded the same kinds of artifacts. That residents would have organized their working and living spaces should come as no great surprise considering how well organized the architecture was.

I depend on gear from entire ring-arc segments to provide a picture of how the town was arranged; individual household and activity space was below detection limits. While tools did not make the person or household, they helped make the town, and looking at gear and appliances helps to show what kind of settlement they made. By all appearances, the rings were a well-appointed place.

Poverty Point residents had many portable items that helped them work, play, dress, and worship. While much of this gear was not new functionally, it was new stylistically. It was varied and bountiful, which vouched for the many activities conducted at and from Poverty Point compared with surrounding encampments. Residents also made many stationary devices, or appliances, to help with daily jobs.

Cooking Gear and Appliances

Poverty Point Objects

Poverty Point objects (or PPOs) were baked earthenware objects used in cooking. They were so abundant at Poverty Point and nearby residential encampments that they have become a hallmark of Poverty Point culture. Whole and broken PPOs made up ninety-seven out of every hundred artifacts found at most spots on the rings, but other encampments had fewer, some considerably so. Surrounding field camps sometimes had as few as one PPO for every 150 stone objects found.

They were made out of the most abundant resource available at Poverty Point—löess. They were made from löess even when it was not available underfoot, and that vouched for its usefulness. PPOs found in the swamp between three and fifteen miles from Maçon Ridge, the source of

Fig. 6.1. Biconical Poverty Point Objects (PPOs) are generally the smallest of the cooking objects. The object on the left side of the bottom row is over two inches in height. Photography by Steven Carricut.

löess, show just how far some were carried. There is no löess in the swamp.

Usually, makers took one to three ounces of moist löess, rolled it around in their hands until they formed a rope, ball, or bicone, and then they often squeezed it, leaving impressions of their fingers. Moving hands back and forth produced a rope (a squatty cylinder), and rolling it onto spread fingers created grooves. Rolling a lump around in the cupped palms produced a ball (or melon), and a rotary motion with the lump held between heels of the hands created a bicone. After forming the basic shape, makers loosed their creative juices and squeezed, twisted, compressed, punched holes, drew lines, or otherwise manipulated generic forms into dozens of minor varieties. Other than constraints imposed by use, I often wonder whether such free expression was not like play, something like our paper/rock/scissors or shell games, or perhaps competition to make the fanciest objects, art for art's sake, or anxiety therapy.

Take bicones, for example. There are more than two dozen variations. They include plain, plain with longitudinal perforation, extruded, folded, longitudinally grooved, longitudinally grooved and end-grooved, vertically incised, vertically incised with longitudinal perforation, notched carina, circular end impressed, circular end impressed and notched carina, circular end impressed and vertically incised, carinally grooved, carinally grooved and vertically incised, multiple circle impressed, vertically and horizontally incised, cross incised, fingernail impressed, plain and diagonally grooved, alternating vertically and horizontally grooved, apically grooved, deeply grooved, grooved and folded, grooved and mat imprinted, grooved and multiple punched, grooved and cane punched, grooved and transversely grooved, and grooved and diagonally grooved. In addition, a few objects were large, many were small, but most were medium-sized, one to two inches in diameter.

Such bewildering variety did not mean that they had as many different uses. More than 98 percent of the PPOs represented some modification of the three main shapes: ropes, balls, and bicones. Separate experiments conducted by Don Hunter and me showed that objects of all three shapes, when heated and transferred to earth ovens, cooked food as well as modern stoves and with just as little monitoring. But plain old dirt clods or gravel would have done that. So, why make shaped forms?

My experiments suggested that shape affected oven temperature when other conditions were held constant. Forty cylindrical grooved objects that were heated in a bonfire for one hour and then transferred to a water-bucket-sized pit heated the pit to a maximum of 300° Fahrenheit. Within twenty-five minutes, temperature dropped to 150°. On the other hand, forty cross-grooved balls heated for an hour produced a maximum pit temperature of 427°, which cooled to 200° fifty minutes later. Forty melon-shaped objects heated for an hour produced a pit temperature of

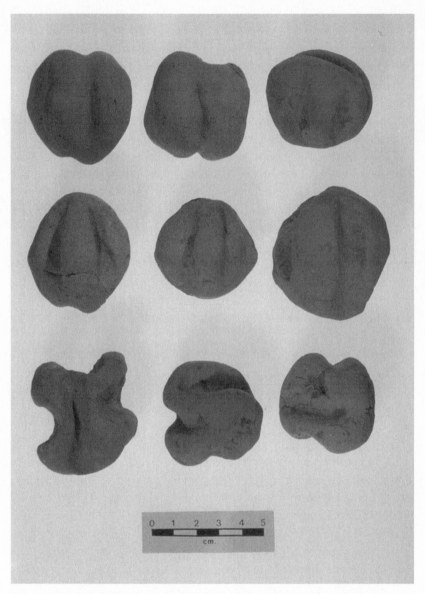

Fig. 6.2. Rounded, finger-grooved PPOs include melons with end grooves (*top row*), melons (*middle row*), and cross-grooved (*bottom row*). Differences are recognized by the placement of finger grooves. Photography by Steven Carricut.

500°, which fell to 200° after forty minutes. Forty biscuit-shaped objects sent the pit to 325°, but it fell off to 157° after forty minutes. A control cooking using forty disc-shaped objects—a shape not encountered at Poverty Point—approximated cylindrical grooved results. Admittedly, these were field tests often conducted while libations flowed and good times rolled, lacking some of the rigorous controls of laboratory experiments. But Poverty Point chefs did not cook in a lab, either. The only thing I intentionally changed during each cooking was the shape of objects dumped into the pit. Foods even remained the same.

Using differently shaped objects changed pit temperatures every time, both temperature maximums and durations, prompting me to conclude that form was functional. Counterarguments based on engineering principles and evolutionary theory and lacking the benefit of practical experiments opined that style alone was responsible. I agree that style is important but cannot go along with it being the sole determinant. By my count, there are well over 100 varieties, but I suspect that 95 percent of them differ in mass and surface area by less than 5 percent. This means that about 95 percent of the heat-conducting and -radiating potential can be attributed to very few general size and shape differences; that is, to the three primary shapes—ropes, balls, and bicones—and three major size classes—small, medium, and large. Hence, style probably did account for the lion's share of PPO variability, but function determined the differences that mattered most. Experienced cooks knew precisely how many and which kinds of PPOs were needed to bake a meal.

Fire-Cracked Rock

The old time-honored method of heating, cooking, and rendering nut oil and grease was with local gravel and sandstone. But rock evidently was not used in pit baking or roasting as none of the discovered pits were filled with or surrounded by fire-cracked rock (or FCR). No concentrations of FCR were found, period. FCR amounts to less than 0.5 percent of the items taken from nearly every excavated section of the rings, and its wide scatter suggests that it probably constituted dregs dumped when portable cooking containers were emptied.

Pottery

Ford, Phillips, and notable mid-twentieth-century archaeologists denied that pottery had been made by Poverty Point people, but now archaeolo-

Fig. 6.3. All three major shapes of PPOs—biconical, cylindrical, and rounded—occasionally were decorated. Decorated PPOs were usually smaller than undecorated objects and probably suggest functions other than everyday cooking. Courtesy of Clarence Webb; rephotography by Steven Carricut.

gists know some was made. Although uncommon, pottery was produced before, during, and after ring construction. Four wares (or fabrics)—fiber-tempered, sand-tempered, clay-grit-tempered, and untempered—and two design groups—Wheeler and Old Floyd Tchefuncte—were made. Old Floyd decorations were applied to all wares except fiber-tempered, which bore Wheeler decoration.

Fiber-tempered Wheeler pottery was mostly undecorated, but Wheeler Punctated exhibited haphazard or linear punctates made with blunt- or sharp-pointed styluses and with fingernails; Wheeler Simple Stamped had roughly parallel indentations made by the edge of a square-sided tool. Sand-tempered ware, often classified as Alexander, also was primarily plain, although about one in six sherds had haphazard tool punctates or fingernail pinches. The rare untempered pottery was so soft and powdery that Webb and his colleagues doubted that the small cup-shaped vessels were serviceable and instead suggested they were toys.

Clay-grit-tempered ware was a catch-all grouping for all early pottery that was not predominantly fiber-tempered, sand-tempered, or untemp-

ered. Decorations on this fabric were called Old Floyd Tchefuncte in order to distinguish them from later Tchefuncte pottery, which had practically identical decorations. Clay-grit-tempered ware made up half of Poverty Point's pottery, and Webb noted that every two in five sherds were
decorated.

Tammany Punctated was the most common Old Floyd decoration, occurring on about one of six sherds. Webb noted several designs: linear or
haphazard fingernail impressions, finger noding, rows of pinched ridges,
hollow circular-tool punctates, linear or haphazard solid, blunt-tool
punctates, and haphazard pointed-tool stipples. Tchefuncte Stamped
made up about one of ten sherds and came in two designs: (a) rows or
columns made by walking a two-pronged tool across vessel walls, and (b)
rows or columns made by employing a solid bar in the same fashion.
Tchefuncte Incised comprised less than one of thirty-three sherds and included plain-line and wiggled-line patterns forming horizontal and vertical panels with parallel horizontal lines, slanting lines, concentric triangles, nested rectangles, alternating triangles and nested diamonds, and
alternating slanting and cross-hatched lines. About one in 100 sherds was
Orleans Punctated, which depicted line-bordered zones of tool punctates.

Information on vessel sizes and shapes was limited. Wheeler vessels
included thick-walled, deep bowls and jars of unknown capacity. They
usually had small, flat, round, and thick bases, although annular (or
ringed) and convex bases occasionally occurred. No vessel form or size
data were available for sand-tempered ware. Untempered ware included
the only known whole vessel, a miniature bowl less than an inch high and
wide and bearing three podal supports—hardly more than a cooking ball
with a hole in it and little nodes pulled out for feet. Other reconstructed
forms included a small bowl about the size of a soup bowl and a cup about
the size of a coffee cup. Medium-sized bowls, jars with straight out-slanting walls, and tecomates (pots with bulbous bodies and small mouths)
were made of clay-grit-tempered ware. Bowl and jar mouths were up to a
foot wide. At least one vessel had a square base, some had small flat disc
bases, and many had bases with teat-shaped legs or encircling flutes. Their
walls were usually thinner than Wheeler's.

In terms of heating performance, Wheeler vessels were better suited for
indirect cooking. They had thicker walls and fiber tempering, which acted
as insulation against escaping heat and heated better from within than
from without. Their wide mouths made it easier to put in hot gravels and

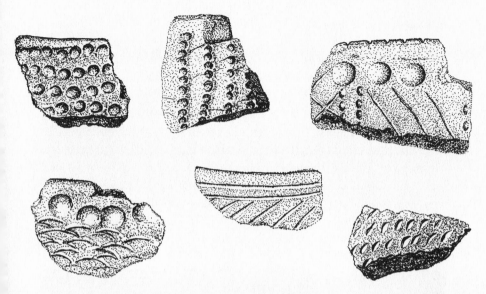

Fig. 6.4. Old Floyd Tchefuncte pottery incorporated several decorations: linear tool punctating (*top row, left and middle*); linear tool punctating separating alternating panels of cross-hatched and hachured incising (*top row, right*); rocker stamping (*bottom row, left*); incising (*bottom row, middle*); and fingernail punctating (*bottom row, right*). Vertical positions (or stratigraphy) suggests that Tchefuncte-like pottery was common before fiber-tempered Wheeler ceramic and soapstone vessels reached their peak. This does not make it any older than the other two types of containers but does suggest an equally early age and an earlier moment of popularity.

take them out after they cooled. They were not as good as clay-grit vessels for cooking directly over the fire. The thinner walls and nonorganic temper of clay-grit containers heated up more quickly. Their deep bowl and jar shapes retained heat that otherwise would have been lost through convection had vessels had wider mouths. Narrow-mouthed tecomates were the best of all shapes for rapid cooking over open flame. Another asset was the four-lobed/legged base. Not only did four-lobe vessel architecture better support the weight of wet clay walls, enabling taller vessels to be created, but it distributed heat more effectively during firing and later during cooking. Such efficiency cut down on differential heat absorption, a common cause of vessel failure. Pot legs helped resolve that problem, too, and enhanced vessel thermal efficiency by raising the main body of the pot above the cooler ash bed and permitting flames to circulate under the bottom. Over the long term, efficient pots conserved firewood. In spite of these design features, clay-grit vessels were not very good from a survivability standpoint. Ceramicist Doyle Gertjejansen and associates contend in their 1983 article in *Southeastern Archaeology* that "cooking was possible in Tchefuncte ware but it had a definite negative effect on longevity. The cooking vessels had to be relatively free from defects to begin with, a case that did not often exist. Repeatedly subjecting the pots to reheating and rehydrating conditions associated with food preparation causes pronounced carbon accumulation on the vessel exterior, a definite increase in cracking, and an accelerated degeneration of the vessel surface (cracking and flaking). The vessels would have been best suited for dry or damp collection and storage." Nevertheless, clay was cheap, and making pottery required minimal skill and know-how.

Fig. 6.5. Tchefuncte vessels have been simulated by contemporary ceramicist Doyle Gertjejansen. He proposed that they had a limited shelf life because low firing left them vulnerable to rehydration but suggested that ease of replacement may have given them an advantage over hard-to-replace stone pots, which had to be imported from the Appalachian piedmont. Photography by Charles Parker.

For another thing, low-fired löessial pottery like fiber-tempered and untempered wares made poor boilers. Even when well compacted and firm, low-fired fabric would have broken down and muddied liquid boiled within. On the other hand, a floated (or wet-smoothed) surface on clay-grit vessels would have formed a tight skin and limited mud flavoring. This raises the possibility that clay-grit vessels may have been used directly over fire while other wares may have been used for hot-rock cooking.

All wares were made while construction was ongoing and probably helped resolve meal-preparation schedule problems created by building. Fast food cooked in reusable, portable clay-grit containers would have kept hungry workers from having to dig a new earth oven every time they covered up an old one with a new layer of dirt. Time and labor also would have been conserved by reusing portable Wheeler pots to render nut oil and animal grease. How? By making it possible for rendering to be carried out by people actively engaged in building. In addition, Wheeler pots were much lighter than soapstone pots. And if one got broken at a busy construction site, it would have caused no major problem; another could be brought from home later or even made on the spot. On the other hand, breaking a soapstone pot must have been a calamity. Sad owners would have had to go 300 miles or more to get another or give up their favorite daughter in exchange.

I believe the four wares served different purposes. They were not vying for the same spot in the cupboard or competing for stylistic one-upmanship. I think pottery vessels of all kinds caught on as labor-saving devices during busy construction moments and stayed around afterwards because they simplified food preparation. That they turned out some pretty tasty mulligans and courtbouillons helped, too; besides, these new watery dishes did not have all those little crunchy pieces of FCR in the bottom of the pot.

Stone Vessels

Stone vessels were ten times more common than pottery vessels. That says a lot about the assumed dictum that people always choose the path of least effort, because pottery vessels embodied far less effort than stone containers: They were homemade, while soapstone vessels had to be brought in from eastern Alabama or western Georgia. Even a few sand-

Fig. 6.6. A soapstone pan was found at Lower Jackson Mound about one and one-third miles south of the rings. Lower Jackson Mound was probably built long before the rings and other mounds but seems to have been incorporated into the complex's main north-south alignment. Photography by Charles Parker.

stone vessels were used, but they were poor imitations since they did not wear nearly as well as soapstone ones.

Stone vessels were used for cooking and general containing. Two basic vessel shapes were indicated by fragments as well as by a few complete examples. The most common was an open bowl, circular or oval in outline with out-slanting straight or gently curved walls and a small, flat, circular base. The other form was a bathtub-shaped tray or pan having a rounded bottom and short vertical walls.

They were about the same size as pottery vessels, ranging between cup and boiler size and capable of holding up to three or four quarts. Walls were from a half-inch to an inch thick; when filled with liquid, vessels would have been heavy, weighing up to ten or fifteen pounds. To help with handling, lugs (short tab or strap handles) were carved on some vessels. A small number were decorated with single or multiple horizontal or slanting lines. Bas-relief figures of a straight-beaked bird and a panther adorned at least two vessels.

Soapstone made durable containers because it was resistant to thermal shock—pots could be heated over and over without breaking. It was soft and easily carved, but that may not have meant much to Poverty Point people, except when adding a few decorations, because the vessels themselves were probably made by Alabaman or Georgian stone carvers.

Durability probably replaced thermal efficiency as the major reason why soapstone vessels were successful cooking containers. Being able to

Fig. 6.7. A group of soapstone vessels was buried in a single cache outside the ring at Claiborne, located near the mouth of the Pearl River on the Mississippi Gulf Coast. Some of the larger vessels were stained inside.

withstand direct flame without breaking would have compensated for their reduced capacity to conduct heat as fast as thinner pottery. Throwing an extra piece of wood on the fire or waiting a few minutes longer for stew to cook would have been all that was necessary. Soapstone pots could be left simmering for hours, turned over or knocked around, and even dropped without breaking. Pots made of more thermally efficient löess and clay would have spalled, cracked, or shattered with such handling.

Durability was one of soapstone's major advantages, outweighing drawbacks of weight and distance from outcrops. Having tough cooking pots around made me wonder why breakable pottery containers were made also. Did the demands of construction hold the answer, or rather did the answer lay amid time and efficiency demands in general? Soapstone vessels were resilient, but they were also heavy and hard to replace. They were not your basic disposable cookware, but homemade pottery was. I suspect that light, replaceable clay and löess pots were used more often while busy workers toiled on the rings, and that good heavy stoneware was used after work and away from active construction areas. Both clay-grit and soapstone pots were used to cook on open fires but under different situations.

The average stratigraphic position of soapstone throughout the rings was higher than all potteries except fiber-tempered ware. That can be explained by residents turning to durable cookware as construction wound down. Still, those expedient pottery containers had earned a small but important place in Poverty Point homes.

Despite their durability, soapstone vessels eventually did break. Owners tried to save vessels when cracks first appeared by drilling opposing holes along the cracks and lacing them together, but cracks continued to run until vessels could no longer be used for cooking and eventually fell apart. When they did, pieces often were recycled into beads, pendants, plummets, and other objects or cached for future recycling.

Clarence Webb reported on one such cache located outside the rings about a quarter-mile southwest of the big mound. Hundreds of pounds of soapstone fragments were buried in an oval straight-sided pit, which was large enough to have held a big man comfortably. Only two vessels could be reconstructed from the pieces, and others fit together with fragments scattered across various ring segments. Even though four fires had burned in pit corners, I don't think this was a deposit of ritually smashed vessels but rather a recycler's stash of fragments collected from all over the rings. So much soapstone was removed from the pit and the immediately surrounding area after being discovered in 1925 that it accounts for more than half Poverty Point's entire soapstone sample today. Webb estimated that 300 to 400 vessels were represented among the fragments he excavated. Earlier and later recorded finds in the cache area double those numbers.

Appliances

Cooking was done in hearths and pits. These were small appliances, shallow or deep, and basin- or cylinder-shaped. Some had plastered walls, while others did not. Some were clean, while others were filled with scrap or burned material. Some were used once, while others had been used repeatedly.

The deeper conical or cylindrical pits probably functioned as earth ovens most of the time. Practically speaking, the deeper the pit, the better it was for baking. Some pits were about the size of a two-gallon bucket, while others were twice as big. Some were crammed full of PPOs, but most contained only a few; others were empty. Some had concentrations of PPO fragments around their mouths, left over from when food was removed. Trash was often thrown into abandoned ovens.

Shallow bowl-shaped pits were probably open-fire hearths, although most also contained PPO fragments, suggesting that baking had taken place in the ashes. Generally, they ranged about from one and a half to two feet in diameter and about half as deep, but some were larger. Webb found one burned area on the second southwestern ring that was over four feet across. I found a big pit in the plaza, three feet wide, its bottom covered with irregularly shaped lumps of baked löess. Seven superimposed hearths were dug on successive building layers in the third upper western ring segment. Each was about three feet in diameter.

Did bigger hearths suggest communal eating while construction was in progress? Did hearths prevail during work periods and earth ovens during down times? These are questions that can only be asked and not answered at present.

Excavations uncovered relatively few pits, but, like postmolds, that situation was probably due to the small amount of actual living surface exposed compared with the large amount of construction fill. When modern land-leveling exposed several acres of old ground beneath and just

Fig. 6.8. The bottom of one large fire pit excavated in the southern plaza was covered with a mass of large, irregular lumps of baked löess, not PPOs. These lumps had been placed on the bottom of the pit and were not pieces of a broken lining.

outside the sixth southwestern and southern rings, two clusters of pits, postmolds, and midden stains were recorded. The smaller cluster contained two pits in an area about the size of an average living room, and the second cluster, fifty paces to the east, contained five pits in an area about three times that size. Goad's large excavation on the first northwestern ring revealed an average of one pit for every compact-car-sized area. That may not mean they were more common here than elsewhere in the rings, because they occurred on several temporary surfaces throughout the full vertical extent of the ring. Those in the conjoined south and southwestern section were found on the old ground surface beneath the outer ring. The upper part of the ring had been destroyed by land-leveling.

Firewood

While PPOs transferred heat, firewood was ultimately responsible for producing it. For needs as common as cooking and heating, it is logical to think that every scrap of wood around would have been burned, making, in effect, the type of firewood used proportional to composition of tree species in the surrounding woods. Such does not seem to be the case. Gum dominated old timber, but its highest representation as firewood was at Steatite Field, a small core residence lying just outside the rings where Fowke and Webb excavated the soapstone cache. There, archaeobotanist Andrea Shea found that gum comprised less than 3 percent of the identifiable charcoal.

Poverty Point cooks were highly selective about their fuel. Shea identified charcoal from three small surrounding core residences, including Steatite Field, and found that oak comprised three-fourths of the collected samples, hickory and cane smaller amounts, and eleven other species together made up the remaining tiny fraction. Cane may have been chosen because it burns fast and furiously, but dry oak and hickory produce around 5,400–5,500 BTUs per pound, which are low-average heat values. Cottonwood, elm, willow, and especially pine all burn hotter. Still, oak and hickory fires are hot enough to cook on and burn longer. Less firewood would have been needed. In addition, oak and hickory are heavy pruners, frequently shedding limbs and branches. Perhaps most importantly, foods cooked over oak or hickory fires take on a delicious, savory flavor.

Tools for Making Tools

Clarence Webb identified several stone objects as food-grinding gear—mullers, manos, milling stones, pitted stones, and a metate. Rocks used for these grinders were chosen for their natural shapes: loaf shapes for mullers and manos, flat slabs for milling stones and metates, and blocky rocks for pitted stones. Except for the finely ground metate, most modifications resulted from being used rather than being intentionally fabricated.

Such objects probably were not used for cracking and grinding hard-shelled nuts and acorns, as Webb assumed, or, if they were, they certainly didn't produce much ground meal. They were too rare to have been used for such a common household task. Besides, they would have left meal pretty gritty. They would have been better suited for making groundstone tools. Nut and acorn meal probably would have been prepared in hollow wooden mortars.

Other tool-making tools consisted of stone abraders, hammerstones, saws, reamers, polishers, bark beaters, and an anvil. They were used for honing, hammering, sawing, reaming, and polishing all kinds of hard or resilient materials. Like grinding gear, tool-making tools were shaped largely by use but were more common. They outnumbered grinding implements by eighteen to one in one large collection tabulated by Webb in his 1976 study entitled *The Poverty Point Culture*. Still, they were not abundant.

Ford and Webb had even noted that the rarity of hammerstones seemed to be out of sync with the large amount of refuse exposed on the site. A good hammerstone indeed must have been a prized possession, but not having one evidently did not unduly worry knappers. Most of Poverty Point's fine-grained stone seems to have arrived as bifaces, and final shaping or maintenance probably was done with antler or wood billets, not with hammerstones. Hammerstones were not used exclusively for drawing blades, either, because they primarily occurred on ring segments other than where blade cores and blades were concentrated. In fact, hammerstone numbers mirror total artifact numbers throughout the rings.

Tools Designed for Chopping, Digging, and Pounding

Chopping, digging, and pounding were carried out with hafted stone tools having bifacially chipped or ground heads, such as celts, adzes, and hoes. Celts and adzes had poll and bit ends; hoes had bisymmetrical rounded ends and parallel sides. Bit blades on celts were centered; bit blades on adzes were beveled. Celts and adzes were fashioned in both chipped stone and groundstone while hoes were chipped only. Chipped versions were palm- to hand-sized bifaces with large flake scars and little edge refinement. Groundstone celts ranged from matchbook to hand size and in finish from roughly smoothed to finely polished; they were made

Fig. 6.9. Polished celts were common at both residences and field camps, implying that they were used for many tasks. They have been excavated from the middle of fill lenses in the earthworks, showing that they were used in the building of the rings. The specimen in the middle of the bottom row is nearly ten inches long.

of durable granite, basalt, other coarse igneous rock, or of dense magnetic greenstone.

Groundstone celts outnumbered chipped celts by nearly twenty-five to one, but groundstone adzes were outnumbered by chipped adzes by a ratio of thirty-seven to one. Celts and adzes were fairly common, and over half the celts were greenstone forms often referred to as pseudocelts or simulated celts. Hoes, on the other hand, were among the rarest special-ized tools at Poverty Point. Most small encampments on Joes Bayou had more hoes than Poverty Point, both relatively and absolutely.

Clarence Webb's inventoried sample of 11,714 projectile points, which is reported in his monograph *The Poverty Point Culture,* provides a stan-dard measure of just how plentiful these implements were. There was one adz for every 35 points, one hoe for every 434 points, and one celt for every 24 points. Among the celts, there was one pseudocelt for every 63 points.

Morphological resemblances among these implements were superficial and related to general size and weight resemblances as well as resharp-ening similarities, not to the way they were used. Celts were mounted with blades parallel to handles and centered in the eye, leaving both poll and bit ends sticking out past the handle. Bit ends were narrower than poll ends, which was important for keeping heads wedged tightly in the eye when chopping. Heavy polished forms probably were used like axes, and thin-ner chipped forms like hatchets. Blades on groundstone celts were usually bruised and battered, even on pseudocelts; nearly half were broken in two, showing that they saw heavy duty and were not strictly show tools.

Adzes and hoes were hafted with blades perpendicular to handles. Hoes were larger than adzes and were usually rectangular or trapezoidal, while most adzes were triangular. The triangular shape was good for keeping heads immobile when hacking on wood or other hard, nonre-silient materials; the harder the blow, the tighter the head wedged in the eye or binding. As the heavier, wider, rougher chipped tools, hoes were less triangular yet still remained reasonably tight in the binding. How was this possible? Because so much of the surface area was in contact with the binding. Although flake-scarred surfaces could not be bound as tightly as smoothly polished surfaces, binding did not need to be as secure as on adzes or celts because digging generated less resistance than chopping.

Adzes were made with beveled bits. Some were as steep as forty degrees from in-handle resharpening, but steep beveling strengthened cutting

Fig. 6.10. A shiny polish called sickle sheen coats the bits of most hoes, suggesting that they were used for digging in the ground, perhaps for grubbing roots. Their rarity at Poverty Point suggests that they were not employed in earthwork construction. This polished specimen is made of Dover flint and is from Aaron, a field camp on Joes Bayou; its length is 6.2 inches.

edges and improved performance. On the other hand, hoes were made with centered blades, but, like adzes, they were resharpened without taking heads loose from handles, and this sometimes left them asymmetrically beveled also. Angles were not as sharp as on adzes, and often both faces were beveled or bifacially sharpened. Heavily used implements had to be continually resharpened in order to remove dull wood polish from adze bits and sickle-sheen from hoe bits. Sickle-sheen is a dulling coating of opal—a mineral present in grasses—that fuses onto bits and faces of implements used to chop through sod. It resembles a thick coat of shellac.

Hoes were more common at Joes Bayou encampments than at Poverty Point. Clarence Webb's large surface-collected sample from Poverty Point contained one hoe for every 434 projectile points. Excavations in many parts of the rings produced no hoes or hoe fragments whatsoever, although a small area excavated on the eastern end of the third northern ring yielded one hoe for about every 30 points, a ratio comparable to two Joes Bayou encampments, Aaron and Terral Lewis. Other encampments on Joes Bayou had even more hoes: Copes produced one for every 13 points and Arledge one for about every 6 points.

Fig. 6.11. Hoes were usually made of Dover or other kinds of northern gray flint and are most plentiful in field camps and residences along Joes Bayou. The objects shown here are from Poverty Point. The largest is 6.3 inches long. Photography by Charles Parker.

These figures showed that some swampers were doing a lot more hoeing than Poverty Point townfolk. They were not hoeing corn, so what were they hoeing? Digging roots, perhaps? Long after corn was grown, historic Lower Mississippi tribes cooked fry bread and dumplings made from smilax-root flour. They also dug groundnuts, wild potatoes, chufa, swamp cabbage, and at least a half-dozen other roots and tubers for the cooking pot. Many of their medicines and some of their dyes also came from roots. Such widespread use suggested their ancestors had been digging roots for a long time.

Chipped stone hoes were not found outside Poverty Point's immediate vicinity. They do not seem to have been used in the Lower Mississippi Valley after Poverty Point's heyday either, but this didn't stop later people from digging roots. What it means is that they quit bringing in big northern gray flint bifaces to do the hoeing. Wood, bone, and antler hoes took up the slack.

Hoes were most numerous where hoeing took place, and that was primarily in the swamp along Joes Bayou and to a lesser extent in low, wet places up on Maçon Ridge. Hoes were resharpened and repaired at the work site or in nearby field camps. Swampers likely lived at Poverty Point and other nearby residences and returned there with their loads of roots or whatever they had been grubbing for. Such logistics would account for why Poverty Point had so few shiny resharpening flakes as well as so few whole and broken hoes. The paucity of hoe-manufacturing flakes at Poverty Point and everywhere else around Poverty Point, for that matter, can be attributed to foreign production: Hoes or their bifacial preforms were probably fashioned at the flint quarries in Illinois, Indiana, or Tennessee and imported to Poverty Point.

Hoes were not used in earthwork construction, or else they and their resharpening residue would have been far more plentiful in construction fill. Groundstone celts, on the other hand, were employed in earthwork construction. They were sort of like hammer-ended axes or hatchets suitable for just about every heavy-duty pounding or chopping job. Often, they were found buried in the middle of basket-loaded lenses. They also occurred in work camps and other residences, usually in similar proportions—ratios ranging from a hoe for every six to every sixteen points.

Adzes were most prevalent at Poverty Point.

Tools for Scraping, Cutting, and Drilling

Just about anything with a chipped, strongly angled edge was suitable for scraping, just as keen-edged stones were suitable for cutting. Bifacial tools were not shaped specifically for these purposes, although flakes were trimmed along one or more margins in order to facilitate scraping. There were numerous unrefined bifaces, about one for every three points in Webb's collection, which could have been used as scrapers, knives, or drills. Unfortunately, wear studies necessary to confirm such uses were not conducted. Although unrefined bifaces were quite varied—thick to thin, long to short, and triangular to irregular—the overwhelming majority started out to be projectile points but never made it because of material flaws or chipping problems. Rather than waste valuable stone, Poverty Point knappers simply used these irregulars and fragments without much if any reshaping.

Projectile points (thin hafted bifaces) were often pressed into auxiliary uses. Their margins were commonly abraded, polished, denticulated, or notched; sometimes broken haft-bearing sections were recycled into drills. Projectile points were the ultimate all-purpose tool and were heavily used during active construction episodes and other busy moments. For example, at least one out of every ten points from Orvis Scott (a field camp on Joes Bayou and three miles from Poverty Point) had heavy edge wear, and most had a little. Almost every whole point excavated from fill or temporary living surfaces within the rings showed worn edges, while those from the tops of finished rings had not been as heavily used. It looked as though laborers stayed pretty busy when moving dirt and did not stop to resupply tool kits, waiting until they got through to do that. At Orvis Scott, they were too busy hoeing and doing other jobs, or else they were awaiting a pause in the construction at Poverty Point to go get fresh tools or the rock to make them.

Flake tools were used both with and without edge modification. Expedience guided technology. In several excavated sections of the rings, as many as one in ten to fifteen flakes bigger than a thumbnail had been used. In northern sections, they were almost equally divided between slightly used (or nibbled) and retouched tools. In western sections, almost all were retouched. Retouch angle ranged from shallow to steep and form from even to jagged. Occasionally, edges were notched or polished by repeatedly pulling them through hard, unyielding substances or dirty hides.

Scraping and cutting were done both with nonspecialized flakes and with aborted bifacial tools. Neither were intentionally made for these purposes, but when modifications were required, they were confined to edges. So many sharp- and strong-edged pieces of chert abounded or were so easily converted from aborted projectile-point preforms that no specialized tools needed to be made.

Drilling, on the other hand, did require specialized tools. Very few flakes or aborted bifaces just happened to have long- or thick-enough projections to be suitable for drilling holes in stone or other nonresilient materials. Drills had to be made intentionally. A few were converted from broken projectile points, and more were chipped from thick slivers of flint into implements half as long as a little finger, with or without expanding ends. But the most common drills were made on the end of small flakes detached not from bifaces but from prepared-platform cores nearly always of local pebble chert.

A specialized stone-working method was perfected for making these little drills, or Jaketown perforators, as Haag called them. A piece of gravel one-third to one-half the size of a fist had one or more ends knocked off with single or multiple blows from a billet. These fresh surfaces furnished platforms for detaching a series of blades (or narrow parallel-sided flakes). Although several kinds of edge-retouched tools then were made from these blades, Clarence Webb and I in a 1981 study published in *Traces in Prehistory* found that nearly seven out of ten had been converted into Jaketown perforators. Shaped like tiny car keys, perforators had steeply retouched (or backed) margins and blunt points.

So few perforators showed obvious rotary abrasion on their tips that James Ford argued that they were not drills at all. He experimentally made objects that resembled perforators by whittling bone and antler, leading him to conclude that they were scrapers. I have learned since that perforators used as drills do not develop obvious signs of rotary abrasion until they are completely worn out. Functional perforators bear triangular or rectangular cross-sections. When these little drills spin around in the hole, only their edges touch. Wear is limited to their edges only and looks as though it could have been produced by whittling, not spinning. Even perforator ends are often irregularly angular because of the minute flakes being mashed off of the spinning bit. Modern drilling efforts by Mitchell Hillman and David Griffing confirmed how easily and quickly perforators put holes through hard substances—stone, bone, and antler—when mounted in high-speed, hand-pumped bow drills. Even hollow cane bits drilled holes through rock when coated with wet sand and used in pump drills. Actual proof that perforators were used to drill stone came when archaeologist John Connaway dislodged the end of one that had broken off in an unfinished hole in a stone bead.

Although these little specialized drills were found everywhere, over half of them were surface-collected from just two ring segments, the third southwestern ring and the fifth southern ring. When perforators from other southern and southwestern ring segments were counted, too, these two sections alone yielded over 90 percent of the total for the entire ringed enclosure. Yet cores that furnished the blades from which perforators were made were primarily found on different ring segments. The fifth southern ring, which had many perforators, also had lots of blade cores, but the third southwestern ring did not; the lower-third western ring, which had few perforators, produced more than one-fourth of all cores. Perforator concentrations, coupled with the fact that perforators were used apart from where they were made, suggests that making blades and drilling were rather specialized activities engaging few people; otherwise, perforators and blades likely would have occurred uniformly throughout the rings.

Tools for the Chase

Hunting was vitally important economically and socially. It put food on the table, and being a good hunter was as surely a measure of a man's importance in Poverty Point times as it was among Lower Mississippi tribes in historic times. Hunting was a "man thing." It was how boys became men and how men became *real* men. Being a good hunter required skill and familiarity with animal behavior and terrain that came from Great Spirit–given physical attributes, experience, and good medicine. It also demanded an efficient weapon-delivery system.

Projectile Points

Poverty Point's main hunting weapon was the stone-tipped dart and throwing stick (or atlatl). Even though some stone tips (or projectile points) were fairly small, none were arrowheads. They came in a variety of shapes, and six forms—Gary, Motley, Ellis, Pontchartrain, Delhi, and Kent—made up nearly three-quarters of the classified points. Twenty-eight more forms were represented among the remainder.

Garys were prevalent, comprising more than one out of every five points. They had contracting stems, which usually formed one-fourth to one-third of the total length, and small sloping or straight shoulders. They were widest at the body-stem contact. Lengths ranged between 1.3 and 5.5 inches, and they were consistently twice as long as they were wide. They were thicker than other major kinds of points, between 0.35 and 0.39 inch, and usually weighed about 0.6 ounce. A little over half were chipped from local pebble chert and the rest mainly from exotic novaculite and Crescent Hills chert. Northern gray flints were hardly ever used to make Garys.

Motleys were slender, well-made points. They were common, making up one out of every seven points. Motleys were barbed, and notches were

Fig. 6.12. Few projectile-point types are as culturally exclusive as are Motley points. Overwhelmingly made of northern gray flint, these large points have large, rounded corner notches that leave narrow (and fragile) stem necks. The example on the lower right is about 4.5 inches long.

big and semicircular, creating stems with narrow necks. Stem lengths averaged about one-sixth of point lengths. They were normally more than two and a half times as long as wide, ranging from 2.8 to 4.7 inches long, 1.1 to 1.5 inches in maximum width, and averaging 0.31 inches thick. They normally weighed around 0.5 ounce, slightly less than Garys. More than eight in ten were made of exotic flint, predominantly northern gray flint.

Ellis points were also corner-notched but were shorter, thicker, and not as well made as Motleys. Over one in nine points was an Ellis. Notching was shallower than Motleys, and resulting barbs were not as prominent. Stem lengths averaged a third of point lengths, and stem necks were 0.4 to 0.6 inch wide. Ellises were 1.3 to 1.8 inches long, 0.8 to 1.3 inches in maximum width, averaged 0.35 inch thick, and weighed around 0.3 ounce. More than three-quarters were made from local pebble chert and the others predominantly from quartzite and novaculite. Northern gray flint was not used.

Pontchartrain points also numbered about one in every nine points recovered. They were slender like Motleys, but had a three-to-one stem-length ratio, half that of Motleys. They had squared shoulders, rectangular stems with straight bases, and were characterized by ripple flaking, which left bodies with thick diamond- or triangular-shaped sections. They ranged between 1.9 and 3.6 inches long, 0.6 to 1.1 inches in maximum width, and stem necks were between 0.5 and 0.6 inch wide. They normally weighed about 0.6 ounce, about the same as Garys. Nearly nine in ten were made from local gravel chert, and the remainder were chipped from quartzite and Crescent Hills chert. I know of only one of northern gray flint.

Delhi points were next in frequency comprising nearly one in twelve. They resembled Motleys in being well made and having symmetrical bodies with barbs but were unlike Motleys because stems were rectangular instead of flared. They were generally shorter than Motleys—ranging between 2.1 and 3.5 inches long—but were about the same width—1.1 to 1.6 inches. Stem necks were wider, between 0.5 and 0.7 inch, and they were between 0.28 and 0.39 inch thick. They were heavier than Motleys by an average of one-tenth of an ounce, 0.6 compared with 0.5 ounce. Nearly three-fourths were made from exotic flint, 30 percent being northern gray flint. Quartzite, novaculite, Crescent Hills flint, and other foreign cherts furnished the other materials.

Fig. 6.13. Pontchartrain points are common at Poverty Point and elsewhere in the Lower Mississippi Valley. They are usually long and skinny and are characterized by regularized "ripple" flaking. Pontchartrains are not culturally or geographically exclusive like Motleys. The specimen on the right is 3.3 inches long. Photography by Steven Carricut.

Kent points were the last major type making up one in thirteen points. They were roughly chipped, and large flake scars were not paired or otherwise consistently arranged. Slight to distinct shoulders were asymmetrical, and stems were generally rectangular, often with pebble cortex left on the base. Stem length to body length ratios averaged one to four. Bodies were sometimes asymmetrical, too, having one straight and one curved edge. They were 1.4 to 2.9 inches long, 0.7 to 0.8 inch in maximum width, and had stem necks that averaged 0.6 inch wide. Average weight was around 0.6 ounce. Almost seven in ten Kents were made of local pebble chert, and the remaining ones were made from Burlington chert, northern gray flint, and other exotics. Kent points were the ultimate generic brand point, the how-to-succeed-without-really-trying form, the low-average, not-too-good, not-too-bad type. They were the C-minuses of the point world.

Some minority forms were distinctive, like Evans (a double-notched point) and Marcos (a point with a wide, curved-sided body and thick-necked stem), but many others resembled one of the six major forms and differed mainly because they had been resharpened or chipped poorly. But even with all the incidental and reworked forms, there were still many basically different forms. Why? Were creative energies in overdrive? Were points designed for different jobs? Were changes in dart-delivery systems so rapid that new improved models appeared before older versions disappeared? How can archaeologists tell?

As hafted projectiles cast by hand or atlatl, points needed one end for binding, the other for penetrating, and had to be small enough to be thrown. Arm strength probably had little to do with size differences, because big ones weighed only a few tenths of an ounce more than little ones. Nor were small points arrowheads and big ones dart points. All were dart points, according to archaeostatistician David Thomas's criteria. Was raw material responsible for size and shape differences—short, simple ones made from pieces of local gravel and bigger, complex ones from slabs or cobbles of exotic flint? Was the mixture of points a result of various social groups, each having its own unique point styles, coming together periodically for ceremonies or trade fairs?

Some of the largest points were Garys and Pontchartrains, and they were nearly always made of local gravel. Many of these same forms were found at field camps and residences outside but close to Poverty Point, indicating that all styles had been made by Poverty Point knappers. That all but eliminated the possibility that the mixture of types had resulted from converging groups bearing separate weapon traditions. But what about performance differences?

Simple ballistics held that long and/or thick points could not be thrown as far or as accurately as short and/or thin ones, but they packed more of a wallop. In other words, smaller points flew truer but did not hit as hard as bigger ones. Could this principle have been behind design differences? Whether long or short, thick or thin, wide or narrow, most points weighed about a half-ounce, implying that weight was an overriding consideration, a compromise between casting and killing efficiency. But how was weight controlled when shapes varied so much? Very simply: Chipping large, rounded notches reduced the weight of long, wide points such as Motleys, whereas smaller notches left more weight on long, thick, narrow-bodied forms such as Gary Longs and Pontchartrains. Short and wide points such as Ellises and Gary Smalls made up weight by being thick and having wide stem necks.

Neck width may have been how Poverty Point knappers controlled weight, but that begged the question: Why did other features vary so much? To find the answer, I went to Poverty Point Commmemorative Area's own Dennis LaBatt and David Griffing, who throw darts for tourist groups nearly every day of the week. LaBatt and Griffing make their own atlatls and darts, and they chip their own points, too. To me, their firsthand knowledge is more revealing than any scientific arguments that might be mustered.

"Hey, Dennis, tell me about dart points. What do all these different shapes mean?"

"Well," Dennis replied, "wide triangular points don't penetrate as deeply as narrow points, but they would cut more tissue, so I think there was probably a trade-off between wide wounds and deep ones.

"Yeah, but which was best for bringing down a deer?"

"I'm not sure it mattered," he said. "You've got to hit it first. David and I both can hit a deer-sized target consistently at twenty-five yards with all kinds of points, and darts will easily travel up to a hundred yards if you give them a little arc. Besides, the dart travels about 125 feet in the first second of flight, and at that speed it doesn't matter what shape the point has."

"Would they have killed a deer?"

"Uh-huh, easily up to thirty or forty yards. I don't know about much further. You know, what may have been as important as point shape was how quickly darts achieved flight stability. David and I use cane shafts, and when they leave the atlatl, they're bent like a bow. I've noticed that darts with big tips don't ever quit tail-wagging, and they don't go very far, but if you put fletching on them, they'll fly just as far and straight as any others."

"What about the atlatls?"

"David uses a weighted atlatl. I don't, but mine's about four inches longer. I don't notice a great deal of difference between our casts."

"Huh, sounds like there might have been more than one way to skin a cat," I pontificated.

"Maybe so. You know, though, some points might have been made for stabbing spears instead of darts. Skinny points could be pulled out easier."

"Yeah," I responded, "they probably wouldn't have barbs or wide shoulders. Do you think skinny ones might have been used for fish instead of deer? Naw, probably not. You wouldn't want fish to slip off your gig, would you?"

After talking with Dennis, I decided that point forms were compromises between function and style. They all incorporated basic ballistic design, and, beyond that, I think Poverty Point knappers simply let their imagination be their guide.

Atlatl Parts

Darts were thrown with atlatls. An atlatl was a wooden lever with a hooked end. The dart was nocked in the hook, steadied with the fingers, and then cast like a football while still holding onto the atlatl. Besides providing greater knock-down power than an arrow delivered with a fifty-pound compound bow, atlatls enabled darts to be launched with a quick, simple throwing motion. Hunters did not have to wind up or take several running steps. A quick release was probably the difference between putting venison in the soapstone or warming up yesterday's fish soup.

Atlatls had several parts. The launcher was probably wooden, and the hook on the end was either carved directly on the launcher or was an attached piece of antler or bone. Groundstone objects may have been tied to launcher shafts to facilitate energy transfers during the throwing motion or to quickly stabilize vibrations caused by the sudden violent release of kinetic energy. Tail-wagging, bouncing, and other kinds of flight instability were the bane of larger, more-powerful darts, and although fletching helped, stabilizing vibration at the source—the atlatl itself—was necessary to ensure smooth short casts, which did most of the killing.

Clarence Webb described several kinds of groundstone atlatl weights, or stabilizers—bannerstones, boatstones, stone bars, tablets, and gorgets. All weights except gorgets were uncommon and probably were used on any contraption that needed sturdy or weighted braces or arms. Bannerstones were perforated cylinders, sometimes with opposing disc-shaped ears. Boatstones were shaped like miniature boats with rounded-vee keels. About half were hollowed out and the other half solid. There were flat, rectangular tablets and thicker rectangular objects shaped like candy bars. One tablet form had narrowed rectangular ends and was usually made of red jasper or red/yellow/black-banded Pickwick chert that had been chipped and then smoothed, completely or partially obliterating flake scars.

Gorgets outnumbered all other weights combined by more than three to one and really were the only ones numerous enough to have been part of a commonplace tool like the atlatl. They were usually flat, oval objects with two holes drilled on opposite ends about halfway between midpoint and ends. Ends were either pointed, rounded, or flat, and perforations were counterdrilled with a solid drill, probably a Jaketown perforator. Many limonite gorgets had a shallow groove running lengthwise between the holes, perhaps as experimenter David Griffing suggested to make their flat faces fit better on round-handled atlatls. They ranged from a little less than 2.5 to nearly 7.0 inches long, 1.0 to 2.5 inches in maximum width, and from 0.4 to 1.0 inch thick. Over 90 percent were made out of slate and limonite. Slate gorgets predominated in the northern rings, but those of limonite and other materials were spread uniformly throughout the rings.

Breaks were common and often repaired by drilling holes along the edges and lacing the pieces back together. Other holes, including half-holes along the margins and semiholes (incompletely drilled ones) on faces, were probably for show. Other occasional decorations included marginal notching and facial engraving: cross-hatched and hachured blocks and meanders, zig-zagged lines, composite curvilinear-rectilinear

Fig. 6.14. Polished-stone gorgets were probably weights attached to atlatls to help in transferring kinetic energy into casting power. This group of gorgets is from the Insley encampment; one is made of banded slate, and the other two are made of limonite. The center object is slightly over three inches long. Photography by Steven Carricut.

engraved-punctated designs, conjoined figure eights and Grecian key motifs made with single continuous lines, Fox-Man figures, and turtle shell patterns.

Netting and Fishing Appliances

Plummets were groundstone objects made of hematite and magnetite. Employing these iron ores from the Ouachita Mountains showed that craftsmen wanted heavy materials. Plummets were heavy for their size, weighing a whopping 5.3 ounces on average and ranging from 1.25 to 5.0 inches long and 0.8 to 2.0 inches across their thickest diameter. They came in four main missile shapes—egg, pear, teardrop, and torpedo—and had plain, grooved, or pierced ends. Grooves and perforations revealed that plummets were designed to be tied onto something. Plain-ended objects did not indicate that they were not fit to be tied, only that they would have needed to be encased in an attachable pouch. Holes through magnetite plummets were cylindrical and drilled from one side only, while holes through hematite objects were conical and countersunk. Some plummets with countersunk perforations had constricted ends, which lessened the distance that opposing holes had to be drilled so as to meet halfway through.

Plummets were common objects numbering about one for every four points. Nearly three in five plummets were broken, indicating heavy stresses; another one in five was unfinished, indicating that they were being finished directly on the rings from imported blanks or rocks. The northern rings had a disproportionate number of top and middle fragments, while the southern rings had more bottom and side fragments than expected. The distribution of pieces indicated that broken plummets were untied more frequently in the northern rings than in the southern rings. Pieces were seldom recycled into new plummets, because they apparently were not heavy enough.

About one out of every eighty plummets was decorated. Some decorations involved multiple grooves or raised rings around the collar, while others employed semiholes or simulated fingernail marks on bodies; a few exhibited engraved, intaglio, or bas-relief figures, including stylized owl-human hybrids, owl monsters with deer antlers, owl-masked and costumed performers (shamans?), a nestling with open beak, a "long-tail" (opossum), webbed waterfowl feet, and a running, nested skate-key pat-

Fig. 6.15. Plummets were made of hematite and magnetite and probably functioned as sinkers for fishnets. The object on the bottom row, lower right, is 4.7 inches long. Photography by Gordon Maxey; courtesy of Clarence Webb.

tern. Designs were often duplicated in reverse on opposite sides, and sometimes the single continuous-line technique was used.

Workmanship was good, bad, and sometimes plain ugly. Often grinding was indifferent, failing to smooth out pecking scars or even to round objects. Still, rough objects often were perforated or grooved and were broken just like their better-made counterparts, suggesting that having a heavy, streamlined, and attachable weight was paramount to makers. On the other hand, some plummets were works of art. Virtually all decorated and many plain ones were ground into smooth symmetrical shapes and were so highly polished that they gleamed in the sun. Why such a gap in workmanship? If finish was not absolutely essential for performance, then differences might reflect aptitude or skill levels or folks just getting by with as little effort as possible. On the other hand, finely decorated plummets not only were made by talented artisans but may have conveyed special, probably magical, meaning.

James Ford's adventures in Alaska led him to propose that plummets were components for bolas, which Eskimo used to hunt waterfowl. Avid duck hunter Clarence Webb agreed and pointed to the vast flights of ducks and geese that migrated along the Mississippi flyway and to the occurrence of plummets on the banks of old oxbows and other lakes where waterfowl flocked. Having once been an avid duck hunter myself led me to question the bola notion. I just could not imagine plummets—which were made from long-distance exchange rock, which were often refined and polished, and which sometimes bore elaborate engraved decorations—being thrown at speedy teal or strong Canada geese flying over open water or even rafting on swamp lakes. I always had trouble bringing them down with number five or double-ought shot at close range. Would duck hunters have been willing to risk losing objects that were made of imported material and that took so much time to fabricate every time they were cast? Ford's Eskimo friends could afford to miss. Their bola weights were carved or chopped from abundant bone and ivory and were subjected to minimal shaping. No, Poverty Point plummets just could not be bola weights.

I contend that they were fishnet sinkers. Both tie-down and floating nets and seines had to have weights along the bottom strand in order to remain stretched out; otherwise, they would have rolled up in the slowest current or while being dragged along the bottom. Modern gill and trammel nets have lead weights attached every one, two, or four feet, and seine

Fig. 6.16. Plummet-weighted nets would have stayed stretched out, allowing fish to be caught in fast-flowing water which came during winter rises and spring floods, normally the toughest food-getting times for hunter-gatherers. Even flooded swamps could have been fished productively with weighted nets.

mudlines have them every foot or less. Fewer plummets would have done the job of many lead weights, especially since they were ten to twenty times heavier.

Being attached to fishnets meant plummets were not bound for quick, certain loss on the job. Fishnet sinkers were retrievable, so the hours spent in grinding and polishing and in going to the mountains or trading with mountain men did not disappear in a single splash. But why were some plummets so finely made and decorated when practically any heavy, rough, missile-shaped rock would have kept nets unfurled? Could they have been invoking good luck, like the eighteenth-century Chipewyans of the Canadian subarctic, who placed charms on their fishnets in order to coax fish to swim into them? Since decorations on Poverty Point plummets are compatible with traditional themes of supernatural beings, spiritual power (orenda), and news carrying, they would have been perfect for coaxing fish into getting caught.

Other fishing gear was not recognized, but I suspect much of it—nets, traps, listers, and gorges—was probably made from perishable fiber, wood, antler, and bone. A few bone and antler pins, awls, spatulas, and flakers dredged from the bottom muds of Bayou Maçon may have been used in fishing or in making fishing equipment. In particular, bone pins with their grooved ends were the proper size and shape required for netting needles, but making fishnets probably was not their only purpose.

Adornment and Power Objects

Stone beads and pendants were fairly common. Clarence Webb tabulated one bead for nearly every 10 projectile points at Poverty Point, although nearby encampments had fewer ranging from a low of one for every 110 points at Terral Lewis to a high of one for every 34 points at Arledge.

Simple beads were shaped like tubes, barrels, globes, discs, or hourglasses and were usually fashioned from red jasper, other hard red and green rocks, copper, and a few other drab-colored rocks, including crinoid-stem fossils. Hard-stone, copper, and galena pendants included miniature replicas of larger objects: a perforated plummet, a bannerstone, a narrow-ended tablet, and several grooved-ax simulations. In addition, geometrically shaped pendants included ovoid, rectangular, cylindrical, geniculate, triangular, Y-shaped, rattle-shaped, spade-shaped, and anchor-shaped forms. Naturalistically shaped objects included claw (or talon), geniculate, butterfly, open clamshell, and bird-head cutouts (silhouettes). Fat-bellied owl pendants were carved in-the-round. Red jasper, galena, and brownstone buttons with hidden perforations were also crafted. A few perforated or notched human and animal teeth were found in spoil dirt dredged from Bayou Maçon. Natural and smoothed quartz crystals were grooved for suspension.

Blanks, cut and partially drilled objects, and other manufacturing failures revealed that ornaments were made at Poverty Point. King Harris found a buried bead-maker's cache consisting of more than four dozen sawed and incompletely drilled pieces of red and green slate, a small bifacial drill, and an edge-polished Pogo biface used to saw the slate. No finished beads of this material have been found at Poverty Point, but identical material has turned up at the Slate site in Mississippi nearly 100 miles east of Poverty Point.

Lapidaries generally used two means of initializing simple beads. Practically all of Poverty Point's beads started out as natural pebbles or lumps. By starting with bead-sized pieces, bead makers avoided having to cut and snap larger blocks, which often broke the rock before shaping ever commenced. Only a few cut-and-snap blanks were found. Holes in longer beads were usually drilled from both ends (counterdrilled), while those in shorter beads were counterdrilled about half the time and drilled from one end the other half. Length was not the only factor determining how beads were drilled (some of the thinnest beads had counterdrilled holes), but the fact that the longest beads were countersunk indicated that short, solid drills, probably Jaketown perforators, were used. How far perforators protruded from drill shafts determined whether or not beads had to be counterdrilled. Obviously, if a bead was too long to be drilled completely through from one end, it had to be turned over and a second hole run in from the other end. Long, hollow or solid drills, which were used to bore long, cylindrical holes in bannerstones, magnetite plummets, stone pipes, and other groundstone objects, were not used for beads.

Copper beads were produced by hammering copper nuggets into thin sheets and winding them around copper wire. Usually two or three wraps gave the desired thickness, and then the wire was pulled out, leaving the beads hollow. Wire evidently withstood the pounding needed to crimp sheet layers together better than small sticks or cane. Wire was also hammered, and segments were short and straight like thick needles. They were too flexible for sewing, but I just cannot imagine so much labor being expended on making something as mundane as hole spacers. Wire would have taken nearly as much time to make as beads, leading me to believe that wire needles were ornamental, sacred, or both. They would have made excellent lancets for bloodletting. Body piercing and scratching enjoyed wide popularity among historic southern natives.

Carved zoomorphic (stylized animal-effigy) pendants suggested supernatural beliefs. Small perched owls were carved in the round, usually from red jasper. They ranged from a quarter inch to just over an inch tall and less than an inch in maximum diameter. Oval faces had semidrilled eyes and thick projecting beaks. Necks were pierced, and small feet were usually turned away from the way heads faced, capturing the owl's unique ability to turn its head almost completely around. Heads were smooth and rounded, with none bearing projections that would have mimicked the ear tufts of great horned owls. Yet size differences suggested that different species were intended—great horned, barred, and screech owls. Each species represented different powers and values in the lore of historic southern natives. Owls, particularly screech owls, were tied to death and witchcraft, but others symbolized night vision, hunting prowess, wisdom, and raw power—symbolic connections rooted deep in antiquity.

Such symbolism was borne out by their pan-southeastern distribution. Although only a handful of owl pendants was found, they reached all the way from a river bottom in central Florida to a red clay hill in the pineywoods of northwestern Louisiana, more than 500 miles. Most were found at Poverty Point. Others were recovered from small, undistinguished encampments, several of which bore Late Archaic materials that only generally resembled Poverty Point's. Even in Poverty Point's own hinterland, owl pendants came from temporary field camps and not residences.

Owl pendants were not identical but were technically and stylistically similar enough to suggest that the few people who made them all knew the stories behind them. Did that mean they all came from Poverty Point or the Poverty Point area? Probably. Did it mean that they all carried the same message, that they worked the same magic on peoples from Louisiana to Florida? Possibly, if they remained in the same hands that carried them that far; possibly not, if they changed hands. I simply cannot imagine a generalized, multicultural owl symbolism producing such similar items across so large an area, even if it did come down from one ancient mother tongue and a singular worldview.

Owl pendants were found at Poverty Point. They were found at nearby field camps, and they were found at far-off places. But nowhere were they found in contexts suggesting that they only belonged to elites; they were not found in cache pits or in association with other status objects. They were not found in burials—no Poverty Point burials have ever been identified. They occurred in many situations that were seemingly quite mundane and secular. Yet objects so important that they were carried from home to campgrounds, as well as far out on the trail, suggested that they conveyed power and magic, that they were fetishes.

In a 1971 article in *American Antiquity,* Clarence Webb proposed that other zoomorphs which he identified as locust effigies were magical, too. I agree with the magical part but suspect that they represented creatures besides locusts, a point that bead experts John Connaway and Samuel Brookes have been making for years. Webb realized that the effigy bead tradition was rooted deep in the Archaic but was unaware that its physical portrayal with hard stone was finished by Poverty Point times. Only two effigy beads, both probably owls rather than locusts, are known to have been recovered from Poverty Point. One came from inside the plaza and the other from an unknown location. They could have been heirlooms, but since neither certainly derived from Poverty Point cultural deposits, they may simply have been lost by earlier Middle Archaic residents, perhaps the generation responsible for Lower Jackson Mound.

Other polished stone objects included small geometrics such as cubes, discs, ovals, spheres, cylinders, cones, and triangles, as well as a crescent, a tetrahedron, and a small cup. The lack of perforations or grooves lessened the likelihood that they were ornaments meant to be worn in public and raised the likelihood that they were charms or fetishes meant to be encased in medicine bundles. Other than being extraordinary testaments to artistic freedom and lapidary skill, these objects did not display a common theme or recognizable link with cosmic symbols. Lack of uniformity divulged that they were created by different lapidaries and not some subsidized artist.

A few elongated, teardrop-shaped objects of fired löess are included here with the other power objects, although how they were used is a mystery. These objects were finger-fluted, leaving four ribs or fins down the long axis. Narrow ends were rounded and plain, not intended for suspension.

Solid human figurines made of fired löess were not very common, about one for every eighty-eight projectile points. They were small, ranging from slightly less than 1.0 to 2.5 inches tall and from just under 1.0 to just over 2.0 inches across the hips. Most were headless torsos lacking arms and legs. Legs sometimes were suggested by rounded nodes or short peglike projections. Shoulders usually ended in rounded bumps, although arms were occasionally depicted in a folded position across the stomach. Most figures were androgynous, but some clearly were female, with breasts, wide hips, and distended bellies reflecting pregnancy. Others were flat-chested but had big buttocks and belly rolls, indicating a need for workouts or stomach tucks. Genitalia were not shown. Heads had been attached, but most had been broken off at the neck. Whether this had been intentional or accidental is an oft-asked question. Facial features were crudely rendered: slits or punctations for eyes and mouths and pinched-up bumps for noses. On some, noses were so beaklike that Webb referred to them as "bird women." Happy faces were the rule, and some were actually smiling. One even wore a mystic smile, Poverty Point's very own Mona Lisa. Middle-parted hairdos occasionally were indicated.

Most figurines were naked, or else clothing was not shown. One figure did have a single line around the neck and cross-hatching on the chest,

Fig. 6.17. Baked löess figurines were mainly androgynous, although some clearly represented females. Their use is a mystery, but if they were associated with fertility rites they had nothing to do with corn planting because corn was not grown. The headless figure on the lower left is three inches tall. Photography by Gordon Maxey; courtesy of Clarence Webb.

indicating a necklace and some kind of neckpiece or tattooing. Another wore a beaded collar, and Webb noted belts or kirtles on others.

The little figures were too stylized to be portraits, and they were too morphologically varied to have been made by one or a few individuals. Yet they were similar enough, at least in abstract, to show that they adhered to a central concept of manufacture if not meaning. Unless they were children's playthings, they probably served a cause higher than routine hearthside work, a likelihood borne out by their dominant presence atop one ring, the third northern segment. One thing for sure was that they were not charms for making gardens grow, as was the case in many Mesoamerican cultures. Poverty Point did not have gardens, at least not maize plots. But statuettes, especially those of pregnant women, are usually considered fertility symbols and, as such, are potentially relevant to every living and breathing thing—plant or animal.

Tubes of löess and stone were less common than figurines occurring in a ratio of one for every 112 points. Those of löess were about the length of half-smoked cigars and were tapering, bigger at one end than the other. Most were thick-walled, and about a third to a half of the bore was enlarged for bowls. These bowls had been blackened from slow burning and were coated with soot. Opposite ends often were flattened and occasionally showed bite marks. A minority of the specimens were thin walled, had fairly uniform bores, and showed no sign of smoking. Stone tubes were made from claystone, siltstone, limestone, steatite, and red jasper. They were generally thicker and shorter than their löess counterparts and actually formed elongated cones with slightly swollen outlines. Their bores had bowls, and in both löess and stone tubes, bores ran full length.

What were they? Pipes? Sucking tubes? Perforated ceremonial cylinders? Yes, they were probably all these things. Among historic southern natives, tubes and cones were indispensable medical instruments used for sucking illness-causing objects from patients' bodies, blowing curing smoke on hurting places, or applying healing heat to affected spots. Dispelled objects usually were spat in bowls of ill-neutralizing water, which was then carried away and thrown out in a secret place. Smoking pipes also were used for healing and cleansing. Ethnologist John Swanton quoted sixteenth-century Virginia colonist Thomas Hariot: "[pipe smoking] purgeth superfluous fleame & other grosse humors, openeth all the pores & passages of the body; by which meanes the vse thereof . . . preserueth the body from obstructions." No matter whether made of löess or stone or whether sucked, blown, or applied fire-hot, tubes were almost certainly healing aids used by shamans to cure the sick and by others for self-healing and purification.

Poverty Point smokers did not light up with tobacco, which did not spread from Mexico or the Caribbean islands until long after Poverty Point. *Kinnikinnick,* a mixture probably made with smooth sumac leaves, had a long history of being used alone or later mixed with tobacco in order to cut the strong taste. Sumac made perfect *kinnikinnick.* Not only were its autumn leaves blood red, a powerful color, but they turned before the rest of the woods, which surely accorded them greater power.

Organization of Technology

How technology was organized said worlds about Poverty Point culture. The most obvious aspect of stone technology—choosing between local or foreign raw materials—apparently did not matter when it came to making bifaces. Usually, the proportions of projectile points and other bifaces made of local gravel were similar to the overall proportion of local gravel in the collection; the proportions made of foreign flint were similar to the overall representation of foreign flint. Flake tools were also made in numbers proportional to the amounts of local and foreign material represented, suggesting that size, thickness, shape, edge length, and feel were more important than rock type when it came to selecting flakes for further modification and use.

On the other hand, local gravel nearly always was selected for making blades and Jaketown perforators, probably because pebbles with knocked-off ends made better cores than did bifaces. Bifaces simply did not possess the steep edge angles necessary to yield good blades, and foreign flints usually arrived at Poverty Point already prefabricated as bifaces.

Similar material use prevailed at Poverty Point encampments on Joes Bayou. At Orvis Scott, a field camp, 36 percent of the flakes, 38 percent of the flake tools, and 38 percent of the bifaces were made of local pebble chert. At nearby Aaron, another field camp, 52 percent of the flakes, 36 percent of the flake tools, and 49 percent of the bifaces were fashioned from local pebble chert. At Copes, a residence, 41 percent of the flakes, 48 percent of the flake tools, and 56 percent of the points were of local chert.

Such similar percentages showed that folks were not very choosy about what kind of rock they used. How much local rock occurred in an encampment determined how much was used for points and flake tools, or perhaps it was the other way around. The same held for foreign flint. If points and other bifaces were carried out to camps, instead of being made out there, then how many there were of a given rock type predetermined how many flakes and flake tools there would be of that rock type. Bifaces required a lot of maintenance, and that always resulted in a pile of flakes. If a flake tool had been needed for some small task that popped up and a suitable flake could not be found lying around on the ground, one could have been knocked off a biface without damaging the biface. Bifaces made convenient cores, especially for sojourners who probably could not expect to replenish rock supplies and formal tools until they returned to Poverty Point or some other residence.

Whether working out in a field camp or in a residence did not seem to make any difference in how many flake tools were used. I expect campers would have used more, relatively, in an effort to save raw material and travel lightly. By using flake tools, campers could have served both ends, carrying out jobs with makeshift tools instead of having to tote full tool kits along with all the camping gear. Apparently, that was not the case.

Use of flake tools was so variable that considerations other than frugality or worry about heavy backpacks must have dictated use. Maybe field camps were too close to Poverty Point or other residences for material conservation or traveling light to have been major considerations. Maybe, if more rock and new tools had been needed, workers knew all they had to do was just skip over to Poverty Point, Copes, or Terral Lewis and get them. It wasn't a problem that a short hike or pirogue pull couldn't have resolved in an hour or so. Or maybe, just maybe, a super tool eliminated such worries. Such a tool, if nothing else, would have eliminated inconvenience. I believe bifaces were that super tool.

Not only could bifaces be used for many jobs, but they made useful expedient cores, too. Flakes were struck off during routine maintenance or could be knocked off intentionally in a pinch. Field camps had more hafted bifaces (projectile points) than residences by a six-to-one margin. They made the ideal Ginsu knife. Besides being light and easy to carry, they could be used to stab, cut, scrape, saw, drill, and do just about anything else. Their general utility made them excellent choices for field equipment. Although uneven data inhibit complete encampment-to-encampment comparisons, there seem to be more points with signs of heavy secondary use and extensive repair in those situations where people happened to be really busy (such as when working on the rings) or outside easy resupply range (more than a day or two from Poverty Point). Bifaces were the ultimate means for making ends meet.

There was an overriding simplicity to all of this. To be sure, some materials were preferred for making certain kinds of tools. Hoes and Motley points, for example, were chipped overwhelmingly from northern gray flint. Local pebble chert was nearly always used for making Jaketown perforators. Stone vessels were carved of soapstone. PPOs were molded from löess instead of river clay. The list of favored materials was long. Such choices reflected material suitability and/or availability. There was nothing in any of these preferences to indicate that certain rocks were destined for the hands of an elite few. Raw materials got into callused working hands as needed. Access to raw material and tools was unrestricted and probably guided by labor demands. For example, the fact that Aaron had so much northern gray flint was not because so many socially prominent people gathered there but because a lot of hoeing went on, and most hoes were made from northern gray flint. That a red jasper owl statuette was found at Aaron but not at Copes did not suggest that a VIP lived at Aaron. It merely indicated that magic worked at field camps, just as in other places. Having unimpeded access to raw materials or tools made from both local and exotic rock did not mean that there was no social gain at stake. Making sure that all those in need got what they needed was a surefire way of building prestige. To be loved and respected by all also guaranteed a power base. Gratitude was the flip side of earned leadership—payback, the stuff of which mounds were made.

Fancy Fox-Man plummets, owl statuettes, finely made gorgets, Jaketown perforators, and dozens of other objects raised the possibility that craft specialists were responsible. Many of these were exquisite pieces, and others, like Jaketown perforators, were used for a task so specialized— drilling holes in rock—that many people probably never did it. Yet drilling per se did not make the craft itself specialized. In the case of exquisitely crafted objects, there were others of the same genre that were not so finely crafted. Excellent to poor workmanship pervaded every single class of polished stonework. If the best objects had been made by specialists, their handiwork should have stood out, but instead fine items reflected wide-ranging individualism, not uniformity or repeated incorporation of stylistic peculiarities, which having only an artisan or two would have ensured. Perforators were used when something needed to be drilled, and although that may not have involved everyone, it did not make drilling a task for specialists alone. It simply meant that drilling was a specialized technical task. In my view, exceptionally fine objects were made by exceptionally talented people, not subsidized artisans. There were no operators who ran drill presses for a living. Too many holes had to be put in too many objects for such a widespread need to be left to a few specialists.

A Wealth of Many Materials

If I had to sum up Poverty Point's gear and appliances in a single word, it would be *abundant*. If I could use two words, I would say *abundant* and *rich*. Poverty Point had a wealth of many materials. Tools, tool fragments, residue from making tools, residue from other living activities, hearths, earth ovens, other pits, postmolds, and other built-feature remains were scattered across town. Million and millions of items were left on the old ground surface before rings were built; they were left in rings while under construction and during breaks in construction; and they were left atop rings after construction was finished.

Having so much stuff and so many classes of implements indicated Poverty Point was a place of residence. There were cooking aids and maintenance gear. There were tools for chopping, digging, and pounding, as well as implements for scraping, cutting, and drilling. Hunting and fishing equipment was plentiful, and symbolic objects for show and magical use were common. Much of Poverty Point's equipment was made at home. Some was brought in already wholly or partially fabricated. A lot of it was used on the rings, and some was used out in the field but returned for repair. Some items were used to manipulate omnipresent spirit forces, ensuring supernatural help and protection. Field camps or vacant ceremonial centers would not have sported such wealth, but what numbers and classes of objects don't show was whether or not the Place of the Rings was occupied for every single moment in its duration. Even if work parties or large numbers of families left home for extended periods, as so often happened with hunter-gatherers and some horticultural groups, such temporarily diminished occupancy would not have detracted from Poverty Point's basically residential character.

7

Fishing, Hunting and Gathering, and Table Fare

"As You Live and Fish"

How do you catch fish? You asked the question: How do you know where they are? Really you don't have the ability to know exactly where they are, but if you're fishing in the daytime you'll find the fish out astirring . . . the same way your fish gets up close to the bank at night, and they feed close to the bank—and that's the way you catch them in your gill nets.

Trammel nets I used, too. We'd drive fish all night. I caught 1,500 pounds, 2,000 pounds, me and another fellow, many nights.

But with a seine you get out there and catch maybe an 800- or 900-pound set and maybe make two more sets [only] catch 200 pounds, and next thing you'd hit another big set. We hand-knitted these seines.

Hoop nets was fished when we had a current, most of the time. They'd catch a few if you tied them up, but they wouldn't catch . . . like they would in a current.

We had traps and things like this, and weather had a terrible lot to do with fishing, [with] fish being in certain places. And as you live and fish, you learn a lot. . . . With certain weather conditions, you fish in certain places, and it makes it a lot easier for a man that's fished all his life than a man that's just started yesterday.

Vernie Gibson, unpublished audiotaped interview, 1994

If Not Maize, What?

Poverty Point ran on its belly. Food lit its fires, shaped its PPOs, set its work schedule, filled out its social calendar, and quite literally influenced its whole being and course of development.

For a while, archaeologists assumed maize was behind its supercharged growth, and many heads turned toward Mesoamerica, particularly the Olmec coast of Vera Cruz, as the most likely source for both maize and cultural inspiration. Maize, monumental architecture, and ornaments and tools similar to those at Poverty Point were found there and were believed to have originated earlier, sparking a punctuated rush toward civilization which at first included but then outstripped Poverty Point. But Poverty Point excavations have never turned up the maize remains everybody was expecting. So if it was not maize, then it must have been wild foods or perhaps locally domesticated starchy and oily seed plants such as goosefoot, sumpweed, knotweed, maygrass, little barley, and sunflower that fed Poverty Point's achievements. Right? Well, yes and no. No cultivated native seeds were ever found, although a few normal-sized seeds from their wild counterparts were. That leaves only wild food, and some archaeologists found this hard to swallow. The idea that Poverty Point might have grown out of hunting and gathering ran against the grain of traditional thinking. Now, it does not.

Poverty Point's list of foods is far from complete. The problem is most acute at Poverty Point itself, where poor preservation conditions combine with only a handful of processed samples to produce a short list. Poor preservation was due to rapid earthwork construction, prolonged weathering, and over a century of modern plowing, which left few situations in which perishable food remains could have survived. Pollen did not survive well, either; centuries and centuries of alternate wetting and drying hastened its loss. So the place from where the very best information is needed has the skimpiest. Some small encampments just outside the rings where there had been no earth-moving provided additional food remains, and Copes, a residential camp located seven miles southeast of Poverty Point on Joes Bayou, furnished the most complete set of table scraps of any Poverty Point camp.

Appetizers, Entrees, and Catch of the Day

Few orts have been identified from Poverty Point's rings. They represent only a small sample, because they came from general fill and temporary living surfaces atop fill layers where food remains were likely to have been fewest. Samples from dozens of pits and building strata still remain unanalyzed, but biological remains recovered by Goad's excavations on the eastern end of the first northwestern ring have been studied. Heather Ward found hickory nut shell in four-fifths of twenty individual samples, cane fragments in nearly half, and acorn hulls in almost a quarter. She also identified persimmon seeds and cucurbit rind in nearly a quarter of the samples and seeds from little barley in about a fifth. Other plants she recognized in fewer than an eighth of the samples included goosefoot seeds, black walnut shell, hackberry or holly seeds, spurge seeds, may-grass seeds, *Poaceae* grass seeds, and chestnut shell. From another part of the first northwestern ring, I recovered hickory nut, acorn, and pecan residue, and several sections of the third northern ring yielded remains of hickory nut, acorn, black walnut, honeylocust bean, plum, unidentified seeds, unidentified fish, and deer. Elsewhere, I identified turtle and hickory nut shell from the fourth northern ring; hickory nut shell from the fifth northern ring; hickory nut and acorn shell from the sixth northwestern ring; and hickory nut, acorn, and pecan shell from the third upper western ring. Faunal adept Mike Russo recognized remains of bowfin, freshwater drum, gar, unidentified fish, mud turtle, and large mammal, possibly deer, from the fourth upper western ring.

These remains only give a general and incomplete idea of what was eaten on the rings as a whole during Poverty Point's entire history. There is no way of telling how cuisine differed from household to household, from season to season, or from year to year. Late summer and fall foods dominate sample remains, but this merely shows that foods that ripened during those months were gathered. It does not show that other seasonal foods were neglected or by implication that the rings were vacant in all seasons except the fall. Fall mast (nuts and acorns) and seeds are hard-shelled and survive burning and weathering better than those from other plants.

Thomas and Campbell found charred food remains in cooking and trash pits excavated from other core residences lying outside the rings up to two and a half miles away. Alexander Point sat on the bluff between the outer northern ring and Motley Mound, and there Andrea Shea identified shell from hickory nuts, acorns, walnuts, and pecans as well as seeds from persimmon, grape, goosefoot, doveweed, and knotweed. Wild beans and possibly cucurbit remains also were recognized. The identity of cucurbits was not in question, but their context was; they were found in a cooking pit that contained possibly later pottery and thus may have postdated Poverty Point. Also from the same pits, zooarchaeologist Kathleen Byrd recognized fish, turtle, snake, and squirrel bones. Freshwater drum was the most common fish. North of Alexander Point and a quarter-mile southeast of Motley Mound lay Motley East. Fire pits yielded animal bones including lots of fish and some turtles, small mammals, and snakes. Freshwater drum dominated, followed by bowfin and gar. Plant residues included hickory nuts and acorns as well as some walnuts, pecans, persimmon seeds, doveweed seeds, and fruit from one of the Composites (flowering plants including dandelion, aster, and others). At Steatite Field, Byrd and Shea identified softshell turtle, hickory nut and acorn shell, persimmon and hackberry seeds, and pieces of blackgum, a Composite, and fruits. Locality Two, another residence located within sprinting distance southwest of Ballcourt Mound, had a few unidentified animal bones and some burned hickory nut shell.

Selective preservation resulting from selective preparation may have been partly responsible for such limited recovery, but food habits were responsible for what was there. These foods, though limited, prompt several conclusions. First, Poverty Point residents, as well as people living and camping outside the rings, made use of everything that walked, crawled, crept, swam, fruited, and seeded. In short, just about anything that could be eaten was, and hungry consumers were not too discriminating about whether food came from uplands or lowlands — nuts and acorns from Maçon Ridge or fish and turtles from the swamp. All were eaten. Second, deer bones were rare. Third, just because remains included nuts and acorns does not imply that Poverty Point and other nearby camps were inhabited only during the fall. Mast indicates fall occupancy but does not necessarily exclude other seasons.

Edwin Jackson collected food remains from Copes. He found that sweet pecan/hickory dominated floral remains occurring in three-fourths of the pit and midden samples. Acorn hulls occurred in half the samples, cucurbit rind and seeds in a quarter, grass seeds in a fifth, and persimmon seeds in a few. Minor amounts of honeylocust, goosefoot, marshelder, portulaca (purslane family), wild bean, *Sporobolus,* and *Lithspermum* seeds occasionally showed up. Fish and deer comprised over four-fifths of the animal remains by bone count. Dominant fish included catfish as well as gar, bowfin, sunfish, bass, buffalo, sucker, and freshwater drum. The remainder of the bones came from turtles: mud/musk, snapping, red-eared, and others; small mammals: rabbit, squirrel, raccoon, and others; snakes: water, king, rat, cottonmouth, and others; bullfrogs; and, last and least, birds: duck, turkey, pelican, heron and egret, goose, crow, and others. There is a good possibility that fish were underrepresented because their tiny bones can pass right through quarter-inch screens and not be recovered. Mike Russo found that fish-bone counts sometimes doubled when pinhead-sized mesh was used to screen samples. If that is the case, then fish were by far the main food at Copes, reducing all others including deer to minor importance.

According to Jackson, Copes's foods had wide implications for life in the shadow of Poverty Point. First, foods represented all seasons, suggesting that people lived at Copes year-round. Second, food remains evidenced a pretty solid, well-rounded diet, not one having a lot of second-line resources (or starvation foods). Third, they implied that few people had lived at Copes; otherwise second-line foods probably would have been more plentiful. And fourth, they consisted of local resources obtained within a few miles of home. Only red snapper and brown pelican were long-distance imports, probably sent up from the coast. These things convinced Jackson that Copes residents had managed to eat well without Poverty Point's help and even may have exported some food, possibly to Poverty Point itself. For example, there were insufficient bones from deer shoulders and rumps to complement the number of bones from other parts of the body, and fish vertebra were also underrepresented.

Furthermore, Copes had a wide assortment of exotic exchange rocks, which attests to its involvement with broader Poverty Point economics. Chiefly redistribution was not responsible. Exotics were probably brought in by workers dispersing from Poverty Point or by exchanges originating there.

Poverty Point's foods were acquired by fishing, gathering, and hunting. Farming was either unimportant or nonexistent. Small seeds indicate that cucurbits are probably wild gourds rather than fleshy domestic squash and that goosefoot, maygrass, knotweed, and little barley seeds also come from wild, not cultivated, varieties. Anyway, except for cucurbits, seeds

Fig. 7.1. Acorns, pecans, and other nuts were major foods.

are so scarce that it reduces the question of horticulture to practical insignificance. Polished hoes offer no support either. If they had been garden tools, more hoes and repair residue surely would have been found at Poverty Point and other residences. Being able to step out the door and into the middle of a food patch is an advantage that gardening has over hunting and gathering. But hoes and hoe resharpening flakes were more plentiful at some field camps located at wet spots on Maçon Ridge and particularly along Joes Bayou, suggesting they had been used in some important subsistence activity, probably digging roots. Digging roots was a job that required swampers to go where roots were abundant, and for smilax, chufa, and others used most often by historic natives, that meant down in the swamp or at swampy spots on Maçon Ridge.

Foods varied, not because of different preferences or food-getting methods, but because different seasonal foods were usually represented. Basically, Poverty Point subsistence was broad-based. Although scores of foods were eaten, nuts and acorns furnished the main fall and winter staples, and fish furnished the main spring and summer stores. Hunting, especially deer hunting, was important, but it was more luck-dependent than other pursuits. A single deer had as many calories as a pirogue half full of dressed catfish or two gallon baskets full of shelled pecans, so luck was something hunters counted on. Out in the swamp, where deer were more numerous and people fewer, deer were taken more frequently. Around busy Poverty Point, where fewer deer remained close by, greater emphasis was placed on gathering nuts and acorns and on fishing. After all, if fishes and loaves fed multitudes in a desert halfway around the world, why would they have been any less efficacious in a fishing paradise?

Organization of Economy

Organization was the key to economic success and excess. No matter how plentiful and how easy to get, foods reached people's earth ovens in amounts determined by how well the economy was organized and how smoothly it ran. Even in cornucopian environments like Poverty Point's, there were lean times and flush times during the year, there were bad years and good years, and there were always social do's and don'ts, which kept food collection from reaching maximum potential. How Poverty Point's economy was organized and carried out said a lot about social complexity, too, at least about how one hunter-gatherer population managed to attain and sustain some fairly complex relations.

The economic year was built around fishing. Nuts and acorns were important, and good mast years went down as good food years. But nuts and acorns were seasonal foods and for nine or ten months out of the year did not require any attention. On the other hand, I contend that fishing was done all year long and was the secret to Poverty Point's success. Technology made all-season fishing possible: in high water or low, running water or still, clear water or muddy, or warm weather or cold. Although fishing was done year-in, year-out, it was done mainly in absentee fashion, with nets and traps. It did not demand nearly as much effort or as many resources as hunting, which drained time and energy as fast as a hill creek going down after a heavy rain. Had hunting not been so invigorating and occasionally wildly successful, I am convinced it would have been relegated to a passive activity like absentee fishing. I suspect that plummet-weighted fishing nets were behind the soaring food gain that enabled Poverty Point's achievements.

The Poverty Point community settled in the lap of plenty. New devices and cleverly organized and timed food quests enabled it to take advantage of nature's bounty and level out those times when bounty turned into scarcity. The way encampments were established across the land and their breakdown into permanent and temporary places indicated that Poverty Point's subsistence basically entailed a collector food-getting strategy, or one where people brought food home instead of moving home, spouse, kids, dogs, and belongings to food. People lived at Poverty Point and a few other places like Copes, Stockland Plantation, and Terral Lewis, probably year round. Only at Copes were faunal and floral remains so abundant and thoroughly studied as to indicate year-round occupation directly. The case for Poverty Point, Alexander Point, Steatite Field, Stockland Plantation, Terral Lewis, and other places being year-round residences was indirect: Their tool assemblages generally looked like Copes's but unlike places considered to be temporary camps.

But permanence was a relative condition. There probably were moments when families or labor parties left temporarily for the surrounding woods to dig roots, fish, or hunt deer and left few people at home — maybe even nobody for a while. There conceivably may have been a more general annual or biannual dispersal in which residents broke up into small groups and spread over a wide territory like the Choctaws during autumn nut fall. Such a dispersal would not only have enabled residents to take fuller advantage of seasonally available foods but would have conditioned them for lean seasons or spells of severe food shortages. I think Arledge, Aaron, Orvis Scott, Hendrix, and dozens of other encampments located more than a day's walk or pirogue-poling distance from Poverty Point were short-term campsites and work areas. Not only did their tool assemblages differ from residences, mainly in having fewer PPOs and more points and hoes, but their campgrounds were not as trashed.

Such organized dispersal would not have made Poverty Point, Copes, and other encampments any less residential or any less permanent for that matter. They were homes — places where people returned after camping out. Permanence was not a case of being at home 365 days a year, but a case of being around a lot during all seasons for several years running. On the other hand, Arledge, Aaron, Orvis Scott, and other similar places were field camps used only every once in a while by sojourners from nearby residences. They were temporary, and their tools showed it.

The Fishing Lure

Fishing not only was vital to Poverty Point's subsistence but had a major impact on its social life. Waterside location was a given. Besides satisfying obvious drinking, cooking, and cleaning needs, being alongside water placed people next to their fishing holes, cutting down on travel time. Aaron, Arledge, Copes, Ray's Brake, and other Joes Bayou encampments were on cutoff lakes, not on the main bayou channel, and those camps along the bayou proper were not on its immediate banks but on high relict levees hundreds of yards from it. While there was a possibility that camps close to the bayou were buried by flood deposits, thus producing a fragmented land-use picture, it was a certainty that camps located on levee crests were less vulnerable to inundation. High ground was the one and only practical place in the swamp for staging dry activities during annual backwaters, and while location alone does not prove springtime utilization, it certainly raises the likelihood.

The incompleteness of the food record from Poverty Point and surrounding camps makes it difficult to rate food importance. Besides, foods did not have to be abundant to be important, especially if they bridged lean times. Folks had to eat during January cold and April flood, periods when fresh plant foods were either unavailable or limited. During such spells, meat undoubtedly assumed a relatively greater role, and fish, which dominated food remains anyway, loomed as the major source. Fish was one case in which abundance did mean importance in terms of both quantity and timing, and consistent supply was the bottom line.

Poverty Point and surrounding camps sat either on the edge of the Mississippi River overflow swamp or on narrow ribbons of high ground down in its midst. The floodplain was laced with active and inactive rivers, bayous, lakes, and deep and seasonally flooded swamps. Few other places in North America had as many fish, absolutely or per acre, as these annually rejuvenated waters. Fishery biologists Victor Lambou, Garry Lucas, Michael Powell, Jan Dean, and Kenneth Lantz found that bottomland lakes supported somewhere between 150 and 1,700 pounds of fish per water-surface acre, normally between 300 and 500 pounds. Many places, such as the 500-square-mile swamp fronting and incorporating Poverty Point encampments, had between 30,000 and 1 million pounds of fish per square mile, enough to keep the smell of cooking fish on the smoke of many fires. If a pirogue full of fish had been caught every day of the year by every camp presently known, total annual poundage would still have been less than a fraction of 1 percent of the total available biomass. Add ten times that amount for Poverty Point and still only a small percentage would have been caught, not enough to degrade overall population or create major imbalances in species composition.

Relative abundance by species differed between floodplain waters and middens, revealing intentional selection and effects of fishing methods. In nature, the top ten species included, first, gizzard shad, and then variously depending on water fertility, longear sunfish, redear sunfish, bluegill, largemouth buffalo, largemouth bass, freshwater drum, threadfin shad, channel catfish, and spotted gar. The only midden with adequate abundance information was Copes, and it contained basically the same major species. Catfish, mainly bullhead but including channel and others, made up just under half the catch, yet they were not as common naturally as the other top species. Shad was the most abundant fish naturally but comprised only a trace in the midden. Gar ranked last among the major groups naturally, yet they were second to catfish in the midden. Although bowfin were not among the top ten naturally, they were more abundant than all but catfish and gar in the midden. So at Copes, it was catfish first, followed by gar and bowfin, and then by sunfish, bass, buffalo, and drum—all species at odds with their natural abundance, even allowing for natural fluctuations among bodies of water.

At Copes, remains indicated that most fish caught were between eight and eleven inches long, with numbers declining sharply for bigger fish. The biggest found was a three-foot-long gar. Bones from smaller fish may have gone right through recovery screens. Using baited traps with small openings might account for the narrow size range: Smaller fish could have swum right through, and bigger ones could not have gotten in. But nobody fishing for food instead of trophies would have restricted their catch so drastically, especially when all they had to do was enlarge the size of traps' openings to admit larger individuals. To have taken mostly eight- to eleven-inch fish would have left most catchable fish to swim around for another day. For example, Lucas and Powell's population counts in Tunica Cutoff, a Mississippi River oxbow lake, revealed that the average size of all fish except for minnow and bream species was greater than eleven inches, and not a single channel cat, gar, buffalo, or bowfin was less than fourteen inches long.

Poverty Point fishers probably used traps. They were widely deployed by historic natives up and down the Lower Mississippi Valley and across the South, suggesting that trapping was a proven ancient method. If traps had been used at Copes, they were more likely to have been set out in Joes Bayou or in the flooded woods and not in Beambrier Lake, the old oxbow on which Copes actually sat. Commercial fisherman Vernie Gibson told me that traps worked best in current, particularly when set close to the bank where fish forage at night or in flooded woods frequented by "blabbers." Blabbers, or bottom-feeders like buffalo and drum, leave lines of frothy bubbles on the water surface marking their commonly used trails and feeding areas.

For fishing Breambrier Lake and other swamp lakes and sluggish streams, weighted nets were the best, most efficient way to go. Gill nets would have caught fish in a narrow size range just like traps, but they would have been effective under all kinds of water conditions, including still waters like Breambrier Lake. Small fish would have passed through their mesh, and big ones simply would have run into the net and been turned aside. Those that swam into the net and were too big to get completely through became entangled. So width of mesh openings did predetermine the size of fish that could be caught. Nonetheless, gill nets posed the same problem as traps: They would have let too many available fish go uncaught, and being so selective was simply unthinkable for people who fished for a living.

I think trammel nets or seines—both of which required bottomline weights—were deployed, but they would have caught everything bigger than mesh openings, leaving the same old question: What happened to the big fish? Jackson reported that vertebra were underrepresented among bones in the Copes midden and suggested that some fish had been moved elsewhere. Having so few large fish remains in the midden strengthened that possibility. If fish had been taken to Poverty Point or other camps either fresh, dried, or smoked, there would have been few bones left at Copes to indicate they had ever been caught. The size of fish eaten at Copes was the best eating size anyway, so Copes's fishers not only ate pretty well while they worked, but they may have cared enough to send the second-best to friends and neighbors or laid by stores for themselves for when they broke camp. Alternatively, missing fish might have been what swampers used to barter with stone traffickers or what they gave away to curry favors and loyality.

If they had been used for bartering or leveraging favors, then fish may have been the means swampers used to get imported stone tools to or from Poverty Point and to create social debt, which ultimately translated into labor on the great earthworks.

The Last Mouthful

The warm waters of the lower end of the Lower Mississippi Valley were as close to a horn of plenty as North America had to offer, matched only by lower Florida. Although just about as good as wild America ever got, food bounty still went up and down depending on hurricanes, floods, droughts, bugs, blights, and hosts of other complications as well as nature's own built-in health and vitality. In addition, wild-food abundance and availability fluctuated seasonally, although not as drastically as some areas further inland where terrestrial climate reigned. But peninsular Florida and Lower Mississippi regions were blessed with a superabundant food that enabled crafty and industrious inhabitants to weather hard times. That superabundant food—fish—was available all year long, year in and year out. As long as there were nets to deploy and a share-the-wealth ethic to shape domestic and political economic organization, the cultures in these regions were able to turn one of the consistently richest natural ecosystems anywhere into a writ for cultural elaboration. Small wonder that mound-building first appeared in these regions and that some of the most highly organized fisher-hunter-gatherers in America lived where fishing was good and major feeding times ran around the clock. Gastronomically and political-economically, fish and fishing were on the ground floor of Poverty Point's surge.

8

Exchange

The Reuniting

Ai, listen, *Holata Humma* speaks.

I am very happy that the long travelers return with heavy canoe. The supply of precious gray and white flints will help conduct this year's gathering in the manner the People expect. Runners from many new bands have come to the village this past moon, asking that they be allowed to attend the gathering and pay homage to *Helona.* With this flint we can gift them for their help with the new construction without having to curtail supplies for our own people.

The flint enables the People of the Rings to retain the affluency and respect we have enjoyed since the old village was built under my mother's brother's leadership. Though we cannot speak his name in death, we hold him close in our memories for what he did for the People. The flint allows the People to live his dream the way he wanted.

So now, welcome home, my long travelers. Get out of the canoe and enter the Village of the Rings. Six days hence, the dance fires will burn brightly. Then, we will feast and listen to you sing your stories. May your sweat time pass quickly, so we can embrace you with more than just words.

Ai, I have spoken.

Holata Humma, 1609 B.C., fictional oratory by Jon Gibson, in *Cool Dark Woods, Poison Ivy, and Maringoins,* 1994

Not Even the Smallest Pebble

Native rock was not counted among Poverty Point's many blessings. Not having any rock—not even the smallest pebble—within its 700-square-mile homeland posed a serious technological shortcoming. How Poverty Point dealt with this, its number one problem, and still managed to put essential raw materials into the hands of consumers was a one-way fare to its unprecedented organization and development. If rock had been naturally available, there would have been little premium placed on knowing about stone sources outside Poverty Point's land or on how to get rock delivered. So recognition went to those who knew such things, and I believe they turned that knowledge into corporate action by drawing on a prevailing attitude—to honor and protect their way of life. Protecting home and country was not new, but protecting home and country from so many evil spirits was. Powerful alien spirits and forces came with the stone from strange lands, and I contend that the threat they posed to exchange and to the smooth flow of economy and social relations was directly responsible for the grandiose insurance taken out to combat them—the huge protective earthworks.

Two Sides of Exchange

There were two sides to Poverty Point exchange. One was given to acquiring materials from the immediate locality and the other to acquiring materials from far away. Both required dealing directly or indirectly with peoples at the rock deposits as well as with groups living along delivery routes. So many classic tool styles and forms were linked to foreign exchange materials that a good case can be made for exchange being the prime enabler for Poverty Point's elaborate hard-rock technology. For example, if imported foreign rock had been unavailable, then three of the five primary classes of stone objects, which Webb used to define Poverty Point culture, would be absent. If these objects had been made entirely of local gravel, as some were, there would have been few compelling reasons to distinguish Poverty Point culture from any other Archaic culture. Most of Webb's secondary and tertiary cultural diagnostics were also made of exotic rock, although many had counterparts of local rock. Therefore, exchange was one of the defining aspects of Poverty Point culture and one of the most important drivers of its unique development.

Poverty Point exchange focused on rock, or so it seems. Rock lasts.

Other possible exchange items have left little or no trace. Venison roasts and fish fillets possibly were produced and exchanged on a local level, while items like pelican feathers and smoked red snapper had to be imported from the coast 350 river miles to the south. Sand-tempered, mulberry-shaped PPOs were evidently involved, too; they probably came from the Poverty Point–age Claiborne settlement at the Pearl River mouth on Mississippi's Gulf Coast, ostensibly through the same exchanges that produced pelican and snapper.

But stone was the number one exchange commodity. Local chert gravel probably came from Bastrop Hills through intermediaries living along Bayou Bartholomew, three to six pirogue hours west of Poverty Point. Bartholomew groups came to assimilate features of Poverty Point culture in the process. Evidently, few if any rocks were gotten from gravel- and sandstone-bearing hills the same distance south of Poverty Point, as local Archaic groups there remained culturally distinctive and did not assimilate Poverty Point styles or tool forms. Nonlocal rocks came from several widely separated sections of the Midwest and interior Southeast. The closest source for novaculite, hematite, magnetite, crystal quartz, slate, calcite, hornblende-basalt porphyry, flourite, and other minor minerals was the Ouachita Mountains, near Hot Springs in Central Arkansas, about 150 overland miles northwest of Poverty Point and more than twice that mileage by circuitous waterways. The escarpment of the Ozark Plateau near St. Louis in eastern Missouri was the source of white Burlington chert and of galena, a lead ore. Quarries were more than 450 straight-line miles from Poverty Point or twice that far by way of the Mississippi River. Another source of galena lay farther upriver near the common corner of Iowa, Wisconsin, and Illinois, about 300 overland and 575 river miles from St. Louis. Copper came from glacial drift deposits in the Great Lakes area, which had water links to the Mississippi or Ohio Rivers. The Shawnee Hills of southern Illinois, which were south of St. Louis and across the Mississippi River north of the Ohio River junction, were the source of Mill Creek and Dongola/Cobden cherts as well as more flourite. The hills were 350 overland miles north of Poverty Point or 600 miles by Mississippi River. Wyandotte and Harrodsburg flints were present in the Knobs region of northern Kentucky–southern Indiana along the Ohio River about 365 overland or 650 river miles above Poverty Point. Flint Ridge chert was nearby. Various rocks including Dover, Fort Payne, Camden, and Pickwick cherts, phyllite, and schist were found along the

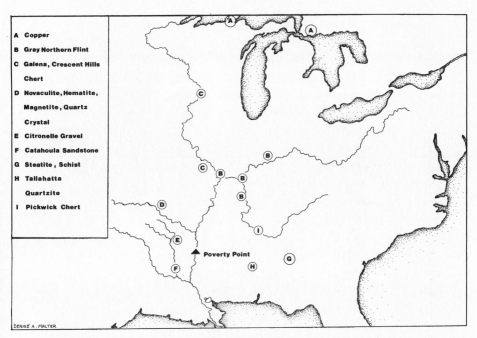

A Copper

B Gray Northern Flint

C Galena, Crescent Hills

   Chert

D Novaculite, Hematite,

   Magnetite, Quartz

   Crystal

E Citronelle Gravel

F Catahoula Sandstone

G Steatite, Schist

H Tallahatta

   Quartzite

I Pickwick Chert

DENISE A. MALTER

Map 8.1. Tons of rock were moved into Poverty Point and other encampments in the Lower Mississippi Valley during the exchange peak. Sources of rock were spread across the midcontinent but were strategically located near the Mississippi River and its primary tributaries. Drawing by Denise Malter.

Tennessee River from near its junction with the Ohio downstream to the Valley and Ridge province in the common corner of Alabama, Georgia, and Tennessee—from 350 to 500 straight-line or up to 1,200 river miles northeast of Poverty Point. Tallahatta quartzite outcropped in eastern Mississippi and western Alabama along the Tennessee-Tombigbee drainages east of Poverty Point. Soapstone and soft greenstone were from the Appalachian piedmont of Alabama and Georgia. If quartzite, soapstone, and greenstone came directly to Poverty Point, they had to traverse 400 long, hard miles, but if they came by way of rivers flowing into the Gulf, across the Gulf, and then up the Mississippi, they had to make one of the longest trips of all the materials, perhaps 1,200 miles. Actually, the longest distance traveled by any material was a piece of obsidian that came from Wyoming.

Most rocks, especially cherts and flints, were identified by visually comparing Poverty Point items with samples of rocks from source areas;

others were linked to sources by testimony of experts; and a few materials were tied to sources by chemical analyses. Chemically analyzed matches included soapstone, galena, copper, hematite, magnetite, and Dover flint. Trace-element comparisons showed that the Wyoming obsidian was not from the Yellowstone locality, although it resembled Yellowstone material, and that the red rock commonly used for beads and ornaments was not the Minnesota pipestone it resembled. Some soapstone did not chemically fit known sources, such as Ouachita Mountains outcrops.

Poverty Point exchange was notable on several accounts. First, trade volume was heavy. Tons and tons of rock made their way to Poverty Point, and most stayed there after arrival. Some seventy metric tons or more of exotic materials wound up incorporated in ring fill, and despite opinions to the contrary, long-distance exchange likely was at a low ebb during busy construction moments compared with before, in between, and afterwards. Some exotic materials got out to hinterland encampments, while some went on to other settlements located hundreds of miles south of Poverty Point. Remember, Poverty Point's community territory had no native rock whatsoever; even local pebble chert had to be brought in, probably through exchange. The absolute amount of rock, both exotic and local, delivered to Poverty Point was staggering.

Second, local gravels arrived in a natural state, but exotic flint and chert had undergone preliminary shaping before coming to Poverty Point. Most exotic flint/chert arrived as bifaces or bifacial foliates and not finished points. Nearly all of Poverty Point's points were either local forms, which lacked lookalikes in the areas where stone originated, or were so generalized (Gary being a prime example) that they were made by practically every Archaic group living between Poverty Point and the rock deposits. Making bifaces at the rock deposits was a smart way to reduce weight for the long trip to Poverty Point without compromising local point-making, except maybe for setting maximum size. For myriad reasons, hundreds of bifaces from the rings never underwent further shaping, although most did. For every biface tabulated in Webb's large studied collection, there were more than six finished points.

Soapstone arrived from Alabama or Georgia as bowls rather than solid blocks. Scrap came from broken vessels, not from manufacturing. Hematite and magnetite used for plummets were also partly shaped or at least size selected at outcrops, because there was a decided lack of large unworked pieces at Poverty Point and surrounding encampments. Although making plummets would not have left much recognizable waste, there surely would have been an unused lump of soapstone somewhere around if it had been delivered to Poverty Point in an unworked condition. So far, unworked lumps are as rare as diamonds. The same can be said for greenstone celts, although being thick and of basic ax shape made them less vulnerable to fabricating mistakes and material flaws than plummets. Generally, small, delicate objects and those that bore drilled holes were more susceptible to production mistakes. Nearly all materials used for ground-stone tools and ornaments had been subjected to some degree of modification. Simply claiming that grinding and polishing did not produce detectable waste failed to explain why natural unworked pieces were so rare. Half-finished objects of all kinds were common, but being partly worked or not being worked presented two different conditions, and both had direct economic organizational implications.

Blanks were probably preprocessed at outcrops for delivery, because no special prefabrication camps have been identified along probable exchange routes. Besides, quarries and deposits have lots of partly worked debris. Another implication is either that quarry workers were familiar with Poverty Point's stone needs or that Poverty Point craftspeople adapted their tools to whatever materials happened to be sent along. But why send along materials of unproven utility? Just the act of choosing a particular resource from among scores and scores of possible candidates suggests a basic familiarity with Poverty Point technology by someone or everyone involved in exchange. How rock dealers gained such familiarity across long miles was the key to Poverty Point's political economic success.

Sources of materials were so far apart and often so far away that there simply would have been no way for Poverty Point people to have found out about them firsthand during their normal food-getting rounds. Thus, I believe Poverty Point exchange was truly an intergroup activity, a real, honest-to-goodness exchange system engaging peoples spread across half the country. What got passed along was what was needed, and what was needed got passed along. The only way for that to happen was for the hand that provided to know what the hand that received was involved with. Rock exchange proceeded on information exchange, and virtually all stone that came to Poverty Point entered into its technology somehow. Even not-so-good materials, like some batches of Burlington chert, were pressed into service despite being flawed.

A third notable aspect of exchange was that exotic materials were used mainly, if not entirely, for general domestic needs, and social standing evidently placed no restrictions on their access. Function determined access, pure and simple. Exchange materials were deployed in everyday activities; they were not channeled solely into special rituals or reserved for dignitaries. In this sense, they were not prestige materials, as were copper earspools circulated during Hopewell times or even gray flint Benton cache bifaces circulated during Middle Archaic days. There was an overriding simplicity to Poverty Point exchange. It was open and responded to common need. No other agenda was involved, although there were some social impacts.

The final aspect of exchange was in many ways the most troubling. Nothing of identifiably Poverty Point cultural origin reached distant sources of exchange materials, and very little of a tangible nature passed along trade routes very far from Poverty Point itself. The lack of reciprocal trade material was what prompted ideas about direct acquisition or about soft goods, either perishable or ideological, being exchanged for hardware. Those ideas never appealed to me. Exchange connections that stretched as far as Poverty Point's would not have involved food, not even preserved stores; distances were simply too great to have created any profit in or dependence on exchange foods. Besides, practically the same foods could have been gotten fresh from home woods and waters with less effort, and Tabasco sauce and crawfish jambalaya were still some time away. Maybe getting a pelican feather was something of a feather in one's bonnet, but as the *raison d'etre* for such a far-reaching and involved exchange system, I have serious doubts about feather power. To me, long-distance exchange had to provide direct and dependable material benefits to all who participated; otherwise it would not have operated so well, for so long, or over such long distances.

Local Exchange Was Function Driven

Despite its long reach, local Poverty Point exchange was basically simple and practical. For it to have been restricted in some way would have been counterproductive or worse in a land where everyone, not just personages, needed stone to make ends meet. The open nature of exchange was precisely what a stoneless land needed to thrive, and getting stone into everyone's hands was a superlative achievement and a mark of the corporative spirit of exchange.

In a 1994 analysis published in *Louisiana Archaeology*, David Griffing and I found that local exchange was function driven. Field camps had nearly as much as and, in several cases, more exchange material than residential encampments. Topping the list of places with exotic material was Aaron, a field camp, with more than 80 percent; but another field camp, Owens, was at the bottom of the list with only 37 percent. Alexander Point and Terral Lewis, both residences, had 72 and 62 percent, respectively; but Stockland Plantation, also a residence, had but 38 percent. When Griffing and I compared how far camps were from Poverty Point—the presumed local source of exchange rock—we found an overall tendency for amounts of exotics to diminish with distance, but there were several exceptions. The strongest influence of all was assemblage composition. Exotic rock was the preferred material for certain tools; when encampments had large numbers of those particular tools, ergo, they had large amounts of exotic flint.

Exchange materials that decline as distance between source and use area increases is supposed to be evidence for simple, down-the-line trade between groups living next to each other. Since falloff patterns around Poverty Point were inconsistent, Griffing and I considered an alternative—directional (prestige) exchange—reasoning that if exchange had been carried out to deliver goods to personages, then encampments where most elites lived should have received the most exchange materials regardless of how far they were from Poverty Point. Elite encampments, we assumed, would have had the largest grounds, the biggest mounds, or the most status markers. We could not detect any correlations, because we failed to identify elite camps. Apart from Poverty Point itself, the largest places were all temporary field camps and not residences where personages lived most of the time. Apart from Poverty Point, no campsite whether residential or not had mounds that could be attributed definitely to Poverty Point construction; and stone beads and other fancy lapidary items, which probably signaled social standing, were so rare everywhere as to indicate how politically undistinguished Poverty Point encampments were.

What came through loud and clear in our study was that exotic chert and flint were most abundant at places where certain kinds of tools were

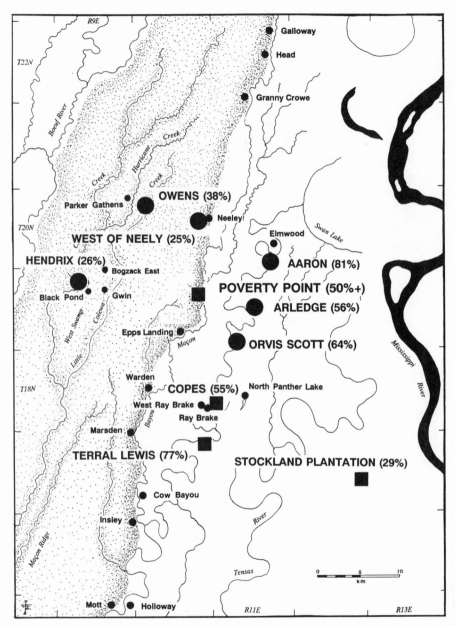

Map 8.2. Foreign flint (*shown in parentheses*), in substantial amounts, made its way to encampments surrounding Poverty Point. It wound up in both residences (*squares*) and field camps (*large dots*). The distance of encampments from Poverty Point often made no difference in the amounts of exotic flint present.

most plentiful. For example, Aaron, Arledge, Terral Lewis, and other wetland camps that had relatively large numbers of hoes had relatively large amounts of northern gray flint, particularly Dover flint. Why? Simply because hoes were made almost entirely of northern gray flint, especially the Dover variety. Hoes were also large bifaces, and resharpening them produced large amounts of gray flint residue. Having lots of Motley, Epps, and Delhi points also meant more gray flint because they were predominantly made of gray flint. Places with large numbers of Gary and Pontchartrain points produced greater amounts of local pebble chert and novaculite. If large numbers of perforators also happened to be present, then local chert representation went even higher, because perforators were overwhelmingly made from local gravel. Places with relatively large numbers of plummets had relatively large amounts of hematite. Hematite was the major plummet material. The list could go on and on, but what it all boiled down to was that amounts of exotic stone depended on what kinds of tools were present, and tools were commonplace domestic gear, not specialized or status-denoting objects.

Long-distance exchange rock went where it was most needed, and that was into the domestic sector. Access was not limited to personages or special events, and that meant that local exchange was infused with practical function and simple access codes. Foreign materials went primarily into activities that put food in the earth oven rather than feathers in the hair or beads around the neck.

Still, there were beads and feathers, and Poverty Point had relatively more ornamentation than other places. Poverty Point had a bead for every 10 points, Stockland Plantation a bead for every 20 points, but other encampments had far fewer—one bead for as many as 35 to 110 points. This is mentioned for two reasons: one, to point out that Poverty Point did have more presumed status-denoting objects than other places and, two, as a reminder that a wide slate of exotic rock was exchanged.

On the first account, having more beadwork underscored Poverty Point's prominence in its locality. Furthermore, there was no consistent association between beads and encampment type. Stockland Plantation was a residence, and it had relatively more beads than any other camp. Yet Terral Lewis was a residence, too, and it had the lowest ratio of all. Arledge was a field camp, and it was second to Stockland Plantation but ahead of Copes, another residence.

On the second account, ornaments and other groundstone objects were made of exotic material, too. Still, they were uncommon compared with chipped-stone tools and were made of rock other than flint, which was usually unidentified or inconsistently recorded. The problem created was that stone typically used for social or ritual objects could not be numerically compared with chert tools to see if distributional patterns were similar. If rock used for nondomestic purposes was circulated differently from rock used for domestic purposes, then local exchange did not have a uniformly simple, unassuming organization.

Regardless of how exchange was organized, the lion's share of exotic exchange material went without major restriction to women and men everywhere who put it to work doing their daily chores. Local chert was used a bit more than foreign flint at neighborhood camps located at increasing distances from Poverty Point, but how it was circulated did not change with increasing distance. Poverty Point reserved greater absolute quantities of nonflint exotics for itself, and it did the same with local pebble cherts. To a large degree, variable amounts of both local and exotic materials at hinterland camps are merely data-recording fluctuations which obscure the real reason behind differences whether that was function, serendipity, or selective access.

The Far Corners

Although exchange focused on Poverty Point, other contemporary places scores and even hundreds of miles from Poverty Point were involved, too. Sources of most circulating materials lay far beyond the Maçon Ridge homeland. For example, novaculite and hematite from the Ouachita Mountains were sent 150 miles or more to Poverty Point; 100 miles to Jaketown, located on a relict Mississippi River course in western Mississippi; 170 miles to Beau Rivage, located on an abandoned Mississippi River course in south-central Louisiana; and 250 miles to Claiborne, also located near a once-used course of the Mississippi River at its outlet into the Gulf of Mexico. Burlington chert was moved 450 miles or more to Poverty Point and at least 600 miles to Beau Rivage. Dover flint moved 350 direct miles to get to Poverty Point and more than 520 direct miles to Beau Rivage, at least twice that far if by river. Other materials had to come even further. But long distances did not keep exotic rock from reaching distant communities, although increasing distances (from Poverty Point) meant decreasing quantities. One-third of the projectile points from Beau Rivage were made from several of the same kinds of exotic rocks as Poverty Point's. At Jaketown, it reached 40 percent. But some of Poverty

Point's own outlying encampments only had amounts comparable to these far-off places. Many other rocks, or rather objects made from those rocks, went on down the line, too, although distributional patterns did not conform precisely to expectations of simple down-the-line exchange. Soapstone, quartz crystal, galena, slates, varied flints and cherts, and other exotic materials reached the far corners of Poverty Point's vast exchange network.

Sizing up the big picture failed to clarify either it or the local picture. In their 1994 study of Arkansas exchange published in *Louisiana Archaeology*, Marvin Jeter and Edwin Jackson reported that Ouachita Mountain rocks were more abundant near the mountains and decreased as they got closer to Poverty Point. Jay Johnson reported a similar situation in western Mississippi's Yazoo Basin, the area around Jaketown. But the fact remained that Ouachita rocks, as well as midwestern and southeastern materials, were superabundant at Poverty Point despite being located farther from the mountains than places studied by these archaeologists. Also, the large percentage of novaculite found at Beau Rivage, near Louisiana's central Gulf Coast, countered the distance-falloff trend. Why or how Beau Rivage got involved with Poverty Point exchange was unclear. Uneven reporting made it impossible to tell how much exotic material wound up at Claiborne, on the east side of the Mississippi Valley opposite Beau Rivage, although at least some did. Claiborne was in a perfect location to have been involved in moving soapstone vessels upriver to Poverty Point—that is, if stone pots had entered the Mississippi River mouth by way of Mobile Bay and the Mississippi Sound, as many archaeologists suspect.

It looked like regional exchange was geared toward getting exotic materials to Poverty Point. Some communities got bypassed in the effort, while some became more involved than others. The same thing happened once exotic rocks were sent southward: Some communities wholeheartedly participated in the trafficking, some did not. Undoubtedly, logistics were important, but community relations probably assumed the lead in establishing and maintaining the strength of exchange connections. Like local exchange, regional exchange benefited the common jobs of house and field; it was not restricted to ceremonial function or dignitaries. Poverty Point exchange, on both local and regional levels, provided rock for needy consumers.

9

Stone and Earth Symbolism

"A Different Fox"

He lay out in the open near the artificial embankment we call the Causeway. . . . He just lay there perfectly still, hind legs spread-eagle cooling his belly on the new dew. . . . We lost sight of him as he bounded into the woods, . . . heading south toward the big ravine. . . .We felt privileged. We had seen the fox once more. The fox had attended our opening ceremony [the first day of field school] and now on our last official day of excavation, the day before we would leave Poverty Point, the fox was there to bid us good-bye.

We entered Mound B Field. The fox was waiting.

"Look," I exclaimed, "There he is."

Everyone turned.

"Where?"

"There, next to the trees."

I pointed. Nobody saw him. Strange, he was standing there in plain view. But the fox we had seen a moment before near the Causeway had run off in the opposite direction. . . . This must be a different fox.

Suddenly, I understood. This was indeed a different fox, he had yellow fur, and he was smiling broadly.

Jon Gibson, memoir of 1989 field-school incident, published in *Search for the Lost Sixth Ridge*, 1990

Spirits and Supernatural Power

Foxes, birds, and the malevolent west and north winds were aspects of a widespread southeastern symbolism portrayed in hard stone and earth at Poverty Point. In the past, archaeologists typically subsumed such symbolism into the ongoing debate about whether or not Poverty Point was solely a place of ceremony. But that argument always missed the point, for ceremony and ritual are inseparable parts of everyday native life. Even if ceremonies had been held on special days and on grounds physically separate from living areas, such as in the plaza, on top of Bird Mound's flat-topped tail, or around Mound B, the fact of the matter is that people lived on the rings. The rings were the boldest expression of their animistic beliefs.

The pertinent issue is not about whether sacred and secular were separate but about how spiritualism and supernaturalism affected everyday living. Rings, mounds, and zoomorphic objects all conveyed powerful subliminal messages, yet massive quantities of domestic refuse vouched for intensive residence of the rings. Symbolic items wound up in the trash. Poverty Point was not solely a huge ceremonial place, but it surely was a hugely spiritual place.

Earthworks, small zoomorphs, and other carvings in hard stone probably represented supernatural images and magical charms, but even so they were only extensions of an everyday world and its natural order. It seems likely to me that if Poverty Point had not engaged in exchange in such a large way, had it not brought so many outlanders together, had it not fished and shared the catch so extensively, had it not done other things in such ambitious ways, then its imposing earthworks probably would not have been built. Had it taken less pride in itself and been less aware of its identity, there would have been little need for ideographic reminders, either. Small, portable, carved reminders were not very common, but they were conspicuous.

I never thought much about the meaning of Poverty Point's iconology and earthworks until one day, while reading missionary Alfred Wright's account of Choctaw religion, I realized that there were parallels. Choctaw tradition held that when a person died, one of the two souls, the *shilup* (or inside shadow), went directly to the Land of Ghosts, but the *Shilombish* (or outside shadow) remained on earth and wandered restlessly around the old haunts, frightening people and trying to make them move away. The *Shilombish* was believed to assume the form of a fox or an owl, the same two creatures that dominated Poverty Point's symbolic hard-stone objects. Was there a connection? My interest was piqued. I voraciously read and reread everything pertaining to native southern traditions, then native eastern traditions, and then Native American beliefs—everything east of the Rockies and south of the Arctic. I found numerous parallels between tribal stories and Poverty Point's stone and earth. Many did not even require an active imagination.

But still, something was missing, a means of tying the shadowy past to traditional stories. I considered the possibility of lore spreading along with rock exchanges but decided that long distances and language barriers were too much for oral literature to overcome. Economic exchange among peoples who were not fluent in each other's language could have been enabled through sign language or a pidgin language, something like Mobilian, but such broken and limited communication would have been unsuitable for telling and understanding cosmic and creation parables. Furthermore, I detected no compelling evidence for mass migrations during Middle or Late Archaic times that might have spread stories. Technological and stylistic continuities indicated general population stability across the Lower Mississippi Valley and other parts of the South for generations and generations, but knowing that earlier dispersals had taken place made me wonder if shared lore might have had roots in common ancestral beginnings when Early Archaic groups were still milling about the land. I reasoned that if languages had diverged during the past several centuries or even millennia, then at least bits and pieces of an ancient cosmology might have survived.

Evidence for just such unity has been discovered. Language expert Mary Haas proposed that many southern languages descended from a Gulf protolanguage thousands of years earlier. Before that, there had been a proto-Gulf language spoken over an even larger area, and preceding that, as language authority Wallace Chaffe claims, there had probably been a parent language spoken by all natives living east of the Rockies.

Of course, how and where Poverty Point's language fit into the larger historical scheme is hard to say. No definite Poverty Point words survive, but other arguments attest to a possible Gulf or pre-Gulf affiliation, probably through a proto-Tunican family connection. Canadian archaeologist Gene Denny, in a 1997 paper presented to the Midwest Archaeological Conference, proposed that Poverty Point and midwestern Algonkian languages were closely related. Linguist Julian Granberry in a 1999 paper published in the *Florida Anthropologist* suggested a Poverty Point–Calusa connection, and again an ancestral Tunican dialect was suspected.

So if Native Americans, including Poverty Point's ancestors, had all spoken the same tongue or related tongues at some long-ago time, it raised the possibility that there had been one world outlook, one slate of cosmic explanations, and maybe even one set of heroic and epic stories. I convinced myself that an essential fidelity was preserved because such beliefs were fundamental to people's feelings about who they were, where they came from, and what their place was in the cosmos. Such fundamental beliefs always were heartfelt and motivational.

That left contexts to be judged for compatibility. So I turned once again to Poverty Point imagery to see whether or not it made any sense when viewed in light of the characters, settings, circumstances, and lessons given in traditional native stories. Lo and behold, I discovered that just about every animal carved in stone had played a role in the stories.

Earthworks as Home and Protection

I suggested earlier that Poverty Point's earthworks were magic. Not only were they large, but they were unlike any built before. I doubted that mounds at surrounding encampments—Ray's Brake, Neeley, Insley, Jackson, and Lower Jackson—were built by Poverty Point hands. Low domed mounds had been erected for at least 2,000 years before Poverty Point's, so merely having domed mounds was insufficient reason to assume they were Poverty Point constructions. None had been recently excavated or radiocarbon dated. Mounds were built at Jaketown, Claiborne, and possibly other places outside Poverty Point's 700-square-mile homeland. But at home, Poverty Point's constructions stood alone, or at least they stood alone in their massiveness.

The layout of Poverty Point's earthworks seemed so compatible with the contemporary cosmic creation story that I take it as a metaphor for the sacred event and its principles. The first principle concerns life itself. The open eastern side of the rings enables the Creator's blazing eye, the sun, to look directly upon the people, and as long as that transpires, life flourishes. The second principle concerns protection. Widespread native lore holds that symmetrical, geometric figures were magical shields against an outside world filled with potentially disorderly beings and evil power. Death, sickness, and other bad problems were believed to come out of the west and social disharmony and witchcraft out of the north; these are the directions shielded by Poverty Point's rings and the partial square of its intersecting mound axes. No earthen barrier would have been needed on the east, where life and vitality originate, or on the south, from whence harmony and wisdom spring forth.

Other features of the earthworks may have offered magical safeguards, too. The earthworks incorporate the sacred number six. There are six rings, six mounds, and six compartments within the rings. In traditional cosmology, the number six corresponds to the upper and lower worlds and the four value-laden directions. If six stands for these divisions of the primal cosmos, then they may signify a spirit time before evil—a safe and secure time. In traditional southeastern cosmology, birds are regarded as spirit helpers and advance scouts. Bird mounds set on the west and north may have added those powers to the protective shielding. Mound form itself may have symbolized the Earth Island, the primordial earth formed by the Creator upon the back of a giant turtle swimming in the great cosmic sea. An earthen mound is linked to where people originated summoned by Creator Sun, who bade them climb forth through a long cave that opened onto a mound summit. Such a figurative account of the natural birth process implies the existence of the Earth Mother concept. Native religion expert Sam Gill argued that the Earth Mother concept developed after European contact, but old mounds deem otherwise. White contact merely amplified the concept. The Earth Mother concept is deeply rooted in native America; otherwise, womb metaphors would not have been so widespread. Even dirt used to construct mounds may have been considered sacred. Some historic southern tribes spread swept-up plaza dirt onto mounds. Such dirt, imbued with supernatural power from personages and sacred activities, was deemed unsafe or improper for common people to walk upon. Mounds as large as Poverty Point's could not have been built solely with plaza sweepings—otherwise the plaza would have been nearly as deep as the mounds were high. This does not detract, however, from the possibility that mound dirt was power-charged. Nonetheless, the rings were safe to walk upon; their fill dirt was taken alongside, not from, the plaza.

Charms and Fetishes

The giant earthworks safeguarded those who gathered within their sanctum, but Poverty Point's food, rocks, and other basic resources came from outside the protection of the earthworks. I suspect that outbound workers carried a little security with them, if not for personal protection, then as insurance for the success of their missions. Small, polished hard-stone objects included several animals and composite animal–human beings, which figured in traditional stories. These objects were the finest of all Poverty Point's creations, and although they seem to represent only a few themes, they all were uniquely executed, attesting to talented stone carvers. If such objects stood for the animals and spirit beings in Gulf-derived lore, then their owners were probably hoping to capture their legendary qualities for themselves or for tasks at hand. They were probably good-luck charms or, if ritually consecrated, fetishes.

Animal, human, and animal-human forms and glyphs all comprise possible links to traditional mythical figures. Birds were portrayed most often. Beads and pendants were made in their image. Flat cutout caricatures of bird heads depict general themes rather than recognizable species; among them are crested, long-billed, and big-headed forms. Other pen-

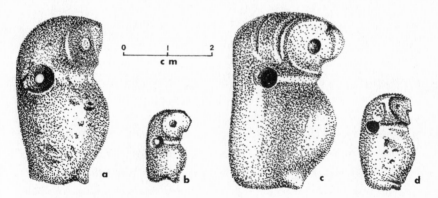

Fig. 9.1. Fat-bellied owl statuettes have been found across the Gulf South from northwestern Louisiana to central Florida. They may have been talismans carried by travelers. The statuettes shown here are from the bottom of the Withlacoochee River in central Florida (*far left*); the Hebe encampment in west Mississippi (*middle left*); the McMullen encampment near Red River in northwest Louisiana (*middle right*); and the Owens encampment on Maçon Ridge a few miles north of Poverty Point. The Owens owl is 0.8 inches long.

dants represented in-the-round owls, but like bird-head cutouts, species were unidentifiable unless size denoted horned, barred, and screech owl species.

I think their abstract nature is in keeping with the general magical meaning of the imagery. Being too specific probably would have restricted their powers. If identifying marks had been important, artisans certainly would have included them. Assuredly, distinct species markings would have been easier to create than the motion that carvers portrayed by turning the feet in a different direction from the head. A similar vagueness pervaded bird designs carved on soapstone vessels, plummets, bannerstones, and gorgets. A flying bird with a crowlike beak, grasping feet, and narrow wings and tail was raised in bas relief on a soapstone pot. A single-line figure of a songbird was scratched on a tubular stone bead, and an open-mouthed nestling receiving food berries was engraved on a polished plummet. Specific species were not recognizable.

Actually, vagueness gave way to downright conflation of some forms. Webb referred to one style of mixed imagery as the Fox-Man design, but the pointed-ear elements presumed to depict fox ears just as readily could have been ear tufts of horned owls, the imagery portraying an Owl-Man design instead. Maybe—just maybe—inseparability was really what was intended. Only plummets and bannerstones displayed Fox-Man or Owl-Man designs. Owl or fox monsters with deer antlers, owl- or fox-masked/costumed performers or shamans, and owl/fox/human hybrids were depicted, or perhaps they represented one spirit being variously clad.

Objects bearing bird decorations were portable and meant to be worn or attached, since all except the vessel and possibly a bannerstone were fitted with perforations. Animal decorations probably were placed on objects for the chase rather than for the home or the nut grove, the latter displaying geometric patterns when any decoration at all was applied. Having an animal decoration did not mean necessarily that the object was meant to be used solely away from Poverty Point, but it did suggest that activities such as hunting, fishing, and long-distance exchange conducted outside the protective earthen shield carried their protection and luck with them.

Other animal imagery was displayed, too: a panther on a soapstone vessel, a periwinkle on a gorget, a "long-tail" (possibly an opossum) on a plummet, and webbed waterfowl feet on plummets. Free forms included open clamshell pendants, musk turtle and tortoise gorgets, and claw or talon pendants. Birds were depicted predominantly, other animals only occasionally. Decorated objects were rare, but then power and magic did not need to be displayed often to be effective and all-pervasive.

These charms reminded me of a small flourite crystal I got in a rock shop in Arkansas when I was eleven years old. The crystal was yellow with one purple end but had absolutely no intrinsic or associational value. It was merely a pretty rock, but it was so different from anything we gravel-road country kids had ever seen before that it became a good luck charm for us all—and an effective one, too. All of us on the elementary

Fig. 9.2. Plummets, gorgets, and even soapstone vessels sometimes were engraved with figures that had supernatural qualities or played important roles in traditional stories of historic and contemporary Native Americans. Adding figures was probably done for luck and transformed otherwise common utensils into charms or fetishes. Bird representations were the most prevalent and included horned owl (or Fox-Man design), hungry nestling, songbird, and "crow" figures and were combined, rarely, with deer antlers to depict costumed performers or supernaturals. Turtles and unique engravings such as the Long-Tail (possibly an opossum) and panther also occurred.

school football and basketball teams rubbed the crystal before every game. We won every game, pulled together as one, and took pride in being the Tullos Rebels, the best in the parish. All on account of a pretty rock. Its magic worked because we believed it would. Being good ball players had absolutely nothing to do with it.

How did these Poverty Point images possibly reflect the ancient traditions? Birds were prominent in native lore. Thunder and lightning were thought to be great birds—Thunderers, male and female, instrumental in bringing weather, good and bad. Crows were associated with bad luck. One story had a crow flying about the primordial watery expanse when the Earth Island was created, so disinterested in creation that it simply flew by without announcing the great miracle. A Thunderer connection is evident (water, flood, and weather being interconnected), but other magical attributes of supernaturals are apparent, too. One is that spirits—any spirit, bird or otherwise—could be either good or bad depending on circumstances; another is that spirit birds were news-carriers. Having the crow fail to deliver a message as important as the creation of the earth emphatically casts the Thunderer as a negative force. The weather link is maintained by wild "canaries," possibly Carolina parakeets or perhaps goldfinches or yellowish warblers. These little yellow birds—*tcintc* to the Chitimacha, a South Louisiana tribe—foretold the weather and "talked" to people. Pigeons or doves symbolized kindness, because they were the winged beings thought to have announced the creation of the Earth Island. The Choctaws considered woodpeckers—flickers, sapsuckers, and red-headed woodpeckers—as guardians; they brought news, announced ball games, and warned war parties of impending danger. For the Chitimacha, wrens (or *kich*) were informants. The connection between birds and news-carrying and weather is only natural: Bird calls announce someone's or something's presence in the woods, and flocking behavior is one of the first signs of approaching bad weather.

Owls, especially screech owls, were omens of death and evil among the Choctaws and Chickasaws, probably because of their association with witches. Southern tribes thought horned owls actually killed men and animals, and hoots of screech and barred owls were believed to portend the imminent death of a small child among family or friends or else the death of a relative. Remember, the Choctaws believed the *Shilombish* (or the deceased's second soul) assumed owl or fox form and was distinguishable from real animals only because *Shilombish* did not respond to hoots or barks. On the other hand, wearing owl feathers was believed to help Creek shamans see at night, so even owls had some positive attributes depending on circumstances.

Owls or foxes? It probably didn't matter, since ghosts and witches assumed both forms. Possibly, Fox-Man/Owl-Man designs conjured up the *Nalusa Falaya* (or the Long Black Being—a beady-eyed, long-pointed-eared supernatural who went about frightening hunters) or *Kashehota-palo* (a deer-human ogre who also lived in the woods and scared hunters).

Other animals had prominent roles in traditional stories. The archetypal turtle was important because it carried the primordial Earth Island on its back. Fables linked turtles and turkeys. One told of a turkey borrowing a turtle's shell in order to win a race against turtles, causing turkeys to have bodies like turtles. The other had a turkey step on a turtle, breaking its shell and requiring ants to sew it back together with colored thread, thereby causing it to look cracked and colored. Terrapin bones as well as those of the panther were carried as charms by Creek deer hunters. Web-footed waterfowl and frogs were important in the Choctaw story of how *Aba* (or the Great Spirit) created water. Among the Cherokees, a giant frog was believed to swallow the sun during eclipses. A common fable told how raccoon fooled opossum into burning all the hair off its tail, leaving it forever bare.

Even the locust (or thirteen-year cicada) had traditional importance. The Choctaws tied the cicada to the birth of humans, maintaining that cicadas and newly formed humans emerged from the birth cave (metaphorical womb) together, and after drying out atop the sacred Nanih Waiya mound, scattered across the land, becoming the various Muskogean tribes. Cicada nymphs live underground as brown-faced grubs for nearly thirteen years before metamorphosing into red-eyed, green-bodied adults, which live for a week, sing shrilly, and mate furiously before dying. Cicada metamorphosis presents a compelling analogy with the Choctaw origin story. With the exception of clamshell pendants, all of Poverty Point's natural representative arts have counterparts in native traditional stories.

I will not hazard guesses as to what some one-of-a-kind engraved decorations represented, especially hachured and cross-hatched meanders or single-line "cloud" or "weather" glyphs on bannerstones and gorgets, but one decorative technique is especially denotative. The single continuous-line technique was used to outline complex figures including Fox-Man,

Fig. 9.3. Other engravings included strange glyphs and unique motifs. The merged-eternity (*top left*) and geometric pattern (*lower right*) are single, continuous line figures and may symbolize the road of life theme so common in native mythology. The merged-eternity, skate-key (*upper right*), and cleft-heart (*bottom row, middle right*) seem to be abstractions of the Fox-Man design. The cloud glyph (*lower left*) and other figures cannot be equated readily with lore characters.

"roller skate"-key, Grecian-key, and "merged-eternity" glyphs, all without having to retrace lines or line segments or getting blocked by intersections. Finding the proper starting point and following the line continually in the right direction led back to the starting point. The designs form single-path labyrinths. Sometimes the lines themselves are the maze; sometimes it is the areas enclosed between the lines.

This technique possibly represents the widespread road-of-life theme, often pictorially depicted as a single-path labyrinth. According to ethnologist Sam Gill, the road of life symbolized the path from birth to death, a journey filled with hardships and conflicts but one ever so orderly, because it always returned to its beginning or led to a center. Poverty Point's designs exhibit intertwining and interlocking twists and turns (life's twists and turns), but they are always symmetrical and orderly. By having the end meet the beginning, the continuous line may depict the unity of life and death, the great cosmic singularity of existence.

Finding the same animals represented in stone and story might have been no more significant than having the same animals around for thousands of years, except that presumed functional contexts of stone figures conform to story themes. I imagine bird images were engraved on plummets, not because plummets were used as bolas for fowling, but because birds were message-bringers and were able to persuade fish to swim into nets and other animals and birds to get entangled, too. If some glyphs represented spirit beings, then capturing their images in stone controlled their good-evil persona, allowing them to be manipulated. To me, it is no wonder that nearly all charms were for the hunt or the long exchange trail, where luck and magic were needed most.

Why All the Symbolism and Protection?

Poverty Point needed all the protection it could get. Like any busy place, especially one where traders and visitors from strange lands congregated, Poverty Point was exposed to many foreign influences and spirits, good and bad. Without protection, it was vulnerable. Without reminders of its identity, it was merely a reflection of the many groups involved in its political-economic dealings.

Stone objects told Poverty Point's story, reminding locals and strangers alike who they were and where they belonged. Earthworks kept out dark forces that threatened from the west and north and vented internal disharmony, which inevitably burgeoned as strangers and residents interacted inside their protective shields. Poverty Point was a place with a high recognition profile, a place where people tried to control their animistic world with magic.

10

Community Core–Periphery Relationships

"Boundaries"

> Boundaries—not those drawn by surveyors and cartographers and marked by fences and signs but those superimposed on the land and inscribed in the mind through the daily experience of inhabiting a locality; not those erected fiercely from without but those pushed out gently from within—are frequently an important component of people's lived sense of place. Such borders, more than political demarcations, give geography order and meaning and help carve a place out of undifferentiated space.

Kent C. Ryden, published in *Mapping the Invisible Landscape,* 1993

Poverty Point Community

Once upon a time, there was a Poverty Point community, a social aggregate composed of kinfolk, friends, and neighbors who lived along a narrow strip of Maçon highland and adjoining section of Tensas swamp. The group's technological and stylistic uniformities spread across 700 square miles attesting to commonalities "pushed out gently from within." Although pushed out twenty-two miles from Poverty Point, its nucleus (or core) was at the Place of the Rings and an encircling zone two and a half miles wide. Beyond that small but vibrant center lay the community out-skirts (or periphery), where people lived and worked in scattered encampments.

What kinds of relationships existed between core and periphery? Did they mainly involve style and technology transfer? If so, how were these ideas passed along—from neighbor to neighbor, by residence shifts after marriages, or through attending fairs and festivals at Poverty Point? Were relationships primarily economic? Was the 700-square-mile zone a major trade belt for rocks and food, or was the periphery merely the outermost fishing, hunting, and gathering grounds for core inhabitants, making core and periphery parts of one big, domestic economic supply area? Was the area under sway of charismatic big men from Poverty Point, subject to a political consensus, or influenced by a shared cadre of supernaturals? Even if any of these possibilities characterized core-periphery relation-ships, they need not be alternatives but simply aspects of a complex web of community interactions.

Residences and Field Camps

People lived in some places and worked in others. They lived at work camps, too, but since their stay was shorter and less involved than at home, work camps had field tool-dominated equipment, less organically stained trash areas, and fewer pits and other appliances. In a 1998 study published in *Research in Economic Anthropology*, I analyzed more than five dozen encampments outside Poverty Point and found that field camps generally were characterized by very prevalent projectile points, common microlithic tools, uncommon PPOs and ground celts, rare plummets and hoes, and very rare lapidary objects. Midden was sparse or absent, and so were pits and other constructions. On the other hand, residences were marked by very prevalent PPOs, common microliths, uncommon projec-tile points, rare ground celts, and very rare plummets, hoes, gorgets, and lapidary items. Black earth midden and pits, earth ovens, postmolds, and other features concentrated at residences.

Projectile points dominated at field camps, usually by a six-to-one margin over residences. PPOs dominated at residences, usually by a thir-teen-to-one edge over field camps. Microlithic tools were common at field camps and residences, although camps usually had about twice as many as residences. All other tools were either rare or very rare, but field camps

The incidence of materials found at Poverty Point residences and field camps

Material	Residence	Field camp
PPOs	very prevalent (75%+)	uncommon (≤5%)
Points	common (≤10%)	very prevalent (62%+)
Plummets	very rare (≤1%)	rare (≤3%)
Hoes	very rare (≤1%)	rare (≤2%)
Gorgets	very rare (≤1%)	rare (≤2%)
Microliths	common (≤12%)	common (≤22%)
Celts	rare (≤2%)	uncommon (≤4%)
Lapidary	very rare (≤1%)	very rare (≤1%)
Midden	concentrated	sparse/absent
Pits	concentrated	sparse/absent

Note: Two primary types of encampments occur around Poverty Point. Residences are typified by black-earth midden, pits, abundant PPOs, common projectile points, and variable numbers of other tools. On the other hand, PPOs are uncommon at field camps, but projectile points are very prevalent; other tools are variable. Midden and pits are either sparse or absent.

Residences include Stockland Plantation, Copes, Terral Lewis, Motley East, Alexander Point, Steatite Field, Locality Two, as well as Poverty Point itself. Field Camps include West of Neely, Hendrix, Owens, Aaron, Arledge, Orvis Scott, and Motley North (see map 10.2). Other encampments cannot be assigned because either data recovery is inconsistent or analyses are incomplete. Despite a graph line, which seems to conform to the field camp group, Poverty Point is actually a residence (see fig. 5.13). Graph data for Poverty Point took only whole PPOs into account. If adjustments had been made for the total amount of PPO residue, which invariably amounts to more than 90 percent of the material recovered from excavations everywhere throughout the rings, its graph line would look like those of other residences.

always had relatively more of them. Having few tools was a measure not of how important they were to the work that went on at a particular camp but of how inconsequential their numbers were when compared with overwhelmingly abundant PPOs and projectile points. A job or two may have prevailed at field camps, and may have been responsible for camps being set up where they were, and yet tools used to carry out those prevailing activities may have been relatively few.

Just because two kinds of encampments were recognized does not mean there were *only* two kinds. Residences were places where people lived more or less permanently for all or much of the year, or at least places where they repeatedly returned after sojourning at field camps. Field camps, on the other hand, varied greatly. Their tool compositions and specific locations revealed that campers primarily carried out different

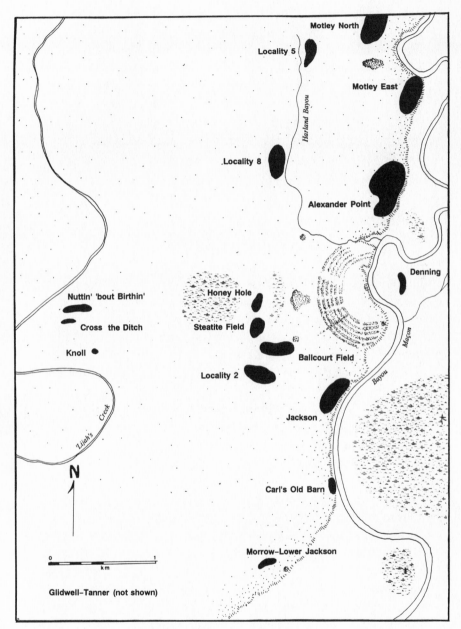

Map 10.1 Core encampments were those that occurred within a two-and-half-mile radius of Poverty Point's rings. Most bore characteristics of residences. Motley North was probably a field camp. Others yielded too few tools to be assigned to one or the other encampment classes.

jobs in different places. Strong seasonal overtones inhered. Hunting and nut/acorn gathering were major activities at field camps on Maçon Ridge, implying fall-winter utilization. Fishing and root-grubbing were major pursuits at swamp field camps, suggesting late spring, summer, and early fall utilization. Residences everywhere were dominated by cooking and nut/acorn processing. Swamp residences usually had more of the same equipment used at swamp field camps, and upland residences more of the same materials found at upland field camps, suggesting that mobility did not solely involve upland-lowland shifting but entailed movement within each of the major ecological zones.

Community Core

While Poverty Point formed the geographic, social, political economic, and cultural heart of the community, more than two dozen encampments and tool scatters were found in the rings' shadow, an umbra two and a half miles wide extending past the rings. All encampments but one were up on the Maçon highland, and Denning, the only one that was not, lay in the swamp immediately across Bayou Maçon from the rings. There was an outer band some two and a half miles wide between the most distant core encampment and the nearest known periphery encampment. Emptiness was real and for good reason. Two and a half miles was about the maximum distance that collectors could have walked to work, put in a hard day on the job, and still managed to get home in time to catch Sun Father entering his cave. Any further and workers would have needed to spend the night in the field, which they often did. So a two-and-a-half-mile-wide empty zone around the outermost core camps was a natural divide between core-generated activities and activities of campers who either were spending time away from home or actually were living out in the woods. Either way, the empty zone separated community core from community periphery.

Except for one field camp, Motley North, all analyzed core encampments were residences. This way hustle and bustle was kept close to the rings and away from food patches and hunting grounds. Nevertheless, Motley North, with its scattered projectile points and a few other isolated tools, revealed that some exploitative activities had taken place on the outer limits of the core area.

Core residences included Alexander Point, Motley East, Steatite Field,

Ballcourt Field, and Locality Two in addition to Poverty Point itself. They contained the usual range of equipment as well as bountiful chipping residue and FCR. Cooking balls dominated shaped tools and included biconical, biconical grooved, cross-grooved, cylindrical grooved, melon-shaped, amorphous, and other shaped forms in varying combinations. Small flake and blade tools were common. Most exhibited regular edge retouch, but some had nibbling or wear more characteristic of expedient use. Projectile points were also common, although less so than at field camps. Like PPOs, the array of points changed from site to site, but of the six prevailing forms at Poverty Point, only three—Garys, Motleys, and Kents—also prevailed at core residences. Two major forms at the rings, Ellis and Delhi, were not identified at all; Pontchartrain, the other major form, was rare. So half of the points found on these core residences were not among the major types of points found on the rings. Other domestic tools, such as ground celts, plummets, and gorgets, occurred in small numbers compared with PPOs, microlithic tools, and points. Hoes or hoe-resharpening flakes were not identified at any of the core residences except Poverty Point, and even there, they were among the rarest of the rare. Polished-stone ornaments and symbolic objects also were very rare, more so than at field camps.

Outside the rings, residue covered between two and twenty-five acres at each encampment, usually strewn across tops of low ridges or knolls and sometimes across several adjoining high spots where terrain was undulating. Grounds were blackened by organic staining, although staining was not uniform. Darker spots usually held shallow basin-shaped cooking pits. Pits produced stone trash, charcoal, ash, charred bones, and nutshell and seed case fragments. Fish, turtle, snake, squirrel, and other small animal bones were identified, and fish—primarily freshwater drum, catfish, and bowfin—were the major menu items. Deer were conspicuous by their absence, just as at the rings. Burned hull fragments of hickory nuts and acorns made up the majority of the plant residue, but pieces of walnuts and pecans were common, too. Charred seed and fruit-rind fragments of persimmon, grape, goosefoot, knotweed, doveweed, wild bean, curcubit, hackberry, blackgum, and *Asteraceae* occurred in minor amounts.

All core residences were fairly close to earthworks, none more distant than 300 to 400 paces. Being close by raised a moot point: whether individual mounds should be considered parts of the nearest core residence or merely parts of the overall Poverty Point layout. Earthworks extended nearly across the entire core anyway, at least they did from north to south. Maybe the more relevant question was: Did it matter? Asking such a question was perhaps more germane to places located in the periphery, where mounds probably implied independent social groups. Since isolated core residences were either within or adjacent to the main earthwork perimeters, they legitimately could be considered outer neighborhoods of the Place of the Rings.

There was nothing unusual about core residences. They were living areas, pure and simple. They were alike in having lots of tools and organic trash, similar in kind and amount. Cooking, stone-tool making, and other domestic activities were sufficiently intensive and long-lasting enough to blacken the soil, hike up the density of artifacts compared with field camps, and warrant digging stationary appliances for repeated use.

Community Periphery

Field camps and a few residences lay outside Poverty Point's core area at distances up to twenty-two miles away. They completely encircled the core area. Of the known encampments, ten occurred along Maçon Ridge bluff both north and south of Poverty Point; two were out in the swamp immediately east of the bluff; seven were in the West Swamp, a poorly drained section of Maçon Ridge upland lying several miles west of Poverty Point; nine were along Joes Bayou, a sluggish stream flowing in an old Arkansas or Mississippi River distributary meander belt several miles east of the bluff; and one was in the swamp on Bull Bayou, an underfit stream occupying an old Mississippi River channel segment well east of the Joes Bayou meander belt.

Of the places with adequate data, three were identified as residences: Stockland Plantation on Bull Bayou and J. W. Copes and Terral Lewis on Joes Bayou; six were field camps: West of Neely, Hendrix, and Owens, all on Maçon Ridge, and Aaron, Arledge, and Orvis Scott, all in the swamp on Joes Bayou. All known periphery residences were in Tensas swamp; none were on Maçon Ridge. Field camps, on the other hand, were located down in the swamp and up on the ridge.

PPOs dominated periphery residences just as they did core residences, and as at core residences, composition varied greatly from place to place. Cross-grooved objects prevailed at Terral Lewis. Melons and grooved bicones were fairly numerous, followed by small numbers of plain

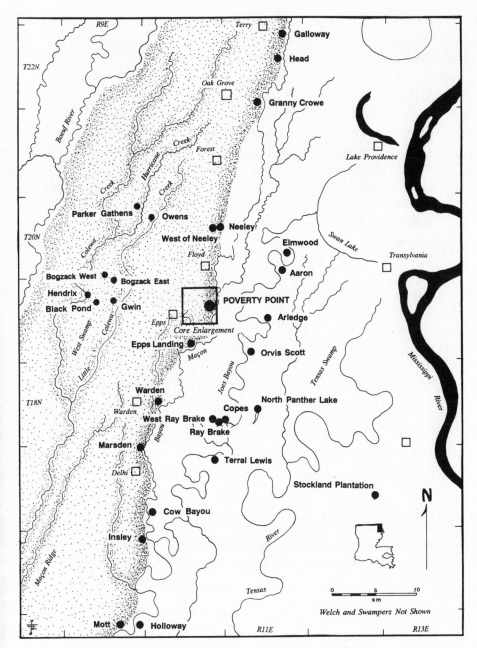

Map 10.2. Almost sixty Poverty Point encampments are known from Poverty Point's periphery, and they include both residences and field camps. They usually occur on the eastern, bluff-lined edge of Maçon Ridge, in the West Swamp (a poorly drained section along Colewa Creek), and on the high meander–belt ridge followed by Joes Bayou in the Tensas swamp.

bicones, tool-punched bicones, biscuit-shaped forms, grooved melons, and globular and spheroidal shapes. Excavator Hiram Gregory did not recognize any grooved cylinders there at all. But at Copes, Edwin Jackson found grooved cylinders to be a major form, along with melons and plain bicones. Minor shapes included melons with end grooves, cross-grooved melons, biscuits, grooved bicones, spheroids, tool-punched bicones, grooved biscuits, and a cone. Stockland Plantation's PPOs were limited to plain bicones, grooved bicones, extruded bicones, melons, and end-grooved melons. Grooved cylinders were uncommon.

My associate David Griffing reminded me that Stockland Plantation's PPOs were made from swamp clay, but Stockland Plantation was way out in the swamp, farther away from Poverty Point than any other known periphery residence, so bringing löess or löessial PPOs out there would have been difficult. Everywhere else PPOs were made of löess, indicating that they were molded up on Maçon Ridge and carried into the swamp. That spoke of a pattern of mobile land use involving both ridge and swamp.

Projectile-point groupings were more consistent than PPOs. Gary points prevailed at all three periphery residences. Next were Kents, at least at Terral Lewis and Copes. They were absent at Stockland Plantation. All other forms were minor occurrences. Terral Lewis had infrequent Pontchartrains and Maçons, small numbers of Motleys and Marcoses, and an occasional Ellis and Bulverde. Copes had a few Pontchartrains, Carrolltons, Ellises, and Delhis. Stockland Plantation had a fair number of Shumlas, which showed up nowhere else, but it also had an occasional Delhi, Epps, Ellis, Carrollton, Motley, or Yarbrough.

These point groupings stacked up pretty well with Poverty Point's. They also conformed fairly well with other core residences. Garys predominated everywhere, just as at Poverty Point, and generally major point types at Poverty Point were also majority forms at periphery residences. Motley was the major exception: Motleys were second in frequency at Poverty Point but were rare at Terral Lewis and Stockland Plantation and apparently absent at Copes.

Other common tools were present, but like PPOs and points, they varied proportionally from place to place. Relative to projectile points, I found that Copes had a lot of small flake tools, thirty times more than Stockland Plantation and nearly eighty times more than Terral Lewis. It also had more plummets and hoes but fewer gorgets. Stockland Plantation had the most gorgets, ground celts, and stone beads. And Terral Lewis did not have a majority of anything.

All periphery residences had sizable numbers of hoe-resharpening flakes, recognizable by opaline glaze coating one face. Edwin Jackson reported numerous hoe flakes at Copes; Hiram Gregory and his colleagues found that about one in four flakes from Terral Lewis were from hoes; and I found that one in sixteen flakes from Stockland Plantation came from resharpened hoes. Each residence also had hoes: Copes had approximately one for every thirteen points; Stockland Plantation, one for every twenty-one; and Terral Lewis, one for every twenty-eight. If the ratio of hoes to hoe-resharpening flakes accurately reflected the amount of hoe maintenance that went on, then Terral Lewis either had the sharpest hoes around or people lived there longer.

Periphery residences were not very big. Stockland Plantation was the biggest, covering a total area about the size of ten football fields, although tools were concentrated in two sections covering less than a quarter of that area altogether. Terral Lewis and Copes both were about the size of two football fields each, but their main trash areas covered only about half that. Stationary appliances were built at all three places. Copes had cooking and trash pits, hearths with and without linings, hardened clay "flooring," and postmolds. Terral Lewis had pits and postmolds, and clay ball–filled cooking pits were exposed by gullying at Stockland Plantation. All these immovables probably were associated with houses, although house patterns were not uncovered by limited excavation. All residences had large areas where dirt was darkly stained, and Copes's thick, dark midden yielded a rich assortment of plant remains and animal bones. Organic residues were not preserved at Terral Lewis, which had a shallower, long-plowed midden; even pollen had been destroyed by exposure. Preservation was also poor at Stockland Plantation, and besides, no excavations were conducted there. Copes was the only one of the three places with a mound. Clarence Webb reported a small conical mound more than 400 paces south of the main midden area, but whether or not it was built by Copes residents was uncertain.

Edwin Jackson found enough organic signs to indicate that Copes was a camp for all seasons, a permanent residence. Although Terral Lewis and Stockland Plantation did not have the organic indications, they did have physical and technological evidence for year-round occupancy. This did not mean that these country folks never went to town on Saturdays or spent a few weeks at a time somewhere else, but if they did, they always found their way back home.

Field camps out in the periphery were a distinctive lot, too. None had very many PPOs, which was the main reason they were classified as field camps in the first place. The upland camps, Owens and West of Neeley, had only unidentified finger-grooved fragments. Hendrix, the other identified upland field camp, had a wider variety: melons with end grooves, melons, cross-grooved melons, grooved cylinders, and plain bicones as well as grooved bicones, twisted melons, biscuits, and spheroids. Despite having a wide array, they still were uncommon compared with projectile points.

Point associations also varied from field camp to camp. Garys predominated. They were the main type at all three upland field camps and at Aaron in the swamp. They were second at Arledge and third at Orvis Scott, the two remaining swamp field camps with adequate data. Pontchartrain ranked first at Arledge, and Motleys and Delhis exceeded Garys at Orvis Scott. Unlike periphery residences, Motleys were important at Orvis Scott, Owens, West of Neeley, and Aaron, although they were not found at Arledge and Hendrix. Their relatively higher numbers at field camps compared with residences suggested that they represented either superior hunting equipment or superior hunters, a distinction of no small social consequence.

Pounding and grinding equipment was more plentiful at Hendrix than anywhere else, which indicated how important nut and acorn processing was out in West Swamp. No hoes and no hoe-resharpening flakes were found at upland field camps, but they were prominent at lowland field camps. Plummets were scarce at upland camps and were from three to twenty-five times more plentiful at lowland camps. Ground celts were more common at lowland camps, but gorgets showed no tendency to be more common in one place or the other. Neither did beads.

Swamp field camps had about the same ratio of celts, flake tools, and stone beads to projectile points as did swamp residences, but they had more plummets and hoes. Aaron, a swamp field camp, had a solid female figurine of löess. Owens, an upland field camp, produced a red jasper button and an owl pendant. Another owl pendant was recovered at Arledge, a swamp field camp. Soapstone vessel fragments, quartz crystals, and lumps of galena also occurred at both swamp and upland field camps.

From one to more than fifty football fields could have fit inside periphery field camps, but only Arledge was really extensive. The others were all under seven football fields in size; Hendrix, the smallest, was slightly smaller than a football field, or about the size of twenty medium-sized subdivision homes. Every camp was located on a convex landform, usually the highest rise around. Even upland camps were on ridges next to creeks, where drainage was best. Although elevated land was hard to distinguish with the naked eye at Aaron, Arledge, and Orvis Scott, it was easy enough to pick out when waters were high, which may well have been when these camps were utilized. Although only Orvis Scott was tested, immovable appliances were not found. Neither were organic residues: Except for small patches at Aaron and Orvis Scott, stained-earth midden was missing. None of the field camps had earthworks, either.

Logistical Mobility and Other Relationships

The core-periphery pattern implied that an economic strategy known as logistical mobility, an adaptational organization which moved food and other resources to consumers rather than consumers to resources, was used. Poverty Point and other residences generally were sedentary. Workers spent nights at field camps when working out in the woods. They were temporary. Field camps had a lot more points than did residences because points were the perfect, all-around general-utility tool, and campers generally traveled as light as they could. That was why points usually showed more signs of repair and secondary use than at residences. Field camps also had smaller numbers of cooking balls, ostensibly because they were heavy and breakable and were used in earth ovens, which usually were not constructed at temporary camps. In fact, field camps had few immovable appliances of any kind. Signs of tool repair and secondary use were only slightly more frequent than at residences, which suggested that stone was a precious commodity everywhere. After all, Poverty Point's homeland had absolutely none. It did not even have any Citronelle gravels.

Arguments to the effect that Poverty Point must have had a small population or food supplies would have been degraded seriously for miles and miles around were countered by presuming that the full 700-square-mile area around Poverty Point comprised a single fishing-hunting-gathering territory and that encampments were complementary in season or function, sequential, or existed in harmony. Under such circumstances, there would have been enough food within a 700-square-mile section of one of the most bountiful environments in the world to have fed a multitude, even during the worst times.

Did Poverty Point exert political dominion over the entire area? No, at least not as a polity controlled by one government, indivisible, with liberty and justice for all. Did Poverty Point hold religious sway over the whole area? No, not if that entailed yielding to a single clergy sequestered at Poverty Point. Did marriages between community residents take place? You can bet your first sweetheart they did. A 700-square-mile area encompassing a dozen or so fairly permanent residences was necessary to find enough young people who were not kin to each other to provide mates. Couples would have spread their arts and crafts around the community, because marriage required that either one or both partners move from their birth home to their spouse's home or make an entirely new home. With kith and kin scattered throughout community encampments and probably throughout neighboring friendly communities, there would have been a lot to talk about at every festival fire.

Poverty Point's core-periphery relationships were mainly economic, although that probably would have been questioned by true loves and hosts busy with social and ritual events that engaged neighbors from far and wide.

11

Political Economy

I Owed Him One

My T-shirt stuck to my back, and my eyes burned from sweat. I had half-run, half-walked the half-mile between the pickup and the banks of the bayou in less time than it took to smoke a Winston. I hurriedly cast my white H & H into the turbid pool awash with wakes, ripples, and splashes. The two-pound bass hit the lure immediately. I cranked the Johnson Sabre reel hard, yanking the fish out of the water and through the air the last ten feet. It flopped on the muddy bank, and the lure came loose. I cast again, and another bass hit before I turned the handle twice. It was another two-pounder. I jerked the double hook from its lip and noticed how warm it felt. I cast again and again, catching one- to three-pound fish on each cast. The twelfth cast brought in a huge four-pounder that tail-walked onto the bank before it, too, pitched the lure and flopped around in an unsuccessful effort to get back into its watery haven.

I tried to wind up the line that was still played out. It would not spool. I tried to pull out more line. Stuck. My reel handle would not turn. Fish were thrashing the water everywhere. I could see their fins breaking the surface. They voraciously attacked every bug and mosquito that lit on the bayou's agitated surface. My heart was pounding heavily, and my reel wouldn't work. Using the exposed line like it was attached to a cane pole, I swung the lure out into the water and backed quickly up the bank so that the spinners on the shallow-running bait turned properly. The bass struck before I had taken half a dozen steps. Thirteen casts, or actually twelve casts and one tight-line presentation, and I had caught thirteen fish—good, nice, heavy, grease-spattering fish. Two more tight-line presentations, two more fish, one of which was foul-hooked in the gills. Fifteen casts, fifteen fish, the creel limit.

I sat down on the muddy bank, heart still racing, and looked around at the flopping fish. I untied my stringer from my belt and reached for the nearest bass. What a fisherman. Nobody ever did better. They couldn't have. It didn't get any better than perfect. There'd be enough fillets to have Elvin and Elsie over for supper. I owed him one. I'd killed the big seven-point buck in front of his beagles. He liked fried fish. Maybe he'd ask me to go hunting again.

Contemporary memoir based on 1965 incident

One Good Turn Deserves Another

Among the most frequently asked questions were how and why did Poverty Point get to be so big and unusual. It truly was a cut above the rest, and over the years archaeologists presumed that was because it had some exceptional kind of sociopolitical organization and means of labor control that enabled it to outgrow other groups. Archaeologists were only saying what the time allowed them to say. That part has not changed, never will, but just because I presently envision Poverty Point being organized in a more mainstream, less revolutionary fashion does not make it any less imposing. At its peak, Poverty Point was alone in eastern North America, but the point I wish to make was that its solitude was not a result of how and why it started but how far it progressed.

What archaeologists see is only the tip of its domestic and political economies—its basic technology, its food and raw materials, its allotment and organization of private and public labor, and its raw authority relations. In my opinion, Poverty Point burst out of the Archaic pack because it had a need for things and met those needs with a simple, everyday response carried beyond usual limits.

Ah, the merits of good deeds. I contend that large-scale adoption of a general benevolent attitude was the bottom line of Poverty Point's political economy. That other Archaic economies also depended on good deeds said nothing about how many deeds it took to push Poverty Point society very near the maximum integrative limits of such familiar, personal relationships. Beyond favors came sanctioned obligations, and making people do things they did not freely choose to do would have made for a very different Poverty Point.

Corporate Strategy

In a 1996 *Current Anthropology* article, theorist Richard Blanton and associates identified two coexisting processes that drove political economies. One process entailed a networking strategy, which emphasized individual-centered exchange relationships among several groups. By networking with distant groups, individuals sought to build personal prestige by putting on intertribal ceremonies and setting up exchanges for goods, wives, and even information that brought favor and recognition on themselves. The other process, the corporate strategy, emphasized welfare of the group as a whole and discouraged vainglorious behavior. While the processes were opposites, they could and did coexist, presenting alternative and even alternating ways of dealing with outside groups as well as with local ones. Often, the difference between them was a single personality.

The sheer volume of foreign exchange suggests that Poverty Point had embraced a network strategy. After all, most traditional societies throughout the world that supported exchange relationships as far-reaching as Poverty Point's did so largely to fund elites, or at least prestige was right at the top of the list of driving motives. But I found no evidence that foreign rocks were delivered into the hands of a few elites who used them for self-promotion. Foreign rocks were not concentrated around mounds or in special places on the rings, which indicated that important persons disdained these usual showy signs of fame and fortune.

Claiming that status goods were buried with the honored dead was not credible, either, because no cemeteries were found at Poverty Point or anywhere else within the community or for that matter within the entire contemporary Lower Mississippi Valley. Poverty Point evidently disposed of its dead by some means other than burying them in mounds or traditional cemeteries, thereby digging no graves to hold elites' treasures. People from other times and places in the Lower Mississippi region buried their dead in graveyards, and if those groups also happened to use special objects to distinguish personages, those items usually went into graves along with corpses. I dismissed the possibility that the lack of burials was fortuitous and simply a case of not being lucky enough to find them. After Poverty Point, nearly every time span and locale had mound or cemetery burial, and not one of those situations was as thoroughly investigated as Poverty Point and its vicinity. If Poverty Point had buried its dead, some evidence undoubtedly would have been uncovered by now. Combining this argument with the fact that the few human bones found at Poverty Point were not from graves leads me to conclude that high status at Poverty Point was not signified by masses of exotic goods. The absence of this usual means of marking prestige suggests that personal prestige was absorbed by demonstrations of group identity and pride; prestige inheres in the earthworks and in the overall wealth of foreign rocks. There is an overwhelming corporate character to the lack of prestige goods and rich burial.

I found no evidence that an unmistakable Poverty Point style spread along exchange routes. Such styles were tantamount to wearing brand-name clothes or sporting trademark equipment. Poverty Point had nothing like the Turkeytail biface caches, which occurred throughout the mid-South north of Poverty Point during the third millennium B.C., the Hopewellian copper earspool/galena bead/raptor-design mortuary ideography depicted among so many midwestern and southern peoples around the onset of the Christian era, or the southeastern ceremonial iconography and exotic materials noted among several interacting Mississippian polities of the twelfth to fourteenth centuries A.D. A handful of jasper owl statuettes did reach from Florida to northwestern Louisiana, but none occurred along exchange routes. All were off the beaten trail. They were not the elusive exclusive style—or at least they did not follow lines of commerce, where prestige and wealth were earned most readily. Although standard styles ensured wide recognition and promoted visual communication among groups who otherwise were strangers and spoke different languages, they communicated status above all else and likely were restricted to self-appreciating promoters of intertribal enterprises, or "big men," as anthropologists call them. Lack of a trademark style suggested that exchange did not take place strictly between elites looking to amass private holdings or garner awards and recognition. Whether intentional or contrived, Poverty Point promoters got their due but pumped material gains back into the community at large, creating debt and earning loyalty in the process.

All clues pointed to Poverty Point having a corporate-based political economy. Neither corporate nor network strategies inherently restricted population or territory sizes. A huge bird mound might have been built to honor a person, but large integrated earthworks stood as testimony to a group. Colin Renfrew and Gary Feinman, who studied political power relations on a worldwide basis, found that corporate-based societies emphasized communal ritual, public construction, and other ways of tying families together while suppressing preferential access to food and important goods. A group-first mentality thwarted the rise of individuals or lineages absorbing ambition and factional ideology within a groupwide consensus. The prevailing attitude was what was good for the group was good for the individual, and vice versa—a true team approach to community relations.

Mounds were not tombs or temples exclusively. Rings were much more than housing ventures. What earthworks symbolized and what people did on them were separate things. Earlier, I argued that earthworks were metaphors of creation and cosmos, that they conveyed strong messages of peoples' link to their land and that they were permanent showcases of community pride and identity. Such meanings affected everybody, not just one or two individuals. They affected the *whole group,* the corporate entity. If the rings and the axial square formed by mound alignments were magical protective shields, then they guarded everyone, the *whole group* living inside their sanctum. As cosmic symbols and magical statements, earthworks issued the ultimate corporate message; the more of them and the bigger they were, the more protection they conferred.

A strong corporate ethic pervaded exchange relations, too, at least on the local level. At Poverty Point and everywhere within its 700-square-mile community, exchange of foreign rocks was open and unrestricted. Exotic materials reached everybody's hands, not just elites'. They did not wind up solely as prestige goods or ideographs, but most became common work tools. David Griffing and I found them at residences, and we found them at temporary field camps. In a number of instances, camps had higher proportions of exotic materials than residences. If prestige interests had been behind circulation of exotic materials, then finding large percentages of particular exotic flints and symbolic objects out at work camps presented a real dilemma. Work camps deployed under a network (or prestige-goods) political economic strategy should have had smaller percentages of exotic goods, not as much as or more than residences. Why? Not because elites didn't work. They surely had to put in their time just like everybody else, but prestige items usually were worn or used in ceremonials, which were staged more often at residences than at temporary field camps.

When Griffing and I checked quantities of exotic materials against distances, we discovered that an encampment's distance from Poverty Point made little difference in how much exotic material it got, as long as it was part of the community. If an encampment lay outside community territory, distance did make a difference, but even that was not straightforward. What we found instead was that the kinds of tools represented at any given encampment determined how much exotic material was present. Since certain implements such as chipped hoes, Motley points, plummets, and many others were made overwhelmingly from one kind of exotic material or another, it followed that encampments having lots of those tools had lots of exotic materials, clearly demonstrating that function and not prestige was responsible for raw-material circulation within the Poverty Point community. Just the fact that exotics were turned into common everyday tools indicated that they were moved about without social restrictions. Unimpeded access was a sure sign of corporate behavior.

Having wide access to exotic raw materials did not mean Poverty Point was without elites. In fact, I think open access guaranteed their presence. Otherwise, there would not have been such a wide selection of exotic materials. Anytime several people were involved in an enterprise as important as providing basic raw materials, somebody profited. And several people had to be involved, because there were simply too many materials and too many active supply lines for one person or one family to manage them all; therein lay the potential for social inequality.

Patronage of any sort, whether gracious or self-serving, curried debt and brought prestige to those who had either the most giving hearts or the most stuff to give. Patrons needed be none other than family heads, who merely were striving to provide the best for their kin. But if every family head was doing the same thing, competition was inevitable. Human nature aside, making sure family members got the best available raw materials gave them an edge when it came down to keeping larders stocked all year long, all other conditions being equal. The barometer of success for family heads lay somewhere on the scale between getting by and living in style, so competition at this subsistence-grassroots level was deadly serious business. In my view, what kept competition from being disruptive was the likelihood that lineages did not compete directly but vied with some ideal standard of living.

Political economy was diversified but simple. I envisioned good fishers giving away surplus catch. Fresh fish would have spoiled quickly anyway, so sharing was a matter of practicality as much as conniving. Extra catch came from using improved weighted nets, and the heavy ores used for weights probably were made available by rock dealers, who not only supplied rock to netmakers but kept hunters and root-diggers in the flint they needed, too. Contacts with soapstone-vessel makers from Alabama and Georgia likely were maintained by additional personages, and the thinkers, planners, and inspirational orators driving the giant building project were important, too—perhaps the most highly respected of all. Whether a few or many personages were involved in Poverty Point's many enterprises is beyond archaeology's ability to resolve, but with so much happening, more rather than fewer personages were undoubtedly behind it all. Poverty Point needed production from many families in order to sustain an overall high standard of living. Direct self-serving competition certainly would have ensured a Black Tuesday long before the one in 1929. Hoarding exotic goods or being overly selective about who received them would have been contrary to the ethic that created Poverty Point. Generous patrons earned respect and hence gained loyality and prestige, but I believe all that would have been compromised if they had tried to flaunt their successes.

Most prestige generated by sharing wealth got reinvested in the community. When everyone shared the benefits, then keeping domestic-economic enterprises running smoothly rose to the top of every individual's list of priorities. When those enterprises ran into problems, either real or imagined, saving them would have become a rallying cry of the masses. After all, when an economy benefited all, all were willing to work to preserve it. Prestige and loyalty were not converted into showy displays or self-serving gratification for a few personages but into leveraging hard work for the grandest demonstrations of all—building the massive rings and extending trade lines further and further away to get more exotic stone, always more stone.

Why So Big?

The question inevitably asked was how Poverty Point got to be so big if political economy was so simple. Were economic relations founded in a giving spirit and a corporate mentality actually capable of supporting involved enterprises such as long-distance exchange and mound-building without birthing god-chiefs and creating privileged and underprivileged divisions in society? I particularly wondered how Poverty Point differed from earlier mound-building societies. Nearly a dozen Watson Brakes, for example, would have fit inside Poverty Point's outer ring, and Watson Brake had the largest pre–Poverty Point earthworks known. Poverty Point's earthworks incorporated twenty to thirty times more dirt, which meant that a lot more labor had been invested in Poverty Point than in Watson Brake. In addition, neither Watson Brake nor any other pre–Poverty Point mound-building community showed signs of having engaged in long-distance commerce in any large way.

Were differences matters of kind or degree or both? Joe Saunders and his associates uncovered no compelling evidence showing that a prestige-goods, political economy drove Watson Brake or any other early mound-builder community. Watson Brake, like Poverty Point, was based on corporate principles, so differences were those of degree (or scale). John Clark and Michael Blake as well as Jeanne Arnold, Brian Hayden, and other investigators of power and authority in midlevel societies conceived growing social complexity to be a consequence of competition, of family leaders trying to outdo others in a headlong dash to gain prominence and loyal followers. Intentional and possibly even formal competition undoubtedly did produce social inequality. Poverty Point probably saw its share of light competition, but rivalries did not produce arrogant winners who by dress and show tried to relegate others to subordinate positions. At Poverty Point, winning most likely was measured by popular support and not by bells, whistles, or plaques.

In my view, ego and position were subordinated by a cooperative spirit, which rose to the front because stone resources were lacking. Had some rock been available on Maçon Ridge and Tensas swamp, then suppliers might have been apt to set aside more foreign rock for themselves and their families; they could have afforded to wear their prominence, to flaunt their stuff. But because this absolutely basic resource was not at hand, getting stone into everyone's hands became the major motive.

After all, restricting access to a life-providing necessity would not have been a smart way to try to earn laurels, especially when living standards and even simple survival were at stake. Being a well-dressed, well-fed, stingy egoist was hardly an accomplishment if most people were hungry and mad; it was certainly not a good way to get people to work voluntarily on public projects. In fact, public projects would have been out of place under such austere circumstances. Egoists were wont to commission self-stroking statues, burial chambers, dedicated buildings, and the like, and although private monuments such as these would have had to be built at public expense, they could not have been built without *making* people work on them. There was no way for big men among fisher-hunter-gatherers to exert that much coercive force, not even among the most complex sedentary groups. Persuasion, not coercion, was the basis for group action among simple and midlevel hunter-gatherer communities.

If basic necessities had been available locally, then egoists might have been tolerated; they might even have thrived. Brian Hayden found that most contemporary hunter-gatherers were willing to put up with hoarders and egoists as long as their own supplies of food and other materials were not interrupted. But lacking immediately available stone, Poverty Point people were obliged to share and share alike. Still, Poverty Point was able to grow larger than other corporately organized political economies. Why? I believe one reason was because population was larger; second, population was sedentary or tethered to Poverty Point; third, technology was enhanced by using exotic stone; and, fourth, a bustling community had more to lose and hence more to protect than smaller and less interactive communities.

More people needed more foods, goods, and raw materials. Sedentism placed a survival premium on working together as a group; at least it did for fisher-hunter-gatherers living in a swamp where one basic raw material—stone—was missing. But opening trade lines to get stone exposed Poverty Point to many potentially disruptive foreign influences and strange harmful spirits. Maintaining harmony and the status quo required powerful medicine: earthworks, very big earthworks, which upheld tribal values while protecting body and soul. Poverty Point was more complex than other places because more happened there, not because it was organized differently from other communities. Poverty Point was a case of a logistically mobile fisher-hunter-gatherer community corporately bound together, a community where egos were not allowed to get in the way of group welfare and everyone worked toward making the good life available to all.

12

Poverty Point Development

Souse and Chops

"Go ask Uncle Jules if we can use Ol' Lep and Bob Saturday. Tell him we'll bring him some ribs and souse."

The hogs had been rooting in Castor swamp since spring high water and were now fat from eating the huge crop of pin-oak acorns that papa said was the heaviest he had seen since loggers cut out most of the old growth. Papa spotted the young tusker he wanted to butcher while squirrel hunting at the salt lick yesterday morning. We needed meat, and besides he wanted to pay back mamma's cousin Bill Miles for the fresh ham he had brought over Thanksgiving eve.

I ran all the way to Uncle Jules's dog-trot at the end of road and back to our place in the pecan grove on the hill.

"He said we could use his dogs," I panted, "but told me to tell you he wanted some chops, too. I didn't tell him you said you'd fix the leak in his barn so his hay wouldn't mold anymore."

"Don't reckon that would help his disposition, either, leastwise he'd never show it."

"Papa, can I go hog hunting with y'all? I'll keep up this time, I promise, and I can climb fast if the dogs don't keep the hog bayed. I'll carry your 22 for you. Please, papa."

Papa went over to the chiffarobe and removed five 22 shells from the old Roi-Tan cigar box on top. He took the rusty single-shot rifle from the corner behind the rolls of cotton batting and quilting scraps, worked the well-oiled action, and stood the gun by the door next to his lariat and shiny-bladed skinning knife sheathed in the fancy new leather scabbard. Then he limped into the kitchen, poured himself a steamy cup of dark roast and me a glass of freshly churned buttermilk, and we sat down to tin plates heaped with buttery biscuits and homemade cane molasses.

I didn't say another word. I knew my grandpa would answer when he got ready. He pushed his cowhide-bottomed chair back from the table, stuffed his pipe with Prince Albert, and asked me to bring him a kitchen match from the back of the stove.

He lit his pipe and puffed.

"Get your jacket and your galoshes. We've got to wade across the swampy end of Goggleye Lake. Soon as Uncle Johnny gets through milking, we'll go get the dogs and head on over to the lick. Go tell Mamma you're going hog hunting."

Contemporary memoir based on a 1948 incident

Warlords to Home Folks

James Ford claimed Poverty Point developed when a southern Archaic group was subjugated by northern Hopewellian warlords. Later, when radiocarbon dates proved that such an event could not have happened, he and Clarence Webb looked to Vera Cruz and proposed that the mighty Olmecs, who were just coming into their own, inspired Poverty Point's development either through cultural diffusion or actual colonization. Later, I envisioned the richness of Maçon Ridge's woods and waters spontaneously giving birth to a simple chiefdom. In reaction, Edwin Jackson proposed that Poverty Point was merely a fairgrounds and not a closed society at all, a huge meeting place where peoples from all over exchanged goods, built great earthworks on the grounds, and then returned to a simple life back home. Years of digging in the rings restored my impression that Poverty Point was a place of residence. I tried to imagine how its residents and neighbors came to be so different from other Archaic peoples. Why had they invested so monumentally in protecting their way of life? I wanted to know what had caused such responses. If Poverty had arisen out of normal, everyday circumstances and processes, I wanted to know how and why they had reached so far, touched so many people, sponsored such large-scale public works, and then changed so completely within such a short time.

Preconditions

There was nothing inherent or inevitable in Poverty Point's location, adaptation, social relations, or organization that preordained its emergence. Yet when they all came together, the mixture was potent, supercharged by selfless doers who in their tireless travail raised standards of living to new levels.

Being located on the highest ground around ensured flood protection for Poverty Point. Maçon Ridge offered sanctuary for swampers, too. Despite being flood safe, Poverty Point was only twenty miles or so west of the active Mississippi River; Joes Bayou, one of its major distributaries, actually came within a couple of miles of Poverty Point. In fact, Joes Bayou and Bayou Maçon, the bayou at the foot of the rings, were connected right at Poverty Point's doorstep by an old crevasse channel, Grand Ranson Slough. All this means that Poverty Point would have had direct water access to the great river, which flowed hard by most sources of imported exotic rock. And those sources not on its banks—like the Ouachita Mountains and the southern Appalachian piedmont in eastern Alabama and western Georgia—lay on waterways that joined directly with the Mississippi, making long-distance travel to lands of stone possible by express canoe. Logistically, there was no better location for rock-swapping peoples anywhere in the Lower Mississippi Valley.

But before accepting the conclusion that exchange considerations had single-handedly dictated the choice of Poverty Point's location, I gave thought to the effects of having a stupendously food-rich land on hand. Poverty Point sat upon an island risen squarely from the lap of plenty, surrounded on both sides by watery wilderness where seasonal overflows curtailed land use. Poverty Point was the perfect place for finding plenty of easy-to-get food, and although abundance vacillated naturally, I doubted that places any poorer would have been likely to have sparked and sustained developments as involved as Poverty Point's. Hungry people are not apt to tolerate excesses—any excesses. Very few movers and shakers emerge from the masses without plenty of food being available to all.

Poverty Point's grounds were inhabited before Poverty Point culture coalesced. Tools such as pitted stones, Hales, Marcos, Evans, and other big projectile points, small baked löessial blocks, red jasper zoomorphic beads, and other objects revealed that groups had lived on-site previously. Some construction—Lower Jackson Mound and possibly Ballcourt Mound—had even been undertaken by these pre–Poverty Point folks. So Poverty Point's location obviously had been attractive for a long time, and being a flood-safe spot amidst superabundant foods was a major reason.

From a general perspective, I envisioned unexcelled food opportunities attracting lots of people and keeping them around, well before growing demand for rock stimulated long-distance exchange. Such exchange in turn stimulated the political economy, which kept getting bigger and more complex as time went on. An inevitable effect of many people living together in a food-rich but rockless environment was establishing ties with other groups who were able to supply rocks needed to keep up with swelling demand. Links were forged with peoples who had access not to one source but to many, and that probably involved many groups. Poverty Point's location had absolutely no rocks, not even gravel. Thus, getting even the closest rock was no small matter, enjoining many hands including some that lay beyond community land. Getting rocks from sources far beyond Poverty Point territory probably entailed diplomatic successes and intertribal transfer pacts, which facilitated movement of large quantities of rocks over hundreds of miles and earned prestige for movers and shakers.

Long-Distance Exchange

In my opinion, exchange was not a precondition for Poverty Point's origin. It was a founding condition. People were already living on the grounds before Poverty Point culture coalesced. They ate well because Maçon Ridge and Tensas swamp were blessed with abundant wild foods; their technology, especially the fishery, was very good; and their skillful deployment of food-getting pursuits allowed them to live on the same grounds for a long time without having to change residences continually. Maintaining a permanent or near-permanent presence on-site probably was enabled by having unisex work parties or families travel to food patches in order to catch, hunt, or collect seasonal foods, and then bring them back home. Home deliveries kept people from having to eat out all the time and kept people close to the house; it turned a piece of land into home. Familiar faces, close relationships, cooperation, and shared experiences gave meaning and history to its land, infusing the ancient löess with one of humankind's strongest sentiments—a sense of *home*.

These conditions existed well before exchange started, so the looming question is: If life was so good, why did exchange ever start in the first place? What purpose did it serve? How did it ever get integrated into the domestic economy and become so important?

Exchange was the heartbeat of Poverty Point culture. Exotic exchange rock filled the old ground midden underneath the rings. It occurred at every residence in the community core as well as in the periphery. It occurred at every field camp. Foreign-exchange material defined Poverty Point culture, but it did more than that. It marked its onset and its end, and it was present throughout, in abundance.

My excavations in the old midden underlying two sections of two upper western rings disclosed that exotic rock made up well over half of the chert debris. Exotics made up nearly three-fourths of the chert debris from the ring-top midden in these same excavations. From the old ground midden under the northern third ring, I found that exotic materials comprised more than half of the stone, and from the overlying ring-top midden layer, slightly less than half. They also made up more than half of the stone underneath a section of the sixth northwestern ring and almost three-fourths of the rock in a ring-top stratum in the same test pit. The same kinds of exotic materials that were prominent before the rings were built remained important for a while after they were completed: white Burlington, dull gray Fort Payne, and shiny gray Wyandotte cherts and waxy white novaculite.

Because relative amounts fluctuate among different parts of the rings, general trends or changing patterns are difficult to identify. At least four and possibly more source areas provided these rocks—Ouachita Mountains near Hot Springs; Ozark rim near St. Louis; Shawnee Hills near the Mississippi-Ohio confluence; and somewhere up the Tennessee River in western Tennessee, eastern Mississippi, or northern Alabama. And these were just the main chert/flint sources. Brown and gray sandstone, Catahoula sandstone, granitic rocks, hornblende-basalt porphyry, magnetite, hematite, crystal quartz, limonite, ironstone, slate, greenstone, soapstone, and dozens of minor substances were also imported, from beginning to end. Some of these materials came from the same areas as the cherts and flints, but others came from other spots, which indicated that Poverty

Point traders had a basic familiarity with hard-rock resources along the entire Mississippi River drainage. Whether that familiarity came from actual visits or from intergroup interactions looms as a major question.

One aspect of Poverty Point exchange overarched all others, and that was its timing. Foreign exchange burst upon the scene, full-blown, just before ring construction started. Preconstruction midden, which underlay the rings everywhere, was thin and usually contained only one-twelfth to one-eighth as much stone residue as midden formed in tops of the rings, but both middens had the same kinds of exchange materials. In my view, long-distance exchange, or rather the conditions that precipitated exchange, were behind the emergence of Poverty Point culture. Exchange defined its emergence.

Nowhere else in the Lower Mississippi Valley before, during, or after Poverty Point was long-distance exchange conducted on such a regular basis or grand scale. A few items of novaculite, some quartz crystals, and sometimes another one or two other kinds of foreign rocks showed up in pre–Poverty Point contexts, but they paled by comparison with the tons and tons of materials that later made their way to Poverty Point and surrounding encampments. All of these materials appear to have come from the Ouachita Mountains, the nearest of the sources that Poverty Point later would tap. Whatever was behind the pre–Poverty Point rock movement does not appear to be highly organized or long sustained anywhere. Basic technology would not have been diminished if no exotics had circulated at all.

As I see it, when exchange started, so did Poverty Point culture. I suspect that something as commonplace as a simple technological improvement precipitated exchange and picked up the pace of other aspects of pre–Poverty Point culture. An improvement like making heavy-stone fishnet sinkers (plummets) could have been the impetus. Whatever the nudge—and I use plummets as the figurative example—it surely didn't take long for Poverty Point culture to come together. I suspect that by the time the first plummet rolled off the grinding slab Poverty Point culture was under way.

An idea alone can change culture. An idea like making a plummet would have melded technical skills, basic need, hard work, knowledge of land and resource, personal ambition, intergroup diplomacy, simple organization, and corporate mentality—none of which was really new. Sometimes an idea really catches on and spreads through entire communities like a grass fire in a high wind. Something new can come from old parts. I think this is what happened at Poverty Point. Although I doubt that archaeologists ever will be able to put their finger on the precise motive or moment of cultural creation, I believe it likely that Poverty Point culture developed out of preexisting technological and interpersonal relations which came together through serendipity or design and offered new opportunities and challenges for the future. Such change could have occurred as simply as the following reconstruction implies.

Fishing, Sharing, Obligation, and "Much Obliged"

Fishing was not only an easy way of providing food in a land full of lakes, bayous, and overflow swamps but also a practical means of showing skill and generosity, both of which earned respect and loyality among simple folk. Fishing set up personal obligation and social dependencies, which in turn gave generous fishers some measure of control over the one favor they seem to have accepted in return—labor. To me, trying to figure out whether or not Poverty Point was sedentary or had a greater or lesser degree of social inequality is not as important as trying to find the source of power behind earthwork building. Identifying the power source and how power worked is like taking the pulse of a culture.

The expansive backwater habitats of the Hypsithermal invited fishing on a large scale; the sluggish bayous and overflow lakes and swamps offered a veritable fishing paradise—thousands to nearly a million pounds of fish every square mile. Of course, the trick is catching them. When fish are hungry, good fishers are not. Everyone catches hungry fish. The fish story told earlier describes one adrenaline-filled moment at an old fishing hole in a Mississippi Valley river in 1965. Fifteen bass in fifteen tries, but anyone could have caught those fish. On the other hand, a good fisherman is one who catches fish when fish are not biting. Good fishers fill stringers when flood waters bathe the treetops, when paddles crust over with ice, and when icicles adorn pirogue prows.

I often have wondered what makes some people better fishers. I once watched three people fishing from the same boat, using the same kind of bait, and fishing at the same depth, and only the one wearing the denim shirt caught fish. Another time, I witnessed two cane-pole fishermen side by side, but the one who filled his stringer with crappie pulled from the murky bayou was the one whose pole the dragonfly preferred. On another occasion, I watched one fisherman run an empty trotline, while not three boat lengths away his competitor ran another line and took catfish off nearly every hook. Why some people make better fishers is one of this planet's greatest mysteries. I have heard many explanations: using the right bait, having better tackle, using better presentation, sitting in the front of the boat, sitting in the back of the boat, going with Walt Durham, and watching Bill Dance. Others claim that the best fishers have more information, more skill, more luck, or blind luck; they trust in the Savior; they hold their mouths just right; they spit Red Man or Copenhagen juice on the worm. These explanations are not a complete list, but they do reveal the truth of the matter: Nobody has the foggiest idea, but everybody has an opinion. The best explanation I ever heard came from a Catahoula Lake commercial fisherman I asked about catching fish year-round; it made sense to me. "Got to," he said. "'Em ol' bills comes in winter, same as summer." People had to eat in winter, same as summer.

For whatever reason, some people simply were better fishers. Not only did they gain by keeping their own cooking grills filled, they benefited by giving away extra catch. Sharing fresh fish is almost inevitable, because they spoil quickly. Unless earth ovens were fish smokers, too, fish probably were not widely preserved in the Poverty Point community. Sharing extra catch with less successful kin, kith, and comrades enabled generous fishers to avoid the stench of selfishness and create indebtedness.

In a bygone era, I often heard the expression "much obliged" when folk received favors or gifts. "Much obliged" was their way of saying that they appreciated the favor and recognized an obligation to return the gesture at some later time.

Some archaeologists recently have grown aware of the power vested in sharing and obligation. I suggest that a community as large as Poverty Point's, which probably maintained a heavy load of obligation all the time, had the power to build large earthworks and to sustain social inequalities as long as life remained good and prosperous. And giving did not have to be competitive or conniving in order to create indebtedness and gain loyalty and support. When a compelling sense of esprit d'corps (or a basic corporateness) guided sharing and gifting, being "much obliged" furnished the essential power to carry out sizable public works, encourage continued sharing, and even tolerate some egotism. I contend that the power of kindness (or reciprocity) underlay Poverty Point's rapid development.

Growing the Political Economy

How might the power of kindness have promoted the enormous feats of building such huge earthworks and promoting exchange across half the United States? A version of the essentialist story told below is a possibility.

The people who lived on Poverty Point grounds before the rings managed well enough to settle down and build a mound or two of their own. A collecting economy brought food from surrounding woods and waters onto the grounds, making it unnecessary for all residents to move from food patch to patch with every passing season. For some reason—maybe population growth, perhaps a conscious effort to improve life, possibly pure chance, or conceivably any number of other factors—fishing was boosted by new and improved netting. Heavy stone plummets were added to net mudlines.

Net weights were designed to deal with waters of winter and flood, when traditional netting methods were less productive. Plummet-lined mudlines kept nets and seines from rolling up in current, enabling them to be dragged along the bottom or set out in high water or flowing streams, not just in quiet-water lakes and swamps. Catching fish during these "off"-seasons, when fishing traditionally was poorest or abandoned altogether, enriched the political economy by allowing sharing to continue or, at times when there was no extra, to keep good fishers from having to accept food from family members or friends and become "much obliged" themselves.

Keeping giveaways one-sided was essential to getting past the point of just having enough to eat and onto the level where built-up indebtedness could be manipulated and used for purposes other than eating. Benefactors had to keep clients in debt and "much obliged" by continuing to give and not take, or else their potential to manipulate indebtedness, particularly its labor side, literally would have been eaten up, leaving no means for leveraging labor for earthworks. Sharing food all year long would have used up any seasonal surpluses and selected against preservation and storage technologies, which ordinarily might have been developed for laying by surpluses as hedges against lean times. Year-round food availability provided by a combination of nature and economic reciprocity seems to have a limitless capacity for leveraging labor. Finding a mutually acceptable means of expending that labor was probably an easy matter, too—

whatever was considered highly important to everyone. Earthworks, I contend, furnished that means.

There are additional considerations that even such a seemingly small, innocuous device like fish-net weights had for cultural development in general. The key to making nets work like they were supposed to depended on getting the right stone for the right job. Ouachita hematite and magnetite provided that stone. They were heavy and were readily worked with traditional grinding, polishing, and drilling techniques. Somebody recognized their properties, knew where they could be gotten, and realized that a streamlined teardrop shape was best suited for all kinds of running-water conditions. Someone had to get either the stone or the plummets themselves into the hands of Poverty Point fishers. This was where exchange came in, where doers turned a simple need—food for all seasons—into a diversified economy with ample room for growth and available jobs for those willing to work. The result: creation of yet another set of "much obliged" relationships.

It so happened that many other kinds of rocks outcropped alongside magnetite and hematite or en route to and from their outcrops. Sandstone, slate, shale, diorite, bauxite, greenstone, calcite, novaculite, chert, and others were all available within a hop, skip, and jump of each other— sometimes from the same river gorge, mountainside, or ridgeline. It didn't take a genius to figure out that having so many different kinds of rocks together was a treasure trove sent straight from the Great Spirit. Proximity prompted procurement of all. Materials were sent downriver, not by way of the Ouachita River, which ran directly through most outcrops, but along the Arkansas River and its old channels. Arkansas courses gave direct water access to Poverty Point. The Ouachita did not. In fact, a healthy forty-five-mile portage would have been required to move goods from the nearest arm of the Ouachita overland to Poverty Point, a portage across several major streams and over some of the worst swamp in the entire Lower Mississippi Valley. So bad was the terrain between the Ouachita and Maçon Ridge that well into the nineteenth century it still defied crossing. In their 1939 book entitled *Northeast Louisiana, a Narrative History of the Ouachita River Valley and the Concordia Country*, historians F. W. and L. H. Williamson describe travel conditions between the Ouachita River and Poverty Point: "Between Monroe and the Boeuf was the virtually impenetrable LaFourche swamp, which was covered with a vast canebrake. About 1839 a road was cut through the canebrake. . . . Even after this road was established it was available for use only in dry weather."

Being aware of so many useful materials in the Ouachita Mountains was not a revelation. Novaculite, quartz crystal, and a few other rocks had been circulated for thousands of years previously, so Poverty Point's predecessors already knew about the rock wealth of the Ouachitas. But some rocks such as hematite and magnetite, the two iron ores, would have been of no use to a domestic economy that did not use weighted fishnets. Iron ore simply was not a resource any more than oil, gas, or uranium would have been. Only when a stepped-up fishery supercharged the economy did magnetite/hematite stock soar.

Tapping the wealth of the Ouachitas was no accident. Poverty Point exchange focused on places where more than one kind of rock abounded or where several kinds of rock outcropped along a single route. This was the case for the Ozark Plateau rim near St. Louis, Shawnee Hills, Kentucky Knobs, Tennessee River Valley, and all other places where exchange rocks came from. Many kinds of materials made their way to Poverty Point, but they came by way of very few routes or actually just one big one—the Mississippi River and its tributaries. Only rocks that outcropped along the river and its main arteries wound up at Poverty Point. Sources of rock located far from the river lay untapped. Trail trade, rather than river trade, remained only a dream in the eyes of padded-moccasin makers and foot masseuses.

Why? Exotic rock was an everyday commodity used by everyone for all purposes, and it was brought to Poverty Point en masse, making the pirogue the most convenient means of transport. Backpacking simply was inadequate for moving so much rock so far. Considerable effort from quite a few people would have been required just to carry a few lumps of this and that—three bags full of Dover flint bifaces or galena cubes—year after year. Poverty Point's hard-stone technology depended on a large continuous supply of foreign rock, or else rock-hungry consumers would have been left chipping their chips and complaining about business. Backpacking or trail trade simply was inadequate for carrying out an enterprise as enterprising as Poverty Point's. Even if rocks or blanks had been delivered by river peoples in a hand-to-hand manner, cargoes were heavy and frequently delivered, making canoes the most feasible means of transport.

The cost-benefit ratio of having several kinds of raw materials in one general spot or along the same river route was one of the keys for successful exchange, or at least for exchange committed to supplying household hardware for the whole Poverty Point community as well as other communities. Exotic rock was used to carry out basic life-sustaining jobs, not merely to drape around a distinguished neck or wave about at midsummer ceremonies. The practical side of Poverty Point exchange was what made it so different from the equally extensive Hopewellian exchange more than a millennium later. Where Poverty Point exchange differed from Hopewell and most other exchange systems was in ensuring the good life in a land absolutely devoid of any kind of hard rock, including local gravel.

Exchange was so thoroughly integrated into the domestic economy that the efforts of many people had to be involved. How rocks were delivered to Poverty Point was anybody's guess, but they told of business relationships among entrepreneurs as well as social relationships among impresarios. Whether fishers were actually responsible for getting Ouachita iron ores themselves or depended on rock dealers is simply not knowable, but realizing what differences plummet-lined mudlines made was easy: Fishers could count the ways in their nets. For rock-desperate people, witnessing the success of magnetite and hematite quite likely fueled a frenzy to bring in other rocks. After all, if iron ores were capable of raising standards of living, just think what other exotic rocks could do. How much simpler root-grubbing would be using big, durable, maintainable Dover flint hoes; how much simpler deer hunting and butchering would be with large Motley points made of Fort Payne flint; how much more efficient cooking would be using soapstone vessels directly over the fire; how good shiny copper beads would look when wearing your finest outfit; and so on. No one doer or family of doers was responsible for setting up and maintaining all the long-distance contacts and interactions that quickly gained a foothold in Poverty Point political economy. There just was too much going on, too many places to go, too many deals to make, too many kinfolks and friends in need. Exchange was not a one-man show. It was big business—so big and expansive that it was limited only by travel logs and by the amount of geological information available to doers.

With business getting bigger and better with every new trade and trader, and with quality hardware helping produce more and more food, the tripwire for population growth was sprung. The spiral of more people, more food—more food, more people, was initiated. So, too, was organization. I remain convinced that exchange was the main reason why the Poverty Point community was able to do what it did. As it expanded and came to provide most of the everyday hardware, it required doers not only to take care of actual hand-to-hand transfers but to carry out foreign diplomatic missions and to manage intergroup affairs within a carefully modulated consensual framework that allowed just the right amount of prestige to be gained without aggravating everyone else. In other words, a delicately balanced political-economic organization lay behind Poverty Point's exchange.

The Genius of Earthworks

If it took many doers to keep the economy going, as I suspect, then some means had to be found to combat competition, which invariably accompanied those activities. Competition did not always undermine social solidarity. In fact, Jeanne Arnold, John Clark, and Brian Hayden, who advocate competition-based processes, found that it actually led to social inequality in societies where personages deliberately strove for social recognition by alternately amassing prestige goods and giving them away. Competition—at least out-front, no-holds-barred, winner-take-all rivalries—would have been counterproductive at Poverty Point, where even simple life-giving necessities were furnished through exchange. Stashing, hoarding, or periodic giveaways were not ways of putting needed hardware into *everyone's hands continually*. And, in my opinion, without the help and concurrence of every man, woman, and child, every personage and plebeian, Poverty Point culture would never have gotten off the ground.

Building earthworks was a stroke of genius. It raised the power of kindness—of being "much obliged"—to a much higher plane. It invested it in a project that not only captured the corporate essence of community—its spirit and pride—but which meant just as much privately to every individual who toted dirt and tamped it in place. With earthen metaphor, builders told the story of genesis. No landmark ever stood taller in its cosmic design, no sign of home ever clearer, and no testament to unity and common resolve ever mightier. Yet the rings, the mounds, and their multiple shields afforded magical protection for each and every person; they kept evil spirits at bay and fostered harmony among all individuals who gathered within their embrace. No greater monument to the power of kindness was ever built.

Why was protection needed and why on such a grand scale? The magnitude and multiple lines of protection were in keeping with Poverty Point's overgrown population as well as with the extent of its dealings with foreigners and with the long line of good and evil supernaturals and orenda that pervaded its animistic world. Exchange dealings with peoples from hard-rock country jeopardized harmony by exposing Poverty Point residents to strange dark forces and malevolent spirits. Working out rock exchanges with foreigners must have seemed like dealing with the devil himself. As transactions became more numerous, so did the number of antisocial forces that assailed the community; bad signs, ominous events, and mysterious deaths increased. Earthworks offered safety and security, *protection for everyone.* The earthworks were big, but so were security needs. The earthworks required a lot of labor. But the power of kindness was up to the task.

Among rural Southerners of the nineteenth and early twentieth centuries, being "much obliged" often carried a further qualifier, *"until you're better paid,"* meaning that a person who benefited from another's largess remained indebted to the benefactor until the favor or gift was returned with one that exceeded the value of the original. Rural folk often repaid such obligation with labor, and the extensive earthworks lead me to expect that Poverty Point people did likewise.

With labor, both gift-giver and recipient knew exactly when an obligation had been satisfied. The secret of the power of kindness was never to pay back in like kind or exact amount but to add a little extra (or lagniappe). Giving lagniappe was more than a goodwill gesture. By giving lagniappe, one party acknowledged that payback had been completed, that obligation was considered fulfilled. By accepting lagniappe, the other party assumed indebtedness. No matter how subtle the act or inconsequential the gift, lagniappe marked a transfer of indebtedness, a shift of obligation, a condition appropriately described by the adage "one good turn deserves another." Such sharing or simple reciprocity was not only self-perpetuating, but I believe it also was capable of generating the raw power behind communal building projects as large as Poverty Point's earthworks.

Earthworks were built with the toil of people who simply were discharging obligations to benefactors while trying to ensure protection for themselves and their families. Labor was payback for every gift of fish or cut of venison, for every foreign biface received, for every soapstone pot gotten, and for every favor extended. The earthworks were a testimonial to the power of kindness—to the potency of being "much obliged." Earthworks were the perfect means of payback, because the labor they embodied not only satisfied obligation to benefactors and raised community pride but satisfied personal desires for security and safety.

The power of kindness required no coaxing, supervising, or quality-inspecting to make sure the earthworks got finished or met specifications. The power of kindness entailed labor freely given. Building the rings and mounds was simple back-breaking work, employing everyone in keeping with his or her strength and talent. No bosses were required, no time clocks were punched, no tally made of the number of baskets carried. People worked until the work was done. They worked because they cared. They worked because they chose to.

Ford and Webb believed a grand blueprint guided construction. Well, it may have, but, if so, the plan was well known to everyone from dim-eyed grandfathers telling ancient stories around winter firesides to bright-eyed grandchildren listening from cozy laps. The plan was told in the story of creation; it was told in the story of the cosmos. Parts of the plan were told in stories of witch birds announcing impending deaths of loved ones and of shape-shifters guarding the earthly remains of the newly departed. From Long Black Beings to White-Skinned Water Monsters, super-naturals invaded the world of the living. Mounds and rings conferred magical protection against their evil acts and established a bastion of harmony. Big mounds and big rings accorded big medicine. They told of the size of the threat confronting the community. Unlike today's magicians, everyone performed magic, everyone knew the secrets, the routines, and how to achieve balance in a world where natural and supernatural dimensions interacted incessantly.

So, in my view, the earthwork protection plan was common folk knowledge (or lore). In my view, no prodding or threatening was needed to enlist labor forces. In my view, there was no need for bosses, gang-pushers, or supervisory personnel. People worked because they wanted to, believed in what they were doing, and knew how the earthworks should look. Gideon Lincecum's story of how the Choctaws constructed Nanih Waiya is the way I imagine Poverty Point's mounds and rings being built. Earth-moving satisfied hundreds and hundreds of obligations at once, but it did more than repay personal favors. The rings provided everyone with spiritual shelter.

Poverty Point's earthworks were built with power generated by being "much obliged." Earthworks were the ultimate issue of a corporately organized society. They embodied an enormous amount of labor, but it was given freely because that was the way things were done when community welfare was put ahead of back-patting and self-glorification.

The Last Ring

By the time the last ring was erected, Poverty Point's development was essentially complete. It had gone about as far as it could with a corporate-oriented, "much obliged" political economy. The same brands of rocks it started with were the ones it finished with. Exchange materials satisfied needs, leaving little to be brought in over and above what already was being used. New technology, such as direct-fire cooking with a wave of imported soapstone pots, proved too costly to maintain in the face of low-cost, locally produced ceramic cookware. Some Burlington chert was imported, even though it was so flawed that it wound up having to be used for hot-rock cooking instead of making bifaces. This revealed just how important exchange dealings had become—more important than the material itself. But the up-welling prosperity that had driven Poverty Point's economy during its glory days had peaked and leveled off, leaving no room for a new generation of would-be doers. Poverty Point no longer provided the land of opportunity. There was nothing left for young people to do except follow their parents' footsteps and try to keep up family businesses in the face of declining returns. The easy-to-get resources had been gotten, and shortly even the trying stopped. The magic of its mounds and rings could not sustain the momentum Poverty Point had grown accustomed to. The drop in standard of living was probably minimal, but to the new generation, it was a disaster. The Place of the Rings became a casualty of its own success.

13

Neighbors and Distant Acquaintances

Sixteen Hateful Miles

Sixteen hateful miles of twisting, chuck-holed blacktop lay between Olla and Jena. Young warriors in these villages grew up hearing legendary tales of battles fought and coups counted in the football wars that had been ongoing between these bitter rivals since the days of their grandfathers. Glory earned in these battles lasted lifetimes and sometimes sent scarred veterans on to fame in college and in state politics.

"Oh, I remember Bobby Lee well," an unfamiliar face replied on being introduced to me at the halftime of the homecoming game. "He got that big interception against Jena but let that Creed boy get behind him for a long gainer. Looked pretty bad until Alvis Lynn Randall made them two quick touchdowns, and Ronald Cruse kept smothering the quarterback before he could hand the ball off. We hadn't lost to Jena the whole time we were in high school, and I sure was hoping this wouldn't be the first time. How you been, Bobby Lee?"

"Good, Tommy, How 'bout you."

"Oh, fine I reckon. Sure good to see all the folks after all these years. Say, do you remember the night those three truckloads of Jena boys tried to pick a fight with us at the Dairy Queen 'cause we were talking to that Impala full of good-looking gals? I remember them ol' boys asking if your real name was Bandylegs, and you told them, no, that it was Mr. Number Twenty to them but that you knew they wouldn't be able to remember it because they couldn't count that high."

Oh, yeah. So this was talkative Tommy and that was the week after the big game, when we figured being victors gave us preening and crowing rights on the south side of the parish, too.

"Yeah, how could I forget? They told us to leave their girls alone and to stay on our side of the parish. It was about ten of them against four of us. We left real quick, right after reminding them of the score and their IQs. Boy, Wayne's old '58 Chevy could scoot."

"You know," Roy piped in, "I tried to buy some worms at that bait stand on Highway 84, and when the man found out I was from Olla, he wouldn't sell me none."

"Y'all ought to be glad your hunting leases don't butt up against theirs," Dewayne complained. "They ain't nothing but a bunch of outlaws, spotlighting deer at night, shooting spotted fawns, does, and my hogs, too. They put nails on our roads all time."

"We had to get this plumber from Jena one time, and he charged triple what old man Snody would have before he had his stroke. Kept us waiting a week, too. No water the whole time," said Coon, shaking his head.

"What you complaining about, Coon? At least you had an excuse for not taking a bath," Tommy pointed out.

"Man, I don't like Jena."

"Me neither."

"Amen."

"Whaddaya mean, Tommy? We had a cistern and a No. 3 wash-tub.

Contemporary memoir based on a 1959 incident

So Near Yet So Far, So Far Yet So Near

The closest communities are often the most blustery, confrontational, and combative. When people live just beyond shouting distance, their paths are destined to cross competitively. They live too far apart for sense of community to bind them together, except perhaps for some shared public multicommunity activity. Yet they live close enough for occasional encounters and incursions on each other's land to be regarded as threatening, even when both communities are merely minding their own business. Nearby communities know enough about each other to be mildly hostile but not enough to overcome their distrust and wariness or to want to. Most often, it is outspoken young men who try to face each other down or incite general belligerence, although women get caught up in inflammatory rhetoric and chest-pounding, too. They just usually have fewer opportunities to showcase their vehemence. On the other hand, men from one community and women from the other usually enjoy amicable, even delightful, relations; after all, they are potential spouses.

Interaction among communities that lie beyond this land of a thousand disagreements generally is characterized by tolerant, less emotionally revved up, give-and-take dealings. People from this socially neutral zone are apt to strike up free exchange and adopt a tool or idea because it works rather than summarily rejecting it because it comes from a hated community. They are also apt, because of some real affront, to become deadly foes rather than merely name-calling sparring partners pursuing old feuds and petty jealousies. So from one community to the neutral zone is a matter not of miles but of social distance. But once the neutral zone is reached, practicality outweighs abhorrence, and the worth of individuals is judged by deed and personality rather than by where they are from.

Nearby Communities

Nearby communities were often not as materially similar to Poverty Point as more distant ones. Poverty Point's community stretched fifty miles north-south and up to eighteen miles east-west before reaching its nearest neighboring communities. The Big Creek and Turkey Creek communities were on Maçon Ridge: Big Creek some twenty-eight to thirty-five overland miles southwest of the rings and Turkey Creek twenty-eight to forty-five overland miles south. West and northwest of Maçon Ridge, some thirteen to thirty-four overland miles from the rings, was the Bonne Idee–Bartholomew community. There was no community out in the Tensas swamp east of Joes Bayou, or else evidence for it was erased by millennia of river shifts or buried by backwater deposits. The swamp was the domain of the fickle Mississippi River, a perennially inundated lowland ill-suited for residence and year-round use. Stockland Plantation, a residence, did lie east of Joes Bayou, perhaps on the east side of the

Mississippi River, but it was on a high natural levee of a relict Mississippi River channel higher than all but the worst floods and backwaters.

Bonne Idee–Bartholomew Community

The Bonne Idee–Bartholomew community was closest to the Poverty Point community's outskirts. Its encampments were scattered along relict Arkansas River meander belts lying off the elevated portion of the Maçon Ridge west of the Poverty Point community and northwest and north of the Big Creek community. Some two dozen encampments, among them Lake Enterprise, Neimeyer-Dare, Pollard, Parks, and Brodenax, shared some general similarities with materials from Poverty Point. With the exception of Lake Enterprise, cooking balls were relatively infrequent and usually consisted of bicones; finger-grooved forms were almost nonexistent. Projectile points dominated collections; Garys prevailed as they did almost everywhere, but Motleys, Ellises, Pontchartrains, Delhis, Kents, and other minor forms also occurred. Ouachita Mountain exotics were common. Novaculite comprised 65 percent of the chipped stone at Neimeyer-Dare and 40 percent at Lake Enterprise; magnetite, hematite, and quartz crystals were also represented. The abundance of novaculite and the occurrence of other Ouachita materials were in keeping with the community's logistically favorable location along old interconnected courses of the Arkansas River, which flowed by the eastern foot of the mountains where these rocks were obtained. The community centered at the point where the Bayou Bonne Idee meander belt came closest to Poverty Point. But the community employed other exotic materials besides those from the Ouachitas. Northern gray flint, including Dover and Fort Payne, made up 27 percent of the chipped stone from Lake Enterprise, and Burlington chert, soapstone, and a few other exotics also made their way along the stream. Two red jasper owl pendants were recovered from culturally undistinguished encampments, but generally Bonne Idee–Bartholomew encampments were bereft of ideographic or ornamental objects. Edwin Jackson and Marvin Jeter's excavations in a small domed mound at Lake Enterprise confirmed that it was built by people who used a lot of cooking objects on the mound but precious few in the adjoining occupation area. Small mounds at Neimeyer-Dare and possibly at other places probably were erected about the same time. Like the Turkey Creek and Big Creek communities, the Bonne Idee–Bartholomew community possessed its own identity but enjoyed good exchange relations with the Ouachitas and evidently with Poverty Point.

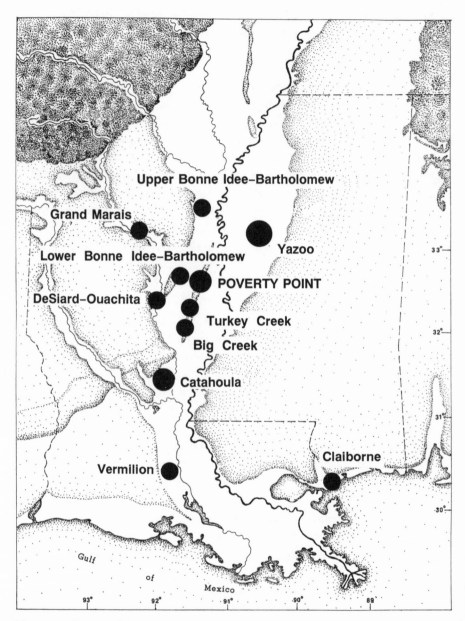

Map 13.1. Groups of Poverty Point–age encampments occur on Poverty Point's periphery, in the so-called neutral zone, and in more distant sections of the Lower Mississippi Valley. Some are more similar to Poverty Point than others; some groups, including nearby ones, are not similar at all.

Upper Bartholomew Community

Marvin Jeter and Edwin Jackson reported several similar encampments further up the Bayou Bonne Idee–Bayou Bartholomew course. Lloyd's Bayou, Stark, Woods Place No. 3, Deep Bayou, and some three dozen other encampments were strung out along a fifty-linear-mile stretch from a point about fifty straight-line miles north of Poverty Point to Deep Bayou, about forty miles below the eastern scarp of the Ouachitas at Little Rock and about 100 miles from Poverty Point. Like the Bonne Idee–Bartholomew community on the lower reaches of the same course, these places showed some material similarities but plenty of differences with Poverty Point. Several encampments had biconical and biscuit-shaped PPOs, but a few cylindrical grooved, melon-shaped, and twisted forms also occurred. Projectile points included Garys, Bulverdes, Williams, Pontchartrains, Kents, Joes Bayou Pontchartrains, Delhis, and others, but round-notched forms with narrow necks, so typical of Poverty Point, were rare or missing. Plummets, especially of magnetite, were common and even plentiful at some encampments but were absent at others. When present, slate and limonite gorgets, greenstone and hard-stone celts, chipped hoes, and occasionally other polished-stone implements looked like ones from the Poverty Point community.

Novaculite dominated chipped stone, but along this stretch of bayou (especially the upper reaches), novaculite was essentially a local material. Still the upper Bayou Bonne Idee–Bayou Bartholomew course, with the numerous Poverty Point–age encampments on its banks, was the main water route by which novaculite made its way downstream into the Poverty Point heartland. Other important Ouachita resources—magnetite, hematite, slate, and quartz crystal—also moved past and perhaps through these Upper Bartholomew encampments. The Ouachita River, which ran through the Felsenthal swamp (or Grand Marais), seemed at first to offer a more direct route down into Poverty Point country, but the Ouachita had no intervening Poverty Point–age encampments between Grand Marais and the old junction of Bayou Bartholomew at its Bayou DeSiard mouth. In addition, once at the Poverty Point latitude, cross-country bearers would have been left with a difficult, fifty-mile-long, wade-and-swim trek to Poverty Point. Jeter and Jackson detected a north to south decrease in the amount of novaculite coming downstream, but such a fall-off pattern was countermanded by healthy relative increases further on down the line, especially at encampments in the Bonne Idee–Bartholomew community, the western Poverty Point encampments, and even the Vermilion community near the Gulf. Soapstone and Tallahatta quartzite were the only two exotic non-Ouachita materials that showed up along the bayou upstream from the Bonne Idee–Bartholomew community; since both originated in eastern Alabama, they must have entered exchange networks via the Mississippi River and one of the river encampments, either Jaketown or Poverty Point. Tallahatta quartzite was not identified among Bonne Idee–Bartholomew encampments but was present in trace amounts at Poverty Point and in minor amounts at Jaketown, where it amounted to almost 5 percent of the chipped stone.

The Upper Bartholomew encampments were located too far from Poverty Point to engage in daily face-to-face interaction. They had uncertain connections with the Bonne Idee–Bartholomew community. What role they played in actually quarrying and moving Ouachita resources on downstream was unclear, too, although unquestionably they were involved somehow. For that matter, it was uncertain what kinds of connections they maintained with each other and whether they shared a sense of affiliation with the same community. But one thing was crystal clear: Without them, Ouachita Mountain rocks would not have reached Poverty Point, and the entire exchange network either would have been shifted around geographically or never would have happened.

Big Creek and Turkey Creek Communities

West and southwest of the Bonne Idee–Bartholomew community on the Maçon Ridge was the Big Creek community. Its half-dozen or so encampments had few cooking balls, especially finger-grooved forms that were typical of the Poverty Point community. Bicones predominated, but even they were uncommon compared with bifaces. Of the six major classes of points at Poverty Point, only Gary points were well represented, and Garys were the least culturally diagnostic of all Late Archaic points because the form was so long-lasting and widespread. Long-distance exotic materials were rare, amounting generally to less than a few percent of the chipped stone.

Turkey Creek assemblages were more like those from the Big Creek community than from Poverty Point. PPOs were scarce, and finger-impressed forms nearly nonexistent. Garys predominated, and Ellises, Maçons, Delhis, and Joes Bayou Pontchartrains were minor forms. Exotic exchange materials were rare, usually amounting to a few percent of the worked stone; novaculite, the major exotic, appeared to diminish from north to south. Burlington chert was not identified, and Dover and other northern gray flints were nearly nonexistent. Soapstone was not recognized, and quartz crystals, slate gorgets, and hematite plummets were rare. One recovered hematite plummet had an intaglio lizard design, and at least one red jasper owl pendant was found at an encampment on the western outskirts of the community or possibly in the adjoining Big Creek community. Stone beads usually were made of greenish, grayish, or reddish hard stone, not red jasper, and typically were cylindrical with tapering holes. No mounds were identified.

Ouachita Mountain novaculite and crystal quartz were the only materials recognized as foreign. But since both materials circulated before and after, as well as during, Poverty Point times, all they really suggested was that the Big Creek and Turkey Creek communities engaged in a low-level, pan–Lower Mississippi Valley circulation. Other presumed exchange rocks such as slate, hematite, chalcedony, petrified wood, and quartzite probably were acquired through local arrangements, either by means of individual efforts or more likely through dealings with the Bonne Idee–Bartholomew community. None of these materials naturally occurred on Maçon Ridge, but except for slate and hematite, they were all present in hill gravels a short distance to the west. The Bonne Idee–Bartholomew community bordered the hills. The southwestern side of the Maçon Ridge simply did not participate actively in exchange with the Poverty Point community.

Diminished exchange along with stylistic differences showed that the Big Creek and Turkey Creek communities were isolated and largely self-contained and had little, infrequent, or negative interaction with Poverty Point. They suggested the kind of puffed-up relationships that often existed between nearby communities—communities that were close enough to have stepped on each other's toes yet far enough away to have been brash and brazen about it. The Turkey Creek and Big Creek communities were to Poverty Point as Ollas were to Jenas.

On the other hand, my impression of the relationships that existed between the Bonne Idee–Bartholomew community and Poverty Point was that they were less strained but still socially limited, probably involving exchange of bifaces, plummets, and other tools of exotic rocks, some style sharing (especially of projectile points), and perhaps courtship and marriage, which permitted movement of spouses, primarily husbands, between communities. As far as upper Bayou Bartholomew encampments were concerned, I suspect relationships were economically sustained and socially restricted to emissary visits with accompanying pomp and circumstance. There may even have been a steamy affair or two, but at some point, exchange soured, friendly contacts ended, and populations living on Bartholomew and Mississippi mainlines went their separate ways.

The Neutral Zone

Between 50 and 150 overland miles from the rings were several other communities having varying degrees of similarity with Poverty Point. The DeSiard-Ouachita, Grand Marais, and Catahoula communities lay west of Poverty Point and the present-day Mississippi River, and the Yazoo community lay to the east. Contrasts depicted both strong and attenuated relations with Poverty Point, and to a large extent, intensity of exchange colored these neutral-zone communities into pale and paler reflections of the Place of the Rings.

Geography was important in establishing the intensity of exchange of materials and information. Both the DeSiard-Ouachita and Grand Marais communities were on the Ouachita River, which despite its course through the resource-rich Ouachita Mountains was not the best way to reach Poverty Point. The Grand Marais community occupied the big bend where the Ouachita River turned and made its run southward toward the DeSiard-Ouachita community 45 miles downstream. The DeSiard-Ouachita community was confined to the Bayou DeSiard-Ouachita River confluence, and Bayou DeSiard followed an abandoned Bayou Bartholomew meander belt. No matter what water routes were followed, both communities lay beyond other communities that were closer to Maçon Ridge and Poverty Point; the Bonne Idee–Bartholomew community intervened between the DeSiard-Ouachita settlement and Poverty Point, and both it and the encampments along the upper Bayou Bartholomew lay between the Grand Marais community and Poverty Point. The Yazoo community lay between 105 and 150 miles east-northeast of Poverty Point measured along the general axis of interconnecting Mississippi, Arkansas, and local meander belts. A traveler could have poled his pirogue from Jaketown, Teoc Creek, and other Yazoo encampments to Poverty Point without having to pull over, but the journey would have been long and arduous and made much further by water than by foot because of the mighty twists and turns of the rivers. Well-heeled swampers and guides were needed to cross this watery wilderness because crossovers and short-cuts from one meander belt to another were required at almost every turn. There was no intervening community between Jaketown and Poverty Point, but there were a lot of places where travelers could be drowned by *Oka Nahullo* (White-Skinned Water People), abducted by *Nalusa Falaya*, or scared to death by *Kashehotapa*. The Catahoula community lay be-tween 90 and 105 miles south of Poverty Point by way of a relict Arkansas River meander belt that hugged the east side of Maçon Ridge, and about the same distance downstream along the Ouachita and other Arkansas River meander belts lying west of Maçon Ridge. Several Arkansas and Mississippi meander belts as well as then-active courses of those rivers all came together in this lowland. Another 10 to 15 miles down those me-ander belts was the Avoyelles Prairie, an island of high ground bordering the Mississippi Valley. It supported a few encampments bearing a few materials that resembled Poverty Point's. Below that, there was nothing for miles.

Grand Marais Community

The Grand Marais community consisted of a dozen or so known en-campments, namely, Calion, Marie Saline, Bang's Slough, Hoover Levee, Green's Island, Woodard Lake, Stringfellow Field, and others. Archaeolo-gist Frank Schambach characterized this extensive river swamp as being much like Lower Mississippi lowlands (it was, in geomorphic fact), but his point was that Grand Marais was quite different from the upper Ouachita River, which was entrenched in a narrow, steep-walled valley. Calion, one of the larger residences, had two low mounds and a Poverty Point–looking assemblage that included PPOs, hematite plummets, soap-stone vessel fragments, and a cache pit filled with greenstone celts. At Marie Saline, more than four in ten cooking balls were plain bicones, but grooved and tool-punched bicones and melons, biscuits, and a block also appeared. Among all encampments, biconical PPOs prevailed, and finger-grooved, spheroidal, tetrahedral, and amorphous forms were infrequent occurrences. Gorgets, bannerstones, tubular pipes, and jasper beads were rare items, but without detailed comparisons they could not be deter-mined to be anything other than Poverty Point namesakes (objects be-longing to the same general classes). Projectile points were uncommon or numerous and usually included Garys and Bulverdes. Delhis, Ellises, Edge-woods, Williams, Hickory Ridges, and Johnsons occasionally were represented. Classic Poverty Point styles with big round notches and narrow necks were either missing or modified to suit local tastes, and they were not made of northern gray flint because there evidently wasn't any. Novaculite and local gravel chert dominated chipped stone, and novaculite typically was more prominent. Investigators Richard Weinstein and David Kelley found that it made up over half of the chipped stone from Poverty Point levels in their excavations at Bang's Slough; local chert constituted another third, and quartzite and quartz flakes made up the rest. Hematite plummets and gravel were common at some camps, magnetite plummets and gravel at others; some places had both, others had neither. A few pieces of sandstone, sphalarite, petrified wood, and shale rounded out the stone resources. Stone was gotten from the nearby Ouachita Mountains and surrounding hills. So what was considered exotic at most other places was really local here and probably was not acquired through exchange—not through long-distance exchange, anyway. Only a piece or two of soapstone, perhaps from broken vessels, did not hail from these mountains. Or maybe they did. The Grand Marais community was close to Ouachita bedrock sources but did not participate wholeheartedly or even half-heartedly in Poverty Point exchange. It was on the right river for rocks but the wrong one for moving them downstream to Poverty Point. Its general Poverty Point appearance was created by the times, its ripirian orientation, and its probable contacts and communication with groups from the mountains and neighboring Arkansas River Valley who did participate.

DeSiard-Ouachita Community

Some forty-five miles on down the axis of the Ouachita River from the last Grand Marais encampment lay the DeSiard-Ouachita community. Several searches of the river banks between these communities turned up no Poverty Point–age encampments, not even the backwoodsy sort. Choice of location was well advised. The three known encampments—McGuire, Zeigen Point, and McHenry—that formed this community occurred where three streams converged. Bayou DeSiard entered the Ouachita from the east, and Bayou Darbonne, the major drainage of the hilly divide lying between the Ouachita and the Red Rivers, joined the Ouachita from the west. In addition, an extensive gravel deposit lay a few hundred yards back from the Ouachita River. Local collector Manning Durham dug these places in the 1930s before they were destroyed by urban expansion. He recalled that McGuire, which was located at the gravel deposit, produced scores of sandy textured PPOs, including biconical plain, cylindrical grooved, cross-grooved, and amorphous forms, as well as tubular clay pipes, broken clay figurines, and a soapstone vessel and several fragments. At Zeigen Point, located directly across the Ouachita from McGuire, he found three sandy biconical PPOs. A few miles downstream, he recovered dozens of PPOs at McHenry. Reca Jones, who recorded Durham's collections, identified cylindrical grooved, melon-shaped, biconical grooved, biconical plain, and atypical forms among the surviving objects.

Additional investigations along the Ouachita River below these encampments revealed no other Poverty Point encampments, suggesting that the large gravel bed strategically located at the confluence of the Ouachita River and Bayous DeSiard and Darbonne may have been a major attraction. If occupants had come from the nearby Bonne Idee–Bartholomew community or from the more distant Poverty Point community itself, I would expect them to have left campgrounds near the quarry, grounds like the DeSiard-Ouachita cluster. Such temporary encampments would not necessarily bear large numbers of tested pebbles, partially finished bifaces, or other signs of quarrying if campers had carried gravels away instead of working them on-site. Close stylistic resemblances with Poverty Point materials make me wonder if the DeSiard-Ouachita group might have been like a home away from home, an isolated island of identity in a foreign land.

Yazoo Community

The Yazoo community sprawled across the Yazoo swamp, across the Mississippi River from Poverty Point. Its three dozen or so encampments were strung out along the Sunflower, Yazoo, and tributaries that coursed through abandoned Mississippi River channels and that were interconnected by a network of bayous, cutoff lakes, deep swamps, and backwaters and floods. In the classic 1951 study *Archaeological Survey in the Lower Mississippi Alluvial Valley, 1940–1947*, archaeologist Philip Phillips noted: "This all adds up to a very interesting, not to say peculiar, environment, one which might be assumed to have fostered, aboriginally, an amphibious type of culture. . . . The dominant note in the landscape is muddy water. Along the courses of present and former meander belts are scores of oxbow lakes in various stages of degeneration into swamp—in this country almost every group of trees conceals a body of water—which, with their connecting waterways into the backswamp, spread a labyrinthine pattern of 'lakes,' 'old rivers,' 'bayous,' 'bogues,' 'sloughs,' 'brakes,' etc., across the almost level plain. These frequently intersect in such a way as to convert large areas into 'islands.'"

A canoe embarking from any pier could have docked at nearly every other encampment in the community. Although Jaketown itself was only 105 miles from Poverty Point (the mileage measured along the axis of intersecting meander belts), the miles were hard. Despite having water connections with Poverty Point and probably with each other, the Yazoo encampments were a varied lot. Jaketown itself was the main residence. It was large—the equivalent of more than 4,000 homes of 2,000 square feet. Seven or eight low mounds ringed the western edge of an old half-moon-shaped point bar, which extended back from the shoreline of an oxbow lake, Wasp Lake. Ford and his comrades William Haag and Philip Phillips dug one of the small mounds in 1951 and discovered a circular pattern of postmolds beneath it. Evidently, a preexisting, wall-posted house had been torn down and dirt piled in its place. Teoc Creek was a second major residence. It was excavated at different times by James Ford, Robert Neitzel, Clarence Webb, Thomas Koehler, John Connaway, and Sam McGahey with a little help from landowner Eugene Neill and others. It proved to be a midden ring, or rather half-ring, about three football fields across, which accumulated at least partially while flooding raised the natural levee on which it sat. Flooding also affected Jaketown deposits as clean layers of water-laid sediment covered layers containing living debris. James Lauro and Geoffrey Lehmann documented a third major encampment, Slate, by means of systematic surface-collecting, not excavation. Webb reported Poverty Point tools and other cultural characteristics at a number of Yazoo encampments—Page, Goss, Choctaw, Tackett, Norman, Paxton Brake, Neill, Garner, and others. Lehmann identified and analyzed exotic materials at these encampments, and Jay Johnson compared their chipped-stone technologies, especially blade-making. Slate's materials were confined to the plow crust, revealing that it somehow escaped the flooding that frequently drowned Jaketown and Teoc Creek.

Like other communities, the Yazoo encampments were a varied lot. For example, PPOs were plentiful at Jaketown and Teoc Creek, and at both encampments, the same forms occurred in nearly equal percentages: cylindrical grooved forms about 60 percent, biconical forms about 17 percent, and cross-grooved forms about 20 percent. A few melons, spheroids, and other types were also present. No PPOs were found at Slate. Early pottery was rare at Jaketown and Teoc Creek. Ford and his associates argued that pottery came after the Poverty Point occupation at Jaketown, but their excavation data indicated otherwise. Slate apparently had no pottery whatsoever. Tubular clay pipes occurred at Jaketown but were not reported at Teoc Creek or Slate.

Pontchartrain was the major projectile-point type at all three encampments, especially at Teoc Creek, where it accounted for over six out of every ten specimens; it made up about three of every ten at the other two encampments. At all three places, Pontchartrains, Garys, and Kents totaled almost three-quarters or more of the points. Like other communities in the neutral zone and beyond, classic Poverty Point point forms fashioned from northern gray flint and sporting narrow stem necks were minor occurrences. Nearly six out of ten points from Teoc Creek showed edge wear indicating they had been used for cutting. Polished-bit adzes chipped of local pebble chert were present at all three places, and polished-bit chipped celts occurred at Jaketown. Hoes of Dover flint were unreported. Jaketown, Slate, and Paxton Brake (an encampment only four miles north of Jaketown) yielded prepared-platform cores and blades, but they differed technologically. Nonetheless, differences are no greater than expected in any nonstandardized folk skill. There are many ways to do the same thing. Jay Johnson, noting the absence of perforators at Paxton Brake, suggested that Paxton's blades were carried to nearby Jaketown, where they were converted into perforators—a potential case of functional separation.

Hard-stone and soft greenstone celts were used at the three encampments. Hematite plummets were recorded at Jaketown and Teoc Creek, but three-quarters of Jaketown's numerous plummets were made of magnetite, exactly opposite of Poverty Point's plummets. Other kinds of rocks were used for Slate's few plummets. Limonite and slate gorgets and soapstone vessel fragments occurred at Jaketown and Teoc Creek but apparently not at Slate. Slate was unusual because of the large number of slate beads and other ornaments in various stages of manufacture; forms included disc, tubular, and barrel-shaped beads, a few pendants, tablets, miniature representations of larger tools, effigies, other unique items, and hundreds of unfinished pieces. About 80 percent of the recovered items were unfinished, having been aborted both before and during drilling. Blanks often were ruined while being snapped along guide incisions. Most finished specimens were thin, disc-shaped beads with short holes, indicating that drilling was an onerous step in completing beads. Slate's particular kind of slate was not represented at Jaketown or elsewhere in the Yazoo community and was unknown at Poverty Point except for a single bead-maker's cache. A soapstone bead was recovered from Teoc Creek. Tubular and disc beads of red jasper and other stone, flat disc-shaped, claw, bird-effigy, and grooved crystal pendants, narrow-ended rectangular tablets of red jasper, and a narrow-ended tablet bearing an engraved human face occurred at Jaketown. Hebe, a small encampment located twenty-five miles northwest of Jaketown, produced a fat-bellied owl pendant.

Lehmann reported that exotic chert was abundant at Jaketown making up some 56 percent of the flakes and 40 percent of the projectile points. About 40 percent of the flakes were Burlington chert but only 7 percent of the points. Northern gray flint, including Fort Payne, made up just 6 percent of the flakes but nearly 20 percent of the points. Tallahatta quartzite, novaculite, Kosciusko quartzite, and Pickwick cherts constituted less than 10 percent of the flakes but over 20 percent of the points. John Connaway and his associates noted that exotic cherts comprised less than 2 percent of the flakes at Teoc Creek, but they included the same materials as at Jaketown: Fort Payne, northern gray, and Burlington cherts, Tallahatta quartzite, novaculite, and crystal quartz. Slate's chipped stone was 20 percent exotic, but only novaculite with 14 percent, Tallahatta quartzite with 4 percent, and crystalline quartz with 2 percent were recognized. The major part of Slate's ground-stone material was exotic and came from the Ouachitas. Lauro and Lehmann identified slate, quartz crystal, quartz diorite, phyllite, bauxite, hornblende basalt, nepheline syenite, garnet schist, magnetite, hematite, and opalized shale. Johnson observed that novaculite percentages from a dozen Delta encampments ranged from 0 to 42 percent of the chipped stone and generally lessened as distance from their sources in the Ouachitas increased.

Lauro and Lehmann doubted that distance fall-off was meaningful in the case of novaculite; once it reached the Yazoo community, only a few dozen miles separated encampments, and they could have been easily canoed. They also questioned whether or not novaculite was treated like other rocks since it was only used to make commonplace simple-hafted projectile points, mainly Garys. Their main point was that novaculite was a poor example to use as a counterargument for exchange having been run by elites or under their self-promoting eyes, because it was destined for such everyday use. Their point was a good one. Subsequent studies have shown that the lion's share of Poverty Point exchange materials everywhere wound up in the workplace or around the necks of workers, not in the safety-deposit stashes of a small cadre of elites. Poverty Point–age communities throughout the Lower Mississippi Valley had personages, but they did not hoard incoming rocks or siphon off the best material for "strut and prance." I am convinced that Jaketown's personages, like those everywhere in the Lower Mississippi Valley, gained and maintained their status by their generosity, either by making sure rocks got into the hands that needed them or at least by not standing in the way of need-based transactions. Political economies of the era were not yet ready for egoists who sought to enrich themselves or stuff their fringed shirts at the expense of their brothers and sisters. After all, what was to be gained by keeping all the good rock when everyone else was mad and hungry?

The Yazoo community and especially Jaketown itself bore close resemblances to Poverty Point in both tool array and stylistic detail. Jaketown's radiocarbon dates, assayed in the early days of radiocarbon dating, are of questionable value in trying to judge whether it was older than, younger than, or contemporary with Poverty Point. In this instance, tool style and raw-material similarities vouch for contemporaneity more than the statistical probabilities of their radiocarbon dates. Exotic materials at both places came from the same group of rocks that circulated throughout the Lower Mississippi Valley during the life of Poverty Point exchange. What is rather hard to explain is why so much Burlington chert made the long trip south when it was so flawed. Jaketown's traders seemed to have been duped more easily than Poverty Point's. At least, they took in a larger relative share of the white chert, which promptly went to waste. Or maybe quality took a back seat to the act of exchange itself. If that was the case, Burlington chert stood by itself as the only really inferior rock imported in large quantities. Occasionally, fine tools were made from it, but more often it wound up being used like local fire-cracked gravel/sandstone or simply being trashed.

The Yazoo encampments were a variable lot but no more so than those in the Poverty Point community or anywhere else in the neutral zone or beyond for that matter. Fisher-hunter-gatherers moved when they had to or dispatched work parties when that was more expedient. Mobility did not preclude some residences from being more or less permanent, but it did ensure that gender-specific camps, seasonal residences, and year-round residences all generated different tool groups.

In my opinion, Jaketown's and Poverty Point's material culture were similar because these encampments and surrounding communities engaged in face-to-face interaction, at least occasionally. Too close to have been created by long-distance hearsay and too many for fads, resemblances were stronger and more common among cooking balls than among projectile points, atlatl weights, and other tools of the chase. If these communities had followed the long-standing native tradition of getting together periodically, such meetings likely would have included feasting but not food-getting. The men were unlikely to have held joint hunts or fishing tournaments. They probably sat around dark, smoky lodges, puffed on their pipes, haggled over the price of rock, and debated river rises and other issues, while their visiting womenfolk were apt to have shared courtboullion recipes, cooking-ball secrets, and the latest in buckskins. Men were generally less likely to have divulged economically useful information than women. Good fishermen or hunters do not share the secrets of their success with other men. It follows, therefore, that Yazoo and Poverty Point cooking balls—probably women's gear—likely would be more similar than men's hunting and fishing gear. In addition to people's curiosity and compulsion for socializing, exchange could have been a driving force behind potential gatherings. The Yazoo swamp had no more rock than Maçon Ridge. Neither place had any. Since Jaketown and Poverty Point exhibited the same exchange materials—Poverty Point the full array and Jaketown a selection—I can envision stylistic similarities growing out of the socializing that would have accompanied interregional exchange. If such gatherings did take place, women may have been a major impetus. Marriage and bride payment could have prompted intergroup gatherings and precipitated exchange. Even if compensation was not involved, I suspect that women were responsible for most of the similarities between Jaketown and Poverty Point communities. Bring women together under social circumstances, even formalized ones, and they are more likely to talk about domestic matters than men. I am not surprised that Jaketown and Poverty Point cooking ball forms are quite similar: Women probably account for more style and technology transfer than men ever do. If some visiting women had stayed on as wives, the cooking ball similarities would have been practically assured. The more women who shifted residences, the more similar PPOs would have become, because the same hands would have molded them.

Catahoula Community

Downriver on the Louisiana side, the Catahoula community spread along old Arkansas meander belts and the edge of a prominent "island" of even older surface in the Catahoula-Larto swamp some 90 to 105 miles below Poverty Point. A dozen or so encampments were active when Poverty Point was flourishing: Caney Mounds, Mount Bayou, Baker's Overcup, Red and White Pipe, Old Saline, Shoe Bayou, Wild Hog Mound, and Lick Bayou, among them. Located about the same distance away from Poverty Point as the nearest edges of the Yazoo community and in just as wet or wetter terrain, the Catahoula community was radically different. Were it not for a few PPOs and a thermoluminescent date or two, there would be little reason to believe that these encampments dated to Poverty Point times or carried on any truck at all with Poverty Point. Independence and self-reliance seem to have characterized these hardy swampers.

PPOs were common in some encampments and uncommon to rare in others. Biconical and biscuit forms prevailed, but when PPOs were common, they sometimes included a rare cylindrical grooved, cross-grooved, or some other finger-impressed object. They were made from clay and not löess. The omnipresent Gary dominated projectile points, but other usual forms included Maçon and Marcos, and occasionally Kent, Pontchartrain, Ellis, Evans, and Williams as well as a dozen more forms. An essential conservatism pervaded point styles and other tools. In fact, the community appears so steeped in tradition that normal chronological indicators are not useful. Usually pottery provides handy time markers. Not here. The biggest change in Catahoula pottery occurred when decoration was added after a long period of making only plain vessels. The first decorations included the basic Tchefuncte styles, and they persisted relatively unchanged for centuries. Gorgets, bannerstones, plummets, and other groundstone implements were almost nonexistent, and rare quartzite and siltstone beads were made in ancient fashion, using cut and snap techniques and unidirectionally drilled holes.

Stone resources were overwhelmingly local: Citronelle gravel, white and brown sandstone, and gray quartzite from the Catahoula Hills immediately west of the swamp. Local pebble chert amounted to over 90 percent of chipped stone everywhere, and quartzite made up from 2 to 7 percent. Exotic stone consisted of novaculite, which ranged from o to less than 2 percent; fragments of soapstone vessels; a few flakes of white chert, probably Burlington or possibly Boone, and Dover flint.

That tool types and stone resources were so overwhelmingly local revealed that the Catahoula community stood apart from the larger sweep of Poverty Point exchange and interaction going on all around. That it embraced neither Poverty Point's ways and means nor its tool forms and styles and that it did not participate more fully in long-distance exchange suggests an isolationism, probably self-imposed. The main north-south Poverty Point exchange route, the Walnut Bayou–Mississippi River, passed either through or along the eastern border of its territory. The Catahoula community provisioned itself locally. How else could it have afforded to remain so isolated? Its hilly western margin provided nearby rocks (chert gravel, sandstone, and quartzite), and the extraordinary annual reversal of water flow through its two major lakes and myriad bayous created some of the best fishing in the Lower Mississippi Valley.

Catahoula people must have witnessed boats full of goods and strangers paddling past their huts. Yet they seem never to have invited them to supper, never offered them local rocks, and never asked them to drop off any cargo. Although Catahoula swampers probably belonged to a different ethnic group and may even have spoken a different language, such differences only mattered when peoples let them. Being protective of their resources may have been a major reason for their independence. In this sense, they were like Big Creek people, who also had access to local gravel deposits. The local stone wealth of the Catahoula Hills had been exploited for centuries before Poverty Point times. The Catahoula-Larto swamp was one of the few places in the Lower Mississippi Valley where a halfway decent supply of rocks existed within easy walking distance of many encampments. Exotic exchange materials simply were not in demand as they were in absolutely stoneless places like Maçon Ridge.

Marksville Mound Ten

Another dozen miles to the south, where several abandoned and active Arkansas and Mississippi channels converged, was Marksville Mound Ten poised atop the Avoyelles Prairie, an old elevated tableland formed during the Ice Age. The mound, a low domed affair, was dug in 1927 by Smithsonian archaeologist Gerard Fowke, who recovered a few cylindrical grooved PPOs and a magnetite plummet. Otherwise, there was precious little evidence for Poverty Point–age settlement along either the western exchange leg (the Teche-Mississippi meander belt) for the next 55 miles until reaching the Bayou Vermilion–Coteau Ridge vicinity, or the eastern exchange leg (the St. Bernard–Mississippi meander belt) for 175 miles until reaching Claiborne on the banks of the Pearl River near its mouth at the Gulf. Not only was the land along both these Mississippi meander belts evidently thinly settled, but it is likely that more recent river shifts would have destroyed traces of settlement even if they had been present.

Beyond the Neutral Zone

Vermilion Community

The Vermilion community consisted of nearly a dozen or so encampments nestled between the Teche-Mississippi meander belt and the Coteau Ridge, the local name for this South Louisiana section of the Mississippi Valley wall paralleled by Bayou Vermilion and its tributaries. It lay about 170 to 185 miles south-southwest of Poverty Point, down the axis of interconnected waterways. The lower margins of the community were only some 20 miles from the open Gulf, and marsh was closer than that. Beau Rivage, Olivier, Meche-Wilkes Mound, Ruth Canal, Paul Blanchet, Hidden Hills, and possibly other encampments lined the Coteau Ridge and a second, lower bluffline that paralleled the first between it and the Teche-Mississippi meander belt ridge. Some places, like Beau Rivage and Meche-Wilkes Mound, had abundant PPOs, while others had few or none. Cylindrical grooved, cross-grooved, and other grooved objects were rare, and so were biconical forms. At Beau Rivage, they were replaced by local forms, primarily plain and decorated objects that resembled small semideflated footballs, rounded penny-match boxes, snuff cans, lumpy golf balls, small thick-crust pizza slices, and alligator eggs. Decorations consisted of irregular tool slashes and marks where fingers had been drawn across wet surfaces. My excavations in the low conical mound at Meche-Wilkes disclosed thousands of PPO fragments but practically none from immediately surrounding residential areas, a situation that reminded me of the Lake Enterprise Mound in the Bonne Idee–Bartholomew community more than 250 miles to the north. Pottery occurred at Meche-Wilkes Mound and Ruth Canal; thick untempered and fiber-tempered fabrics were both present. Most was plain, but random and linear punctating with fingernails and sticks as well as simple stamping adorned both fabrics. Rocker stamping, drag-and-jab incising, and wiggled incising were also added to untempered wares. Although fiber-tempered wares bore designs similar to Wheeler ceramics, they differed in manufacture. Their surfaces were heavily floated or coated with a paper-thin skin of clean clay, which left cores porous but surfaces smooth and unmarked with fiber molds. Although this was not a dramatic technical difference, it indicated that pottery was locally made. Sealed contexts— building levels at Meche-Wilkes Mound and a flood-deposited stratum at Ruth Canal—unambiguously depicted use of both ceramic fabrics at the time when cooking balls were still going strong. Projectile points were a varied lot, too, but generally Garys predominated, followed by Marshalls, Mohrisses, Ellises, Elams (a broad, distinctly shouldered form about half-way between a Gary and a Maçon), and others. Classic Poverty Point

Fig. 13.1. Beau Rivage, an encampment on the Vermilion River in south Louisiana, yielded a few typical PPO forms but had many that did not look like those from Poverty Point. The latter included cane core (*upper row, far left*), tubular pipe (*upper row, middle left*), amorphous PPO (*upper row, middle right*), cylindrical grooved PPOs (*upper row, far right; bottom row, far right*), and flattened rectangular (*bottom row, left*) and ellipsoidal (*bottom row, middle*) PPOs. The cylindrical grooved object (*bottom right*) is 2.2 inches long. Photography by Steven Carricut.

Fig. 13.2. Ruth Canal, upstream from Beau Rivage on the Vermilion River, produced both fiber-tempered and clay-tempered (untempered) pottery. Decorations included simple incising (*upper row, left; second row, middle*), wide incising (*upper row, middle and right*), drag-and-jab incising (*second row, left and right; middle row, middle right*), linear solid-tool punctating (*third row, left, middle left*), linear hollow-tool punctating (*fourth row, right*), rocker stamping (*fourth row, middle*), and fingernail punctating (*third row, far right; bottom row, all*). Photography by Steven Carricut.

styles were not present. My impression is that points were generally smaller than their northern counterparts, although they were not measured or weighed. It would make sense, though, considering the small size of the closest Citronelle gravels and the long trip that exotic flints had to undergo before reaching the area. Pencil-shaped drills, flake tools, Jake-

Fig. 13.3. Ruth Canal also produced other materials of Poverty Point character including a pencil-shaped drill (*upper row, far left*), Kent points (*upper row, three middle specimens*), a reworked point distal fragment of northern gray flint (*upper row, far right*), a grooved hematite plummet (*middle right*), a plain biconical PPO (*middle left*), a plain extruded biconical PPO (*bottom row, left*), and plain grooved biconical PPOs (*bottom row, middle and right*). The drill in the upper right is 1.6 inches long. Photography by Steven Carricut.

town perforators, sandstone and orthoquartzite hones, ground ortho-quartzite celts, a few soapstone and sandstone vessel fragments, and a plummet of galena and one of hematite also were identified. A red jasper bead was excavated at Hidden Hills Lake, and one made of porphyritic basalt was found at Meche-Wilkes Mound. Gorgets and other ground-stone objects were not present in collections. One mound at Meche-Wilkes was a low domed affair, and a similar structure of unknown origin occurred near Hidden Hills.

Local pebble chert dominated stone everywhere, accounting for be-tween six and nine stone artifacts out of ten, but exotic exchange material was well represented. Novaculite made up one-twelfth to one-fifth of the

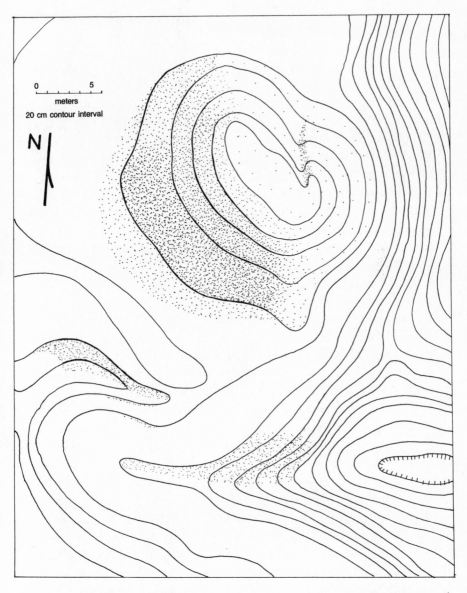

Fig. 13.4. The low, domed mound at Meche-Wilkes on Coulee Des Marks in the Vermil-ion River swamp is only a little over waist high and about eighty feet across. PPO frag-ments are abundant in the mound but are nearly nonexistent in the surrounding living quarters.

stone, except at Olivier where almost three-fourths of the stone consisted of the white, waxy, translucent material. Northern gray flint, including or perhaps exclusively Fort Payne, made up a tiny fraction of all stone at Beau Rivage and at Meche-Wilkes and over one-twelfth of the exotic stone at Olivier. Small amounts of Burlington chert were found at Beau Rivage and at Olivier; it was not identified at Meche-Wilkes. An exotic black flint, probably Pitkin or Big Fork, was the second major exotic at Olivier, comprising a tenth of the stone. It was not identified at Beau Rivage but was represented in a small fraction of the projectile points at Meche-Wilkes although not among the flakes. A single flake of Tallahatta quartzite was recognized at Meche-Wilkes; at Beau Rivage, Kisatchie quartzite made up more than 5 percent of the stone. The quartzite along with Catahoula sandstone, red ochre, soft geodic hematite (or mud-stone), and ironstone suggest ties with the Catahoula community or at least access to rock deposits in the hills that bordered the Catahoula community.

Vermilion material culture was first thought to resemble Poverty Point's more than nearby communities', but subsequent analyses proved that similarities were merely superficial, suggesting that the two communities had little direct contact and not many indirect dealings. With few exceptions, PPOs were radically different; none of the Vermilion forms spread further inland, and their closest counterparts were found at Choctawhatchee Bay in panhandle Florida. That both Poverty Point and Vermilion PPOs were manufactured of löess made them seem more similar than they really were, especially since comparisons were based mainly on fragments. Except for the most generic and culturally least distinctive forms, projectile points were dissimilar as well, and this carried over to size: In general, Poverty Point's were larger. Other implements belonged to the same classes but differed in technological detail. Exotic exchange materials were augmented by relatively large amounts of quartzite and other Catahoula rocks, which only showed up infrequently at Poverty Point and other communities above Catahoula. These materials came from the hills west of the Catahoula community, which were located about halfway between Poverty Point and Vermilion communities. Catahoula rocks apparently moved downstream more easily than upstream. The fact that these materials—in addition to some of the more usual Poverty Point exchange rocks—came down one of the two southern exchange routes makes exchange more of a locality-to-locality enterprise than one sponsored entirely by Poverty Point. No matter how circulated, the volume of exchange material throughout the entire Vermilion community probably would not have filled the aft end of a single pirogue.

What were relations like between Vermilion and Poverty Point communities? I suspect they maintained few if any direct contacts and probably no sustained ones. The material similarities are superficial and probably result from both communities being contemporary (sharing generally similar styles) and having similar domestic economies (sharing generally similar tool forms). They both made PPOs, points, microliths, and a few other tools, but each remained committed to its own fashions. Some tools such as gorgets were not shared, and even plummets, which were so prevalent at Poverty Point, were almost nonexistent at Vermilion. Similarities appear to be compatible with limited and infrequent exchange, suggesting that Poverty Point and Vermilion communities did not reach out and touch each other directly. One bit of evidence for this view is that the total amount of exotic rock in the Vermilion community evidently is small. Another is that novaculite and black flint were major exotics (they are minor occurrences at Poverty Point) and may have come to the Vermilion community by way of a more direct water route from the Ouachitas bypassing Poverty Point altogether. And another is that Kisatchie quartzite and white Catahoula sandstone were important (quartzite being the second most common exotic after novaculite) and implied direct or indirect connections with intractable Catahoula people who seem not to have participated in Poverty Point exchange. What these findings suggest is that the Vermilion community had limited or indirect connections with Poverty Point, attenuated connections that extended through intervening communities that were indifferent, if not openly hostile, toward Poverty Point. Nevertheless, Vermilion people had a compelling need for rock, one stronger perhaps than Catahoula people, who enjoyed the luxury of having nearby rocks, such as they were, and could afford to be independent and maybe even haughty.

The Vermilion community had little or nothing of material value to promote exchange—no superior rock, no wildly popular new tool, and no charming style—and it was too far away to guarantee delivery of fresh seafood very far inland. On the other hand, if exchange relations were less like trade for gain and more akin to gifting, then people themselves may have been the resources that circulated; exotic rock merely could have been compensation for black-eyed beauties from South Louisiana, routine presents among visiting personages, or pecuniary tokens or passports while visiting in foreign lands.

Fig. 13.5. The Claiborne (*right*) and Cedarland (*left*) rings were built near the Pearl River mouth on the Mississippi Gulf Coast. Material culture remains showed considerable differences considering how close these residences were. Some investigators claim that Cedarland was older and that historical changes were responsible for the differences. Others noting their statistically indistinguishable radiocarbon dates speculate that social differences were to blame.

Claiborne Community

The Claiborne community, at the end of the southeastern exchange line along the St. Bernard–Mississippi River, was in many ways the oddest Poverty Point community of all. Claiborne sat on the first high ground rising above the marsh at the Gulf entrance to the river along its Pearl River branch. It was farther away from Poverty Point than any other Poverty Point settlement, yet in terms of tools, styles, and its artificial half-ring, it resembled Poverty Point more than any other place except Jaketown, which was less than a third as far away. Claiborne was also different because it was so isolated. There were a few encampments with PPOs and other Poverty Point–looking tools located a few miles to the west on the St. Bernard–Mississippi River (around the shoreline of today's

Lake Pontchartrain) as well as sixty-five to seventy miles to the east along the Pascagoula Bay shoreline, but any cultural or historical connection they may have had with Claiborne was unclear. Another unusual feature was the presence of Cedarland, a second half-ring north of and almost touching the Claiborne half-ring. Together, Claiborne and Cedarland rings looked like a giant figure eight cut in half lengthwise. Assemblages at both places were so distinctive that investigators Clarence Webb and Sherwood Gagliano concluded the rings dated from different eras and represented a single rapidly evolving community. Yet radiocarbon dates suggested that the rings were occupied at the same time or rather during the same period and prompted investigator James Bruseth to conclude that they were inhabited by two independent groups who lived side by side. Bruseth made a strong case for Claiborne being like a village of eigh-

Fig. 13.6. PPOs from Claiborne included most of the major Poverty Point forms, including biconical grooved (*upper row, left*), plain biconical (*upper row, right*), melon (*bottom row, left*), and cylindrical grooved (*bottom row, right*), but they differed in minor ways. Claiborne PPOs usually had fewer finger impressions, and more had holes through the middle. In addition to these differences, Claiborne PPOs were made of coarse sandy alluvium rather than löess like those from Poverty Point. The cylindrical grooved object on the left is 2.3 inches long. Photography by Steven Carricut.

teenth-century Tunican traders who moved repeatedly from one exchange junction to another as political fortunes changed.

Claiborne was similar to Poverty Point. PPOs dominated Claiborne's assemblage and included all the major forms that occurred at Poverty Point in addition to some unique shapes. Melon-shaped varieties prevailed, followed closely by biconical varieties and then by cross-grooved, cylindrical, spheroidal, barrel-shaped, and several minor shapes. They were made of sandy clay (there was no nearby source of löess), and although slightly smaller on average than Poverty Point's, they were a little heavier. Also, Claiborne had three times as many perforated objects as Poverty Point, although they were rare at both places. Its melons usually had three finger grooves instead of four like Poverty Point's; its end-grooved melons typically were grooved on just one end, whereas Poverty Point's were grooved on both. A few small, solid human figurines were present. They represented headless women and looked like some of Poverty Point's except that they were made of the same sandy clay as PPOs. Undecorated and punctated Wheeler pottery was uncommon, and plain untempered ware was rare. Pontchartrains and Garys made up nearly half of the projectile points, with Maçons, Shumlas, Carrolltons, and Kents comprising most of the rest. Classic Poverty Point types were either rare or absent, and points more at home along the eastern Gulf Coast, such as Morrow Mountains, Kirks, and Levys, also were identified. These "eastern" forms were older than Claiborne and may have been collectibles or relics from an earlier occupation. Actually, Morrow Mountains and Levys had Lower Mississippi counterparts that dated from Poverty Point times, but Kirks did not.

Other chipped-stone tools included various bifaces (mainly projectile-point preforms), drills, adzes, celts, and edge-retouched flakes. Micro-flints including perforators were present, too. Chipping residue was uncommon. Claiborne was far removed from rock sources except for deposits of small Citronelle gravels several miles up the Pearl River, and bone and antler may have taken the place of rock. Deer ulna and split-bone awls occurred, as did polished antler flakers, wedges, float valves, net spacers, handles, spatulas, pins and tubes, pendants, beads, drilled teeth, cut and polished animal mandibles, and other items. Whatever the case, chipped stone included two of the major exotics that circulated in Poverty Point exchange as well as some minor ones. Although local Citronelle gravels constituted seven out of ten chipped stone artifacts, the remainder were Tallahatta quartzite, Burlington chert, and northern gray flint. These three kinds of rock made up nearly three-fourths of the exotic chipped stone; white and gray rock figured prominently in exchange, orthoquartzite did not. Novaculite was important, too, although it only made up a little over 7 percent of the exotic rock. Other foreign rock included opalized shell and tan exotic chert. In addition, imported copper was used to make bracelets, pendants, beads, and pins; soapstone for vessels; hematite and magnetite for plummets,; and greenstone and coarse hard stones for celts. Catahoula sandstone, galena, quartz crystals, limonite, and a few other materials occurred, too. The important thing to remember was that every piece of stone had to be imported.

Objects for dress, show, or good luck included tubular and barrel-shaped red jasper beads, a zoomorphic bead, an owl statuette of galena, a quartz crystal cylinder, drilled jasper pebbles, pendants of various stones, small ground and polished projectile-point representations, and claystone and soapstone tubes and tubular pipes. A deposit of twelve used soapstone vessels was buried in the ring-encircled center section, where a line projected due west from the small conical sand mound that once stood outside the ring would have bisected it. James Bruseth noted that the fragmentary vessels were covered with clean sand, which also held copper bracelets, a copper pendant, a ground piece of galena, and a red jasper bead. He found a second smaller cache of broken vessels northwest of the mound. There were caches of projectile points, usually refined items made of exotic rock and in rare styles, some including classic Poverty Point types that were rare in general midden contexts. Clusters of PPOs, hearths, and a burned spot where a bunch of perforated PPOs had been fired also were found. Earth-moving brought the ring to its final form and raised the sand mound outside the ring.

According to Edwin Jackson, freshwater and marine fish made up a sizable portion of Claiborne's foods, but meats such as venison, cottontail, dog, turkey, sandhill crane, and other cuts were represented, as were Rangia clams and some oysters. Brent Smith suggested that at least some of these animals were taken in fall and winter, but spring and summer hunting and fishing could not be ruled out, because the analyzed sample was so small. Plant food remains have not been identified.

Tool details reflected home production, not specialties imported from Poverty Point or some other place. Although some items resembled Poverty Point forms and styles—PPOs most of all—there can be little doubt that Claiborne made its own things in its own way. Clams and oysters imparted a similar down-home flavor; clams in particular may have been tantamount to fast food because they are so abundant in the immediately adjoining marsh and are easy to collect. Claiborne clams and Cedarland oysters did not necessarily imply, as some investigators have maintained, that marsh was becoming increasingly fresher, suggesting a time lapse between the encampments. Rangia clams and oysters grow side by side. Something as simple as collecting shellfish from tidal channels rather than freshwater streams could have been responsible. Oysters flourish in water as little as two parts per thousand saltier than rangia can tolerate. Hand-collecting at low tide instead of at extremely low tide could have made the difference, since oysters were intertidal and would have been exposed before the subtidal clams. Raking from pirogues would have worked better for clams buried in bottom muds than for oysters, which cemented themselves to each other and had to be forcibly dislodged. Taste was a subjective thing to a hungry collector, but I have no doubt which species would have been collected had equal opportunities availed themselves. The bottom line was that oysters and clams came from the same general area but from waters with slight salinity differences. Neighboring peoples could have exploited either species without getting in each other's way or taking food from the other's mouth.

PPOs made of the sandy clay underfoot also suggest that the community developed in place. Neither raw löess nor already formed löess cooking balls could have been imported in quantities necessary to keep ovens hot. Besides, counting on imports to do something as essential as everyday cooking would have been asking for trouble. Claiborne's assemblage was strictly vintage Claiborne, not that of immigrants recently come to the land. In my opinion, this raises the prospect that Claiborne and Cedarland folks were ethnically separate people who had banded together to promote general welfare. Material items from neither one of the rings had obvious precedents here or afar, making them seem like they simply materialized out of gulf breezes. Lacking clear local ancestry but having technical and stylistic details that affirmed in-place development rules out either ring being founded by immigrants from Poverty Point. Nevertheless, radiocarbon dates and exotic rocks show that both Claiborne and Cedarland were contemporary with Poverty Point, although not necessarily with each other.

Exotic materials from the Ouachita Mountains, the Midwest, and the

Appalachian piedmont occurred at both rings, although Bruseth's inventories showed they varied in both kind and amount. Tallahatta quartzite from the piedmont was common in both places; quartzite possibly from the Ouachitas was common at Cedarland but rare at Claiborne. Northern gray flint from the Midwest was common at Claiborne but rare at Cedarland. Midwestern white chert, Ouachita novaculite and quartz crystals, and Great Lakes copper were rare at both places. Ouachita magnetite and hematite were common at Claiborne and unknown at Cedarland. Midwestern galena and piedmont soapstone and opalized shell were not recognized at Cedarland either, although they did occur rarely at Claiborne. A black flint, presumably Pitkin or Big Fork, showed up rarely at Cedarland but not at Claiborne. Other materials at both encampments were local or rather could have been gotten in the hills alongside the Lower Mississippi or Lower Pearl Rivers; they included abundant Citronelle gravel and common red jasper, ironstone, and limonite. White sandstone from the Catahoula vicinity showed up rarely at Claiborne but not at Cedarland. These materials revealed that inhabitants of both rings were involved in long-distance exchange. Exchange of this particular array of materials happened only once in the entire history of exchange in the Lower Mississippi Valley, and that was only for a generation or two a century or two when Poverty Point was flourishing. There was simply no way to get around this fact: Both Claiborne and Cedarland participated in Poverty Point exchange but did so differently despite being side by side. That neither had demonstrable local precedents was a further indication of their rapid punctuated growth—growth undoubtedly stimulated by exchange.

Claiborne's PPOs looked a lot like Poverty Point's; like Poverty Point, they dominated the assemblage. There were some differences, but they were the sort that came from being made by peoples who lived a long way apart but who shared essentially the same repertory. For example, Claiborne's melons generally had three grooves instead of four and had a groove on one end instead of both. Claiborne had three times as many perforated objects, and there were other minor differences. But the main point was that the miles between Claiborne and Poverty Point did not compromise basic similarities, as they did with Vermilion cooking balls. Claiborne's PPOs were locally made, but they sure looked as though the hands that molded them had crossed Poverty Point palms on occasion. Actually a handful of Claiborne PPOs—sandy spheroids with bumpy surfaces, reminiscent of mulberries—were recovered from Poverty Point's southern rings. Although archaeologists never will be able to tell whether they were carried to Poverty Point by Claiborne visitors, brought back by Poverty Point residents vacationing on the Mississippi Gulf Coast, or passed upriver from group to group, the presence of Claiborne-like objects at Poverty Point vouched for direct or possibly indirect contact between the encampments—contact which ostensibly involved earth-oven cooking and probably feasting. Red Snapper fillets and possibly pelican feathers, which Jackson identified at nearby Copes, also testified to direct contact with coastal people. These circumstantial clues suggest that residents of Claiborne and Poverty Point came face to face occasionally, and rock exchange would have given them an excellent reason for getting together.

Foreign Places

Recognizable Poverty Point culture did not extend past the neutral zone, even though most of its exotic exchange material came from foreign places. Contemporary distant communities such as Hugo, Frierson, O'Bryan Ridge, Nonconnah, Labras Lake, Riverton, Broken Pumpkin, Elliot's Point, and others lying en route to the rocks or at the rocks themselves did not adopt many Poverty Point norms, at least not the fine points. Yet distant peoples either started exchange materials moving on down the line, helped them to get across their lands, or simply enabled them to pass through without incident or toll. Some communities—generally those lying closest to Poverty Point territories—did use PPOs, but those were usually limited to bicones or other simple ungrooved forms. Communities farther away bore fewer Poverty Point resemblances. Such limited material resemblances suggest that many of Poverty Point's basic raw materials came from lands inhabited by strangers. The question that comes to mind is how exchange was conducted across such a vast territory, which encompassed shining Great Lake waters, majestic cloud-clad Appalachians, and even soaring Rockies before reaching steamy bayous. Unless Poverty Point stone knappers quarried rocks directly (a most unlikely job for people with fisher-hunter-gatherer mentality and training to carry out so far from home, especially when so much depended on having unimpeded access to rocks in somebody else's home territory), then intertribal arrangements (exchange) must have pushed rocks toward Poverty

Point and other Lower Mississippi communities. But what kind of arrangements would do that?

As one-directional as they seemed, one-sided they were not. There were no more genuine humanitarians then than there are now. Compassion stopped at community limits. Being generous with kith and kin brought reward; being magnanimous with strangers brought bad Burlington chert and invited bad karma. Poverty Point communities ran on a few percent to greater than 80 percent imported rock, and there simply was no way that peoples so far removed from their basic raw material sources would have placed themselves at the mercy of strangers, nice or not. Whatever arrangements Poverty Point peoples worked out with rock providers worked for a while, long enough for exotic exchange rocks to become an integral part of their basic technology.

In my view, what Poverty Point groups exchanged for foreign rock was nonmaterial. Hugs and handshakes, fun and festivities, wives and husbands, alliance-building and nonaggression pacts, and revivals and rituals would have left little trace, but they would have encouraged get-togethers. Rock suppliers did not aspire to be like Poverty Point people; they were content as they were. Nonetheless, they thought enough of their brothers down the Mississippi (or more likely of their own reputations) to send their very best, except for purveyors of Burlington exports. Long-distance exchange transactions were not tit for tat; they were more akin to gifts, goodwill tokens, and bride payments. Whatever they were, they worked well enough and long enough for Poverty Point and other Lower Mississippi communities to become dependent on them. In a sense, Poverty Point's grandiosity was due to long-distance exchange and its social and political economic fortunes.

14

In Retrospect

"Maybe One More Time"

As always I conclude a Poverty Point project feeling like I know less than I did when I started. It would be frustrating if I didn't also realize how many things I learned in route to knowing less. Knowing less has become relative to the size of our increasing body of data. The more you learn, the more you realize there is to learn. I always enter the analysis and writing phases of each project vowing that this will be my last time, but even as I write these words, I catch myself thinking about where I want to dig next summer. Maybe one more time.

Jon Gibson, in *Cool Dark Woods, Poison Ivy, and Maringoins,* 1994

Before Poverty Point

Thousands of years and thousands of peoples left their marks on the Maçon Ridge before the Place of the Rings rose from the ancient dust. Ancestors of Poverty Point people fine-tuned their hunting, gathering, and fishing skills to the rhythms of land and water. They raised economy, especially fishery, to new levels. Shifting routine and changing custom resulted in new organization and uses of power. Point Point's ancestors had a strong sense of who they were. They showed their pride by building an earthen mound, maybe even two, on Poverty Point grounds. Charged with history and emotion, the land experienced change. Ridge and swamp took on campfire glow, and löess took on the comfort of grandmother's lap. A place on Maçon Ridge became home sweet home, but these changes were minor compared with those that rocked Poverty Point's world during the eighteenth century B.C.

Archaeological Research

A few archaeological investigations took place during the late nineteenth and early twentieth centuries, including Clarence Webb's first visits. But James Ford's work in the early 1950s attracted national attention and still remains a milestone in the history of research. Clarence Webb joined his friend Ford in that endeavor and for decades thereafter was the principal figure in Poverty Point research. Ever the caring physician Webb nurtured research and researcher alike, and his love and respect for Poverty Point infused research with lofty standards. Poverty Point created its own disciple in Mitchell Hillman, an unconventional researcher who was born and raised and died in the shadow of the big mound. Both Webb and Hillman were excellent human scientists, but they were more: They were Poverty Point advocates. They still influence Poverty Point research.

Interpretations of Poverty Point have changed many times during the half-century following Ford's seminal work. Poverty Point has gone from being a settlement of industrious Hopewell captives to a palimpsest resulting from generation after generation of visitors returning to a favored spot; from a vacant ceremonial center with Mesoamerican ties to a large, permanent agricultural village inspired by Olmec holy men; from a self-made chiefdom to a stellar observatory; and from a periodically held trade fair to a large, permanent encampment of harnessed fisher-hunter-gatherers who carried the power of kindness to previously unachieved levels. Which is it? All of these interpretations held sway for a while, but times change, people change, opinions change. Such is Poverty Point's destiny. Its real nature may be forever elusive, but at least future researchers will have better ideas of what it is not.

Genesis

Sometime around 1730 B.C., give or take a decade or two, a metamorphosis took place on Maçon Ridge. Poverty Point culture burst out of a Late Archaic way of life, and two political economic shifts marked its emergence—a massive building program and an extensive long-distance exchange enterprise. A set of six elliptical half-rings was raised, along with several mounds including two huge bird-shaped eminences, a steep-sided dome, and one or two flat-topped platforms. Nearly a million cubic yards of dirt were moved, and even more dirt went into leveling the building site. Building occupied hundreds of people for decades and showed that laborers had more on their minds than just keeping their bellies full. In addition, they imported rock and made sure it was shared with the needy. Rock came from sources as close as a day or two away and as far away as 1,500 miles. Open access was enjoyed. Practical needs determined who got what and how much; exotic exchange rock went to those engaged in everyday work as well as those who gained prestige from the transactions.

Equipment

From exotic and local stone and other substances, Poverty Point folks made their equipment, appliances, and homes. Some of their material things were new in purpose and design. Lumps of löess were hand-shaped into balls used to heat their cooking pits. Referred to as Poverty Point objects, they came in a variety of shapes: bicones, grooved bicones, grooved cylinders, cross-grooved melons, longitudinally grooved melons, end grooved melons, spheroids, and dozens of less common forms. Shapes helped regulate pit temperature and cooking time. Decorated and miniature balls probably were used for other things. I do not believe they were attempts at writing or taking inventory, but I have no doubt they were ideographic on some level.

As important as PPOs were, they were not the only means of cooking. Cooking also was done indirectly with hot rocks, not in pits but in containers. Hot-rock cooking was an old tradition, but containers were new. Soapstone pots were brought in from the southern Appalachians, but fiber-tempered and untempered dishes were produced at Poverty Point. Cooking and rendering nut oil and lard in portable containers facilitated work during construction peaks. Digging semipermanent ovens and cooking pits on temporary building surfaces would not have been practical, since they would have been covered up with the next load of dirt. Ceramic vessels eventually replaced stone ones, but not at Poverty Point. By the time durable stoneware was all broken, Poverty Point was abandoned.

Poverty Point people were gadget-rich. They had tools for making tools, tools for aiding work, and objects for appearance and displaying importance. Hones, saws, reamers, polishers, hammerstones, and other implements were used for preparing and maintaining equipment, but they were uncommon. This scarcity suggests that tool-making tools were coveted and used for a long time and that much gear was fashioned at least partially away from home and finished and repaired with perishable billets at home. Chopping, digging, and pounding were aided with ground-stone and chipped-stone celts, adzes, and hoes. Celts and adzes were commonplace both on Maçon Ridge and at swamp encampments, but hoes were common only at swamp camps. Scraping, cutting, and drilling tasks were carried out with unrefined and refined bifaces, including projectile points, and with blade and flake tools. The main hunting weapon was the dart and atlatl. Garys, Motleys, Ellises, Pontchartrains, Delhis, and Kents were primary types of stone dart tips, and all integrated ballistic design with striking power. Atlatls were weighted in order to stabilize the flight of darts; weights included bannerstones, boatstones, bars, and numerous gorgets. Heavy magnetite and hematite plummets were attached to bottomlines of seines and other nets, which enabled them to be deployed in rising or swiftly flowing waters, making fishing effective year-round. Stone beads, pendants, bangles, and baubles were worn when power dressing or carried when luck was required. Copper lancets and stone and pottery sucking tubes (or pipes) were employed in healing ceremonies. Although exotic rocks were preferred for some tools and local rocks for others, function and not functionary was responsible. One overriding generality that emerged from Poverty Point's wealth of material culture was its basically domestic character.

Subsistence

Poverty Point was essentially a fishing culture. Hunting and gathering were important, but fishing dominated food pursuits and enabled all-year food supply without winter and early spring flood-imposed shortfalls.

Neither Poverty Point nor contemporary settlements cultivated native seed plants or tropical domesticates. Year-round fishing solved food crises, and no terrain favored fishing more than the waters around Poverty Point. Yet Poverty Point developed beyond the point enabled by a few fish and nutbread loaves. Its growth was stimulated by organization.

Exchange

Poverty Point's stone resources came from outside its homeland, even the local chert gravels. Rock was imported from dozens of sources stretching from bedrock outcrops in the Ouachita Mountains to the southern Appalachian Mountains and from local gravel beds to glacial drifts around the Great Lakes. Even a piece of Wyoming obsidian found its way to the rings. Exchange volume was heavy. A lot of local pebble chert arrived in a natural condition, but exotic material generally came in as bifaces or at least in a preshaped condition. What was given in exchange was either perishable or ideological, or else exchange was like gifting among personages or bride compensation. Once at the rings, exotic rock found its way into all kinds of common domestic activities and was not hoarded by elites or used strictly for their glorification. Function determined what kind of rock was needed and how much got into the hinterland. Distance meant little to rock circulation in the Poverty Point community as well as elsewhere in the Lower Mississippi Valley, revealing that occupational needs and social relations were important to exchange interworkings. After all, what difference did a few more miles make after rock had already endured voyages of hundreds and hundreds of miles just to reach Poverty Point? Poverty Point was the major player in exchange, but not in a political sense. Social interactions laid down the ground rules of exchange, charted itineraries, and loaded pirogues.

Spirits and Ghosts

The symbolic and representational world of Poverty Point was revealed by design imagery and earthwork layout. It was a world filled with spirits and power, a world manipulated with magic and good-luck charms. Whether Poverty Point was a secular or hallowed place was a question investigators have repeatedly asked over the years and have never convincingly answered. Why? Because it was not one or the other; it was both. Animism and everyday living were inseparable. Mounds were metaphors of the creation story—of the Earth Island built by an Earth Diver out of muck from the bottom of the primordial sea and of humans who climbed into the light from the underworld. Few monuments praising home, ethnicity, and common action could have been more demonstrative. But what about the rings? Eastern native mythology holds that broken-circle arrangements give protection against death, despair, sickness, and other outside evils, which originated in the west and north. The open east side allowed Creator Sun's blazing eye to bathe inhabitants with warmth and goodness. Disharmony that built up within the rings was vented through the five cross-cutting aisles. But outside evil forces were kept from using the aisles to gain entry into the inner sanctum by the axial alignment formed by five outer mounds, including one (maybe two) that were centuries older than the others. There were six rings, six ring compartments, and six mounds. Six is a sacred number in native beliefs. It corresponds to the parts of the primal cosmos: the upper and lower worlds and four value-laden directions. If the big mounds were intended to be birds, then birds' roles as Thunderers, spirit helpers, and advance scouts added those qualities to the protective shielding of the rings and the mounds. To me, the earthworks have too much cosmic meaning to be coincidental. Their magic warded off supernatural harm, attracted good luck, and uplifted community spirit and ethnicity.

Small, polished, hard-stone objects and glyphs represented animal, human, and composite animal/human figures, which displayed unique or even supernatural abilities in native lore (flight, night vision, weather forecasting, early warning, and news bringing) or which simply played roles in parables and explanatory stories. These charms and fetishes were more than just a rabbit's foot or a lucky flourite crystal; they were powerful medicine embodying the qualities of the story characters they represented. They brought good luck and protection to those who carried them, even beyond the safety of the rings.

Community Core, Periphery, and Beyond

The Poverty Point community spread over 700 square miles. The Place of the Rings was the center, but several small residences encircled the rings for nearly four miles in every direction, except east off the bluff. Beyond this residential core, dozens of field camps and a few more residences stretched for another fifteen to eighteen miles. They formed the community periphery, its economic and social hinterland, which not only provided foods and other resources for the core but succored small nests of people who preferred to live in the country. Joes Bayou paralleled the bluff to the east and attracted numerous swampers and residents. Another group of encampments lined Maçon Ridge bluff north and south of Poverty Point, and others bunched along streams and ponds in the West Swamp more than a day's round-trip from the community core. The core basically was residential and the periphery mainly an economic support zone, although a few residences also were established. Logistical mobility created most of the settlement landscape, but marriage and exchange tied backcountry residents together and with people at the rings.

Some of the communities closest to Poverty Point did not interact as intensively with it as did other communities farther away, or if they did, interaction had little lasting impact. To some extent, this is probably just a "town/country" thing, but I think that social independence was mainly to blame. Since differences encompassed styles as well as exchange and PPOs as well as projectile points, I believe isolation was intentional. I don't think nearby communities liked Poverty Point a lot and showed it by not fawning over exotic rock and not participating in foreign exchange. They didn't need to: They were closer to local gravel beds than Poverty Point and did not have to rely on anybody but themselves for rock.

Some faraway communities had materials, tools, and styles that looked a lot like Poverty Point's, and some did not. Whether or not communities had access to local rock seemed to have a lot to do with similarities. Those with gravels on hand bore fewer similarities than those without handy gravels, but domestic economy was less important than political economy. That was why the Vermilion community shared many exotic rocks but hardly any styles with Poverty Point; why the Catahoula community shared neither; and why Jaketown, Claiborne, and Bonne Idee–Bartholomew communities shared both. Long-distance exchange encouraged social engagement. Even if the situation had been the other way around, and social relations had prompted exchange, outcomes would not have changed. It not only took two to trade; it took two to exchange gifts, to marry, to make babies. The exception to this generalization was the Bonne Idee–Bartholomew community, which had access to local rock but still maintained close ties with Maçon Ridge—probably because Ouachita rock passed through its coffers to the Place of the Rings. While goodwill and friendship were spiritually uplifting, exchange was visceral. Long after Poverty Point, the land included in the old Poverty Point and Bonne Idee–Bartholomew communities was occupied by the Koroa and other Tunican tribes who were entrepreneurs and skilled traders in salt, horses, furs, bear oil, and other in-demand commodities. They probably were direct descendants of Poverty Point people, but the crucial point was that they turned a tidy profit and gained a reputation as businessmen by exploiting their strategic location and providing a needed middleman service.

Political Economy

One of the foundations of Poverty Point culture was its corporate makeup. Prestige and status were as prevalent as in networked society, but in corporately organized society, a group-first mentality replaces an ego-first mentality. Instead of using material profits and obligations for personal enrichment, doers turned them back into the community from whence they came. Patronage was born, and patronage was power. As long as obligations were called in to support projects that benefited both debtors and the community at large, Poverty Point knew no bounds. Once basic resources were provided, patrons would have had access to unbridled labor upon demand or rather upon request. A corporate political economy was responsible for the earthworks as well as their magnitude. Why? Because earthworks were insurance: They protected all who worked and lived on and around them. Exotic exchange rocks came to those who needed them, not just to those who brought them in. Why? What good would rocks have done if not put to practical use? What good was wealth when even the rich still had to starve or live like paupers? Prestige earned by sharing produces loyality and leverages labor; prestige gotten through threat and fear only leads to more threat and fear. Reciprocity built the huge earthworks and promoted widespread exchange. Coercion was as a drop lost in a heavy dew.

Development

Exchange accelerated development of Poverty Point culture, and the power of kindness accelerated exchange. Year-round fishing was the fuel for both. Fishing set up sharing and social dependencies, which in turn were transformed into raw labor—the only universally available means of repaying favors. Sharing came from catches made during the entire year, especially during high waters, when nets with weighted bottomlines were the only guarantee of success. Weights were made of Ouachita iron ores made available through exchange. So fishing, exchange, and sharing were behind Poverty Point's growth.

"Much obliged, until you're better paid" was the prevailing attitude, the process, and the power behind Poverty Point's building and exchange achievements. Sharing—the power of kindness—was enough to push a corporately organized society to levels normally reached only by coercive government. It was a remarkable feat for fisher-hunter-gatherers who settled on Maçon Ridge more than three and a half millennia ago, a people whose home has come to be known as Poverty Point—Place of the Rings.

Glossary

Aba: Great Spirit, in Choctaw language

Adena: burial-mound-building culture of the mid-South and East, partly preceding and partly contemporary with Hopewell culture

Ag-Cat: slow-flying airplane used by crop dusters

animism: native belief that the world is filled with ghosts, spirits, and supernatural power

Archaic: prolonged cultural adaptation to Middle and Late Holocene environments; also a prehorticultural, hunting-gathering way of life

artificial earth: mound fill, dirt used to build earthworks

atlatl: hand-held lever used to throw spears

benchmark: permanent marker tied precisely into a system of land location such as latitude and longitude or an archaeological grid

biface: chipped-stone tool or tool preform chipped on two sides

billet: bone, antler, or wooden baton used to flake rocks; a soft hammer, distinguished from a hammerstone

bladelet: small flake at least twice as long as wide with parallel sides and a striking platform on one end

bride compensation: gifts given to in-laws by groom in payment for their daughter

broken circle: earthen enclosure bearing a gap or opening, often said to be an entrance for good, if on east side, and an exit for evil, if on west or north sides

cap: artificial layer of dirt laid only across the summit of a mound or ring, distinguished from a mantle, which covers both summit and sides chiefdom: sociopolitical organization that integrates social inequality with strong but noncoercive leadership

chops: pork chops

Citronelle gravel: glacial outwash incorporated in Pleistocene uplands flanking the Lower Mississippi alluvial valley

corporate strategy: a consensus-based means of interpersonal relationships that emphasize group welfare over personal ambition and greed

courtboullion: fish stew

crevasse: break in a streamside levee where water exits the main channel during high-water stages

Crowley Stratigraphic Unit: gray clayey upper stratum of Prairie Terrace directly beneath Peoria löess

Cultural Resources Survey: archaeological and historical investigation conducted in order to bring client into compliance with federal legislation protecting and conserving the country's heritage

directional exchange: movement of material between important places and personages, making distance irrelevant

distance-decay: trade or exchange of a commodity that decreases as distance from source increases

dogtrot: old house type of the rural upland South, typified by an open central hallway or breezeway separating two pens or groups of rooms

earthwork: mound, embankment, or other architectural form built of earth

exchange: transaction involving transfer of material from individual to individual and social group to social group

fetish: power object, or charm, sanctified by shaman

field camp: temporary work-staging camp set up near resource patch

floated surface: skin of pottery vessels smoothed by wetting and rubbing; floating aligns clay particles, producing tougher, more impervious outer layers

gorget: flattened, oval-shaped polished-stone object bearing a hole near each end, thought to have been a component of an atlatl or drill

H & H: artificial spinner bait with lead head, double hook, and rubber skirt

Heloha: in Choctaw, the female Thunderer, the giant spirit bird whose flapping wings create thunder

hierarchical settlement: local or regional pattern of residential areas ranging from small simple camps to villages to large community centers

Holahta Humma: Choctaw warrior name: *Holahta* is a ceremonial name for chief, *Humma* means Red, so literally Chief Red

Hopewell: midwestern Middle Woodland culture featuring burial mounds, prestige goods made of exotic exchange materials, and an "international" style

hypsithermal: warm dry climatic episode that claimed much of the North American midcontinent for thousands of years before 3500 B.C.

John Deere: tractor used for cultivation and planting

Kashehotapalo: in Choctaw, a supernatural deer man who delights in frightening hunters

knapper: artisan who makes artifacts by chipping stone

lagniappe: a little extra, a courtesy meant to show appreciation for payment or fulfillment of obligation

land tenure: system of economic land use

liquid limits: point at which soil liquefies, measured in terms of amount of water that must be added

löess: wind-blown silt, a geological layer or deposit of dust

logistical mobility: movement of foods and other basic necessities to consumers by work parties, thereby avoiding frequent relocation of residences

microlith: small chipped-stone tool made from a flake or bladelet

midden: anthropic soil top stratum, usually darkly stained by organic decay

much obliged: acknowledgment of indebtedness, usually spoken after receiving a favor

mulligan: stew made with wild game, especially squirrel

Nalusa Falaya: in Choctaw, the "Long Black Being," a supernatural who resembles a man but has small eyes, long pointed ears, and goes about frightening hunters

Olmec: ancient Mesoamerican culture, dating about the same time as Poverty Point and once considered to have influenced Poverty Point's development

orenda: pervasive mystical power, mana

Paleoindian: the first or one of the first cultures in America, the vanguard in the peopling of America

perforator: small chipped-stone drill shaped like a miniature key

Pine Island Unit: sandy upper stratum of Prairie Terrace below the Crowley Soil Stratigraphic Unit pirogue: dugout canoe

plummet: plain, perforated, or grooved teardrop- or torpedo-shaped polished-stone object, usually made from heavy rock, believed to be fishnet sinkers

political economy: organization of production, exchange, and consumption within and between groups

power of kindness: generalized reciprocal ethic responsible for motivation and power behind large-scale mound building, long-distance exchange, and other elaborations in simple society

PPO: Poverty Point object, small hand-shaped lump of baked löess, used to heat earth ovens

protolanguage: extinct language from which several later languages derived

reciprocity: giving without expectation of immediate return (generalized), with expectation of immediate return of something of equal value (balanced), with hopes of getting something better than what is given (negative)

residential mobility: entire group continually moves living quarters to be near resources

set: deploying and running trotline, net, or trap

Shilombish: in Choctaw, the outside shadow or second soul of the deceased, one that stays near the earthly remains, scaring those who venture too close

souse: hog's head cheese prepared during family hog-killings in the rural upland South in the days before refrigeration

translocation: establishing coordinates of a point by measuring Doppler effect of signals transmitted to and from orbiting satellites

trotline: fishing line bearing many suspended short lines tipped with hooks, meant to be set out and left untended until run (or checked for catch)

For Further Reading

Byrd, Kathleen M., ed. *Recent Research at the Poverty Point Site*. Louisiana Archaeology, no. 13. Lafayette: Louisiana Archaeological Society, 1990.
———. *The Poverty Point Culture, Local Manifestations, Subsistence Practices, and Trade Networks*. Geoscience and Man, vol. 29. Baton Rouge: Louisiana State University, 1991.
Ford, James A., and Clarence H. Webb. *Poverty Point, a Late Archaic Site in Louisiana*. American Museum of Natural History, Anthropological Papers, no. 45(1). New York, 1956.
Gibson, Jon L. *Cool Dark Woods, Poison Ivy, and Maringoins: The 1993 Excavations at Poverty Point, Louisiana*. Report No. 12, Center for Archaeological Studies. Lafayette: University of Southwestern Louisiana, 1994.
———. "Poverty Point and Greater Southeastern Prehistory: The Culture That Did Not Fit." In *Archaeology of the Mid-Holocene Southeast*, edited by Kenneth E. Sassaman and David G. Anderson, 288–305. Gainesville: University Press of Florida, 1996.
———. *Poverty Point, a Terminal Archaic Culture of the Lower Mississippi Valley*. Louisiana Archaeological Survey and Antiquities Commission, Anthropological Study Series, no. 7. Baton Rouge, 1996.
———. "Broken Circles, Owl Monsters, and Black Earth Midden: Separating Sacred and Secular at Poverty Point." In *Ancient Enclosures of the Eastern Woodlands*, edited by Robert C. Mainfort, Jr., and Lynne P. Sullivan, 17–30. Gainesville: University Press of Florida, 1998.
———. "Elements and Organization of Poverty Point Political Economy: High-Water Fish, Exotic Rocks, and Sacred Earth." In *Research in Economic Anthropology*, edited by Barry L. Isaac, vol. 19, 291–340. Stamford, Conn.: JAI Press, 1998.

————, ed. *Exchange in the Lower Mississippi Valley and Contiguous Areas in 1100 B.C.* Louisiana Archaeology, no. 17. Lafayette: Louisiana Archaeological Society, 1994.

Jackson, H. Edwin. "The Trade Fair in Hunter-Gatherer Interaction: The Role of Inter-societal Trade in the Evolution of Poverty Point Culture." In *Between Bands and States: Sedentism, Subsistence, and Interaction in Small Scale Societies*, edited by Susan A. Gregg, 265–86. Southern Illinois University Occasional Paper no. 9. Carbondale, 1991.

Ryden, Kent C. *Mapping the Invisible Landscape.* Iowa City: Univeristy of Iowa Press, 1993.

Webb, Clarence H. *The Poverty Point Culture.* Geoscience and Man, vol. 17. Baton Rouge: Louisiana State University, 1982.

Jon L. Gibson is professor of anthropology at the University of Louisiana at Lafayette. His interests in Poverty Point go back to his earliest childhood. He wrote his dissertation on Poverty Point and has been conducting research there ever since. Gibson collected his first cooking ball from Poverty Point in 1956 and his latest in 1998. He has spent eight field seasons with his students digging in Poverty Point's rings and mounds and has published more than four dozen pieces on Poverty Point in professional journals and books. His drawings of Poverty Point have appeared in many books and have been exhibited in galleries and museums across the country.